Also by Author

Virtual Personal Training Manual, © 2013, 978-0-9883440-9-9, https://www.createspace.com/4428594

Poems...Of Eternal Moments, © 2012, 978-0-9883440-8-2, https://www.createspace.com/3905443

The Fitness Book of Lists, © 2012, 978-0-6156563-0-4, https://www.createspace.com/4007866

Genealogy of Romano, Disimone, Vitale, Viviano..., © 2012, 978-0-9883440-6-8, https://www.createspace.com/4011878

Fitness Quotes of Humorous Inspiration, © 2011, 978-0-9883440-8-2, https://www.createspace.com/4052242,

Genealogy of Wittle, Acri, Stewart, Barbuscio..., © 2011, 978-0-988-3440-5-1, https://www.createspace.com/4040063

Genealogy of Mazo, Curry, Thompson, Mason..., © 2010, 978-0-988-3440-7-5, https://www.createspace.com/4005580

Thompson Family History, © 2005, 978-0-9883440-4-4

Dedication

This book is fondly dedicated to

my grandfather, Harper B. Thompson.

Genealogy of Thompson, Hensel, Goodman, Updegrove, Penman, Brown (2), Workman, Culp, Russell, Stoddart, Guise, Romberger, Reisch, Schneck, Black, Moffatt, Muckle, Lehman, Angst, Schmidt, Cochran, Smith, Keitchen, Wilson, Bowman, Walter, Brucker, Pennypacker, Benfield, Haman et al

Thompson Family History v. 1 of East Lothian & Midlothian, Scotland; Bavaria & Rhineland-Palatinate, Germany; and Berks, Dauphin, Lancaster, Perry, Schuylkill, Union & York Cos, PA

MARC D. THOMPSON

Family histories require constant revision. As this century moves along, more and more information becomes digitally or electronically disposable. If we do not save this information, it may be lost forever. Please contact author with any corrections or additions, marc@VirtuFit.net.

ISBN: 978-0-9883440-4-4

Photography by Marc D. Thompson

MARC D. THOMPSON - VIRTUFIT.NET®
www.VirtuFit.net - marc@VirtuFit.net
Skype: VirtuFit
Ideafit: www.ideafit.com/profile/marc-d-thompson

Foreword

My first memories of my brother, Marc Thompson, are a little boy with an incredible desire to learn, explore the unknown, solve problems or mysteries, and uncover secrets. He studied the stars in the universe, experimented with a better way to hard boil an egg (in the microwave—it didn't work in the 1970s!), collected stamps and examined their history, and had an uncanny knack of finding my sister and me even after we went to extreme measures to ditch him—no we didn't want our baby brother tagging along on our bike rides! While earning his college degree, he delivered pizzas on his off time, to keep afloat financially. Marc drove an old, beat up, 1969 Pontiac Tempest that spewed black exhaust. It was a truly ugly car, sporting forest green paint, with highlights of primer gray. These were not easy times, and essentially, Marc's passion, determination, and hard work are how he achieved this major milestone. From this young boy's early curiosities developed a love of genealogy.

Marc is the author of seven family history volumes, and the detail is remarkable. They are unique and special because the focus is more on the person and their life, with recorded recollections and stories, in addition to name derivation, family medical history, heraldry and coat of arms, birth, marriage, and death records, estate and land records, census records, personal notes and letters, local histories and newspaper articles, and old photographs. They are a special and a genuine treasure. When I take the books to our family reunions, our relatives are delighted to have this record of our family history.

This volume will be a keepsake for future generations. Marc's dedication to researching and preserving family history in words and pictures will take the reader on an exciting journey, into our past, bringing tears, laughter, and wonder!   --Jill D. Thompson, Hagerstown, MD

Preface

Our 30 years journey of knowledge has led to a plethora of information. We have learned much. We have discovered our roots, good and bad. It has molded us. We have found we are related to some famous and infamous folks and there are some areas of the country that are named for our distant families.

We are direct-line descendants of King Philip of France and the Royal families Cleves. We are descended from Civil War servicemen Elijah Anderson, Thomas E. Batdorf, Andrew G. Hensel, Daniel Updegrove, John H. Wert, Louis L. Stewart and Jacob Wittle, War of 1812 servicemen Adam Frantz and Andrew Hensel, and Revolutionary War servicemen William Anderson, John Daniel Angst, Philip Jacob Bordner, Peter Brown (British), John Faber, Casper Hensel, John George Herrold, Jacob Lehman, Michael Leymon, Andrew Messerschmidt, John Miller, John Balthaser Romberger, Jonas Rudy, John George Schupp, John Peter Shaffer, John George Felten and Gottleib Zink. Our ties also include European Mayors John Guerne and John Emmerich, religious leaders John Peter Batdorf, John Batdorf, John George Bager Jr., John George Bager Sr., John Heilferich Lotz , George Gaukel and Entrepreneur Alexander Thompson.

We are direct-line descendants of the some famous homesteads and locations, including the George Bager Homestead, Abbottstown, PA, the Chris Miller Homestead, North Lebanon Township, PA, the George Mennig (Minnich) Homestead, PA,the Thomas Benfield homestead, Berks Co., PA, the Livesey Homestead, Philadelphia, PA, and the Wirth Homestead, Lykens Valley Golf Course, Dauphin Co., PA (demolished 1989). Additionally, our ancestor's names were immortalized at these locations: Bordnersville, Kelly crossroads, Livesey Street, Herrold's

Island, Keefer's Station, Deibler's Gap, Deibler's Dam, Shoemakertown, all in Pennsylvania. Finally, our ancestors had surnames named after the Jura Mountains of Switzerland and Acri, Italy, among other locations.

We are collateral descendants of Presidents Dwight D. Eisenhower and William McKinley and Pennsylvania politicians Samuel Pennypacker, John Morton and Jonas Row. Civil War Brigadier General Galushia Pennypacker, Entertainers Marlon Brando, Les Brown and Ray W Brown, Religious leaders Conrad Weiser and Michael Enderline, Melba Dodge, Jesse Runkle, Enrico Caruso and Galla Curci are all cousins. Lastly, Taylor Wittel lists relations to James Madison, Zachary Taylor, Jefferson Davis and Gene Autry

This volume will serve to honor us with the researched and documented information of our background. Our ancestry was derived from this data, the Thompson Family History (TFH) genealogy, that includes:

7,426	Relatives in TFH
2,047	Marriages in TFH
1,264	Places in TFH
1,227	Sources (over 5,000 Sources not producing information) for TFH
1,164	Surnames in TFH
332	Media in TFH
20	Generations (12 Generations in format) in TFH
95	Age of oldest ancestor at death, Sarah E Wirt & Mrs. M. Curcio
89	Ancestors named John or Albert
85	Ancestors named same male name, John, Johannes, Jean, etc
82	Ancestors names Sophia (4) or Maria (78)
74	Ancestors named same female name, Mary, Maria, Mary Ann, etc.
51	Ancestors named Dolores or Ann
50	Most variations for single surname, Batdorf, Bodorff, Buderff, Pottorf, etc.
38	Ancestors named Mary or Frances
34	Ancestors named Shirley or Mary

27	Number of letters of longest female ancestor's name, Amelia Dorothy Elizabeth Bager
24	Number of letters of longest male ancestor's name, Howard Andrew Carson Hensel
22	Age of youngest ancestor at death, Andrew Morton & Henry Rudin
21	Ancestors named Connor (1) or Adam (20)
17	Ancestors named Andrew (16) or Roman (1)
16	Youngest age when first child born, Myrtle A. Thompson & Fortune Marsico
13	Ancestors named Mary Ann
11	Number of countries ancestors born, DEU, ITA, IRL, SCO, ENG, FIN, SWE, CHE, FRA, HOL, PRT
7	Most different ancestral lines with same surname, Miller, Mueller, etc.
6	Number of states ancestors born in, PA, NY, DE, GA, SC, VA
5	Ancestors named Tyler (1) or Anthony (4)
5	Ancestors named Tiffany (1) or Rachel (4)
4	Ancestors named Paul or Paolo
4	Ancestors named Ed or Edward
3	Ancestors who died at sea, N. Benesch, G. Rieth & G. Shoemaker
2	Ancestors named Ashley (1) or Renae (1)
1	Ancestors named Gerald or Gilbert
49%	relatives born in Pennsylvania
19%	relatives born in Germany
16%	relatives born in Scotland
9%	relatives born in Italy
5%	relatives born in Georgia
5%	relatives born in South Carolina
5%	relatives born in Ireland
2%	relatives born in New York
1%	relatives born in Switzerland
<1%	relatives born in Virginia, Florida & West Indies

Acknowledgments

Thanks to my parents without whom I wouldn't exist, and hence their parents, ad infinitum. Thanks to my sisters, for being there for me and showing interest in our history. Thanks to Joe who tutored me as a teen at the Pennsylvania State Library Genealogy room. Thanks to my hundreds of cousins, close and distant, that have selflessly donated their hard–worked family history to me. Thanks to every clerk and registrar, cemetery manager and LDS employee, who has taken their time to assist me discover our roots. This book is truly the love of thousands, both literally, my family, and figuratively, every one else who selflessly helped.

Table Of Contents

Introduction

Genealogy was created in order for people to know the history of their lineage; to discover their origins; to prove bloodlines and royalty. Responding to their deep desire to understand and discover their past, this volume was compiled. It shall stand as part of the legacy of their ancestry.

Our mission is to document and record all that is available for our direct line and reap the enjoyment that this discovery brings. The first goal of the Thompson Family History (TFH) was to amass photographs of as many ancestors as possible. As a face can tell a thousand tales, so much can be learned from them. The second goal of the TFH was to document the medical background of our ancestors, so our children can lead a healthier life. The third goal of the TFH is to amass documentation of our ancestors in order to extend the lineage and to lead to information about the personality (biography) of our forefathers. Our ancestors are not a mere name. They have tales to tell, journeys to documents. They have accomplishments and set backs. Their have remembrances. They have goals, glories, and personalities. The Irish Kings would orally pass down their regal history. They would recite a list of names, their kin, noting outstanding events associated with the forbearers. The ancient Scottish bards similarly memorized their royal family, reciting the pedigrees of the Old Scot's Kings, regardless of the complexity.

Genealogy is a duty. The day we bear children, we took the responsibility of passing along our history. We are responsible for the knowledge of their grandparents and all the wisdom that comes with this knowledge. Our duty, then, includes our children's heritage, the names and faces of their forefathers and mothers. The medical history and genetic backgrounds of their blood lines; the Princes and the paupers; the photographs and historical areas and properties; the tragedies and joys. This TFH is our heritage and with this information we can be proud of ourselves, our past and aim toward a bright future and better lives. If our duty is neglected, as each generation passes, so will our family history.

Most genealogies tend to trace a descendancy or the paternal line (single ascendancy). Our purpose was to trace all ancestors with equal perseverance. This is a monumental, if not impossible, task. We have compiled a pedigree, beginning with our children and using an ahnentafel format. Our children are generation 1, their parents are generation 2, their grandparents are generation 3, etc. There is a family group sheet for each pair of parents along the pedigree. The emphasis at present is on generations 1 through 10, although we have researched as far back as generation 20. Additional collateral ancestors have begun to be added as of 2005. In most cases, the Anglicized first an middle name were used throughout the TFH. For example, Johann Heinrich is John Henry and Orsala Francesca is Ursula Frances. The most commonly found surname was used, whether Anglicized or not. The majority of the collateral information was derived from the US census records. To preserve privacy, all information on living persons has been removed or privatized.

As genealogists will agree, no family history is 100% accurate. We have made errors as others have before us. As this century moves along, more and more information becomes digitally or electronically disposable. If we do not save this information, it may be lost forever. The TFH is a guide for future generations who may use this information for their own goals, whatever they maybe. We have given our children a foundation. Take it, improve it, embrace it.

The continued excellence of this genealogy will be improved by the following plan.

A. Correct errors and complete Source Citations.

B. Collect photographs and medical history of ancestors.

D. Document more personal information of ancestors leading to a more biographical history of family.

E. Expound on current family group sheets and extend parentage.

F. Begin a written biographical volumes (Narratives)

I have a desire and I have a bond. I have a desire to know from whence we came. I want to know our history, our origins. I want to know what our ancestors did, how they persevered and how the spark of life made it way from Geoffrey Livesay born 1410 in England to Sophia born 2004 in Florida. I feel a bond. I have a strong connection to the late 19th century.

If I were given the opportunity to live in any era, I most certainly would pick the 1860-1880's. The time was simple and the people were honest. People worked hard and took pride in their family, their home and their reputation. When I look into the eyes of our ancestors from this time period, I feel a link. I would have fit nicely in their time. Read and enjoy.

Marc D. Thompson

Chapter One

Our family's pedigree and history.

Our ancestors and their family history, with details of life and times of all of our relatives, including cited sources.

Pedigree Chart

Alexander Thompson

b: October 22, 1805 in...
m: January 01, 1835 in Pottsville,...
d: December 04, 1873 in Tower...

Robert Bruce Thompson

b: September 24, 1847 in York Farm
Burial Grounds, Pottsville, Schuylkill
Co, PA
m: Abt. 1873 in Schuylkill Co, PA
d: October 10, 1907 in Tower City,
Schuylkill Co, PA; Typhoid fever
w/contaminated water

Isabelle Stoddart Penman

b: May 09, 1816 in Newbattle,
Midlothian, Scotland
d: April 18, 1851 in Pottsville,
Schuylkill Co, PA

Abel Robert Thompson

b: November 28, 1880 in Sheridan,
Schuylkill Co, PA
m: June 15, 1904 in Schuylkill Co,
PA
d: October 15, 1918 in Tower City,
Schuylkill Co, PA; Pneumonia
w/influenza

Michael Goodman

b: June 10, 1806 in Berks
(Schuylkill), PA
m: Abt. 1832 in Schuylkill?, PA
d: December 27, 1900 in Rush,
Dauphin Co, PA; Old age

Lydia Ann Goodman

b: February 20, 1856 in Clarks
Valley, Dauphin Co, PA
d: October 09, 1883 in Tower City,
Schuylkill Co, PA; Complications of
pregnancy

Mary Magdalena Brown

b: 1816 in Dauphin Co?, PA
d: December 17, 1884 in Dauphin
Co, PA

Harper Bruce Thompson

b: September 28, 1907 in Sheridan,
Schuylkill Co, PA
m: June 15, 1935 in St. Johns (Hill)
Lutheran, Lykens, Dauphin Co, PA
d: July 23, 1981 in Polyclinic
Hospital, Harrisburg, Dauphin Co,
PA; Cardiorespiratory arrest
w/subdural hematoma

Andrew Guise Hensel

b: February 18, 1831 in Home,...
m: May 17, 1853 in Halifax,...
d: December 14, 1908 in...

**Howard Andrew Carson
Hensel**

b: September 02, 1858 in
Wiconisco, Dauphin Co, PA
m: September 02, 1884 in
Wiconisco, Dauphin Co, PA
d: June 06, 1927 in Tower City,
Schuylkill Co, PA; Arteriosclerosis

Catherine Workman

b: May 17, 1838 in Old Lincoln,
Dauphin Co, PA
d: February 10, 1877 in Joliett,
Schuylkill Co, PA

**Augusta "Gussie" Mae
Hensel**

b: February 16, 1885 in Wiconisco,
Dauphin Co, PA
d: March 27, 1973 in Home, Tower
City, Schuylkill Co, PA; Medullary
paralysis w/thrombosis w/cerebral
hemorrhage & arteriosclerosis

Daniel Updegrove

b: June 28, 1839 in Wiconisco,
Dauphin Co, PA
m: October 09, 1862 in Dauphin Co,
PA
d: March 25, 1899 in Williamstown,
Dauphin Co, PA

Clara Matilda Updegrove

b: November 30, 1866 in Lower
Ranch Creek, Tremont, Schuylkill
Co, PA
d: March 28, 1926 in Tower City,
Schuylkill Co, PA; Metastatic
carcinoma of medial atrium & left
chest w/carcinoma breast

Sarah "Salome" A Culp

b: June 30, 1844 in Union Co, PA
d: July 03, 1923 in Williamstown,
Dauphin Co, PA; ? due to
carcinoma of shoulder (recurrent)
w/secondary ?

Outline Descendant Report for Harper Bruce Thompson

1 Harper Bruce Thompson b: September 28, 1907 in Sheridan, Schuylkill Co, PA, d: July 23, 1981 in Polyclinic Hospital, Harrisburg, Dauphin Co, PA; Cardiorespiratory arrest w/subdural hematoma

... + Myrtle Adeline Batdorf b: January 05, 1918 in Big Run, Dauphin Co, PA, m: June 15, 1935 in St. Johns (Hill) Lutheran, Lykens, Dauphin Co, PA, d: May 08, 1983 in Polyclinic Hospital, Harrisburg, Dauphin Co, PA; Cardiorespiratory arrest w/ASHD w/pacemaker

......2 Living Thompson

...... + Living Duncan

.........3 M Thompson

.... + Living Curry

.... + Living Romano

.... + Living Wittle

.........3 Living St. Thompson

.... + Living Shannon

.........3 Living Thompson

.... + Living

......2 Eugene Robert Thompson b: August 07, 1937 in PA, d: March 21, 2007 in Harrisburg, Dauphin Co, PA

...... + Margaret "Peggy" Evans b: 1935, d: July 31, 2005

.........3 Living Thompson

.... + Living Potteiger

.... + Stephanie Hockley

......2 Living Thompson

...... + Nancy Tutto b: 1938, d: 1988

.........3 Living Thompson

.... + Living Sikora U

...... + Living Cleary

.........3 Living Thompson

.... + Mark McCracken

.........3 Living Thompson

.... + Living Greene

.........3 Living Thompson

.... + Living Landis

...... + Living

Family History

Generation 1

1. **Harper Bruce Thompson** (son of Abel Robert Thompson and Augusta "Gussie" Mae Hensel) was born on September 28, 1907 in Sheridan, Schuylkill Co, PA[1, 2, 3]. He died on July 23, 1981 in Polyclinic Hospital, Harrisburg, Dauphin Co, PA (Cardiorespiratory arrest w/subdural hematoma[2, 3]). He married **Myrtle Adeline Batdorf** (daughter of James "Edward" Batdorf and Beulah Irene Wert) on June 15, 1935 in St. Johns (Hill) Lutheran, Lykens, Dauphin Co, PA[4, 5]. She was born on January 05, 1918 in Big Run, Dauphin Co, PA[4, 6]. She died on May 08, 1983 in Polyclinic Hospital, Harrisburg, Dauphin Co, PA (Cardiorespiratory arrest w/ASHD w/pacemaker[7, 8]).

More About Harper Bruce Thompson:
Burial: 1981 in Woodlawn Memorial Gardens, Harrisburg, Dauphin Co, PA[2]
Census: 1910 in Porter, Schuylkill Co, PA[9]
Census: 1920 in Porter, Schuylkill Co, PA[10, 11]
Census: 1930 in Emmaus, Lehigh Co, PA (Uncle James Knittle)[12]
Census: 1940 in Tower City, Schuylkill Co, PA[13]
Education: 1920 ; School[14]
Funeral: 1981 in Jesse H Geigle, 2100 Linglestown Rd.,Harrisburg, Dauphin Co, PA[2]
Medical Condition: ; cardiac arrest due to clot in brain, cataracts, heart disease, hernia
Occupation: Abt. 1929 ; Boxer
Occupation: 1930 ; Lineman (Telephone Co)[12]
Occupation: 1935 ; Laborer
Occupation: 1981 ; Retired mail handler (Harrisburg Post Office)[2]
Occupation: ; Lineman (Bell Telephone Co)[13]
Political Party: Republican
Religion: 1981 ; Lakeside Lutheran Church[2]
Residence: 1930 in 914 ? St., Emmaus, Lehigh Co, PA[12]
Residence: 1972 in Harrisburg, Dauphin Co, PA[15]
Residence: 1981 in Beaufort Farms, Camp Curtain, Estherton, Fort Hunter, Harrisburg, Hecktown, Lucknow, Rockville, Uptown, Windsor farms, all Dauphin Co, PA[16]
Residence: 1981 in 2600 Green St., Harrisburg, Dauphin Co, PA[3]
Social Security Number: 1981 ; 205-05-3254[16]

Notes for Harper Bruce Thompson:
Harper was named for his grandfather, Robert Bruce Thompson [author,1990] Born Tower City, PA [Gerald Gilbert Thompson birth record, #1170270-1935, 09-23-1935, Dauphin Co, PA, Department of Vital Records, New Castle, PA]

I must tell you a story that I hadn't thought about in years. When I was a little girl we used to watch the Santa Claus Truck first down at Grandmas (Carole's now) and then back to the corner at my uncles. Then we would walk along with the truck up North Street until it got to our house besides the [Batdorf's], your family! My Mom would run and turn on the lights before the Truck got there. And the people would all be hollering "run Vera!" There were always a lot of people on Batdorf's porch and [your grandfather] Harper used to come down the steps to the sidewalk and give Wanda and I a candy cane! Ask your daddy if he remembers that. I hadn't thought about it in years but in the mail last night we got your gift cert and the Upper Dauphin Sentinel. Here was a whole page about our Santa Truck! I guess in my mind it made me remember about the candy canes. I don't remember if he did it every year or one year BUT he did do it at least one year. So, Marc, 55 years ago your grandfather gave me a candy cane and now you gave us [a present] again for Christmas! What a family legacy! I am sooooo glad that I remembered and could share it with you . --Jeanne Romberger, June 1997, Email to Marc D. Thompson

Harper Thompson, 73, died Thursday at Polyclinic Hospital. He was a member of Lakeside Lutheran Church. A former Postal Service employee, Mr. Thompson is survived by his wife Myrtle, and 3 sons Eugene, Gerald and Robert, and 10 grandchildren and 2 great grandchildren. Services will be held...and so on reads the obituary. And that's all it says. But what about the man, the husband, the father, the brother, grandfather and friend? That's the person you and I have known. A tall, rugged-looking man who sometimes cried at movies, who was sensitive to others, and friendly. I only knew Harper for two years, but I won't forget him. Every Sunday when he and Myrtle were in church, I could depend on hearing Harper's deep baritone, 'Hi ya Gregg!' as the tall man walked by and shook my hand. I remember, too, the man in the hospital who got. teary-eyed talking about his sons - 'good sons' he would say; who nearly beamed when Myrtle was near. And who cried when he received communion. You have memories, too. Some fonder than others, I suspect. Some of joy and fun. Others, perhaps, of father angry with erring boys. Of a husband maybe working too hard or worried about bills. Others of Harper's broad smile and great laugh. Of dad playing with his 'boys. You remember, too. That's Harper. For him we grieve. For him we weep. Because we loved him and will miss him. Like Jesus and Lazarus. A good friend. Dead. So he mourned. But the question came "Could not the one who opened the eyes of the blind kept this man from dying?" That's our question too, I think, if we really face up to our grief. "Why couldn't God keep Harper alive and well?" Though death comes to each of us, the timing could usually do better. So we not only weep but we are somewhat angry as well: with hospitals, doctors and a God who didn't seem to help. Yet in the midst of our grief and anger comes a word, a story, of life and hope that overcome death and sorrow."I am the resurrection and the life - unbind him and let him go." Lazarus was raised - a sign to John's church that resurrection is not only for the end-time but happens now - in the midst of life and death, joy and sorrow - new life, restored life comes into our world. As we may loosen and let go of the bonds of death and the past. Harper, unlike Lazarus, will not rise and walk among us. Lazarus was for John's church and for us a sign that life overcomes death. We have the sign. Yet not only that. For Jesus' own death and resurrection stand before us - cross and empty tomb - not only as sign but as gift and power. For we, like Harper, who are baptized have taken part in that death and resurrection - washed in it, enlivened through it, "I am the resurrection and the life" said Jesus. Yet he wept and grieved as we do. But death and grief are not final. God has the last word and the last laugh. We are resurrection and life in the midst of Sorrow and death. For God is with us, inseparable from us and Harper. We remember him. And we untie him, to let him go. For us there is life now. There is more to give and to receive. There is time for joy and laughter.We remember Harper. But we also hope - as the communion of saints and in the resurrection of the dead - for nothing, not even death, can separate him or us from God's love in Christ Jesus. I am the resurrection and the life.Funeral of Harper Thompson, Pastor Gregory Harbaugh, John 11:17-44, July 1981

More About Myrtle Adeline Batdorf:
Baptism: October 11, 1918 in Evangelical Lutheran Circuit, Lykens, Dauphin Co, PA[5]

Burial: May 11, 1983 in Woodlawn Memorial Gardens, Harrisburg, Dauphin Co, PA

Census: 1920 in Washington, Dauphin Co, PA[17]

Census: 1930 in Lykens, Dauphin Co, PA[18]

Census: 1940 in Tower City, Schuylkill Co, PA[13]

Education: 1930 ; School[19]

Funeral: 1983 in Jesse H Geigle, 2100 Linglestown Rd.,Harrisburg, Dauphin Co, PA[20]

Height: ; 5 ft. 9 in.

Medical Condition: ; cardiac arrest due to arteriosclerosis, arthritis, cataracts, diabetes, heart disease, hypertension, obesity

Occupation: 1983 ; Housewife[7]

Political Party: Democrat

Probate: Bet. May 10-19 1983 in Harrisburg, Dauphin Co, PA[21]

Religion: 1983 ; Lakeside Lutheran Church[8, 22]

Residence: 1983 in Beaufort Farms, Camp Curtain, Estherton, Fort Hunter, Harrisburg, Hecktown, Lucknow, Rockville, Uptown, Windsor farms, all Dauphin Co, PA[23]

Residence: 1983 in 2660A Green St., Harrisburg, Dauphin Co, PA[7, 8]

Social Security Number: 1983 ; 165-26-7303[7, 23]

Will: March 30, 1979 in Harrisburg, Dauphin Co, PA[21]

Notes for Myrtle Adeline Batdorf:
Myrtle was named for her grandmother Adeline Row [author,1990]

Born 1917 [Myrtle A Thompson, #3455802, Department of Vital records, New Castle, PA.
Democrat, [Gerald G. Thompson]

My mother Myrtle was 5'9" tall and had brown hair and hazel eyes. She was a housewife but I don't know who Myrtle was named after. She didn't drive or own a car but owned a dog named Domino. She was Lutheran and a Democrat who didn't graduate high school. She taught all 3 of us boys to cook and bake. We took turns doing the dishes. She made sure that we cleaned, dressed for school, etc. She was an outspoken, sometimes loud in correcting our errs. She was the "mother hen," She and dad made sure we children had all the necessities, for they did not have a lot. Bur love and praise took care of the rest. Not knowing the exact date we got our first TV set, maybe 1952. This was part of our education that she wanted us to have
--Myrtle A. Batdorf Thompson as told to Marc D. Thompson by Gerald

Thank you very very much for your informative letter. The news about your mother shocked me. We extend our sincere sympathy to all you boys. We liked Harper and Myrtle very much. At one time, Harper lived with us when he worked in Allentown for the Bell Telephone Co Then the depression came and he was laid off. I met you twice. Once when you were about 2 years old, your mother, father and you visited us on S. 18th St. Your mother wouldn't let you do something and you banged your head against the wall. It scared me but you were not hurt. The second time I saw you was 2 years ago at your father's funeral. Dorothy & Roy Strohecker and Jim & I went to the funeral, the cemetery and back to the church for refreshments. That was the last time I saw Myrtle. At one time we had relatives allover Tower City. Now we have no one; and that is the reason I wrote to your mother to find out if my sister Gussie's house was sold and who bought it. Thanks for giving me the latest news. I have not been in touch with Abel for many years. Thanks for the addresses; I copied them all in my address book. I'm sorry we could not get to Lydia's funeral but we were told the weather was bad up that way. Jim does not drive any more because he had bad operations on his eyes at Wills Eye Hospital. I do the driving but do not take long trips anymore. I am just glad I am able to do the errands and shopping around Allentown, and trips to the doctor, dentist, etc. It keeps me busy. My sister, Myrtie Hensel Sterner, lives in Manheim and we hope to get a trip over that way very soon with Dorothy & Hay. Myrtie will be 90 years old in October. I want to see her soon. For your information, Dorothy is a cousin of Harper's; her mother was Lilly Hensel Yohe. She & Roy live here in Allentown. The Hensel family was a big relation and I am proud to be one of them. It is impossible to keep track of' everybody. Thank you, Gerald, for your informative letter. Best wishes to you. Your great-aunt Edna P.S. Excuse the typing. I hurt my right hand some time ago and now have arthritis in it; and being a secretary for many years, typing is so much easier for me. --Myrtle Batdorf Thompson Letter to Gerald G Thompson by Aunt Edna Hensel, Allentown, PA, June 1983

Myrtle Thompson's death came as a big surprise to me. I'm sure that was true for many of you--especially her family. I was called by Vaughn Miller on Monday morning. The family had asked if I would take care of the funeral services. I said I would and asked who died. 'Myrtle Thompson', he said. The name didn't ring a bell. I thought for a while. 'You took care of her husband's funeral.' Thompson. Harper. Myrtle. I was stunned. I sat down. I had visited her Friday and she was fine. We had a good talk. She had been thinking a lot about her mom, her sons and Harper, with .Mother's Day coming up and all. She shared some stories--and told me her doctor said she was fine but she wanted to lose some weight. She hugged me when I left with the bags she had kept for the Food Pantry. Then on Sunday, I saw Myrtle in church. I was stunned on Monday morning. I liked Myrtle. I will miss her. So will you. A sad Mother's Day for you--Beulah, Gerry, Gene and Bob--for your families, for friends. A sad day--period. We begin to think of the 'what ifs' or the 'might have beens. I know I do. I think: I might have visited Myrtle more often, to talk. She worried a lot. I might have helped. You probably do the same. Perhaps you are somewhat angry--with yourself; with God for taking her; with Myrtle for leaving so suddenly" --and on Mother's Day, no less. Martha was angry with Jesus when Lazarus died. They had called him when their brother became ill. But he had delayed, taken too long. Lazarus died. His friend Jesus--the healer and wonder-worker--had failed him. And Jesus wept. But Martha was angry. Listen to their dialog with some different tones: 'Jesus, where've you been? If you wouldn't have taken so long, Lazarus wouldn't have died. So, why don't you ask God to do something now.' Jesus replied, 'Martha, you know Lazarus will rise again.' 'Of course I know that--on the last day.' But I'm talking about now! Perhaps not. Perhaps Martha was soft and pious in her sorrow. She went out to meet him though. She was aggressive. Perhaps seeking. I suspect angry. And Jesus accepted the confrontation with care and comfort and strength: 'I am the resurrection and the life; whoever believes in me will live and never die.' Yet Myrtle is dead. We know that. The story of her life for us has come to a sudden close. All we have left are the memories. Yet, a sudden unexpected death was just like Myrtle. I mean, it fits the story. The time I've known Myrtle she's been loving, but tough. Caring but straight forward and painfully honest. She said what she thought and meant it. I always knew where I stood with Myrtle. And she told me stories of how she handled I her boys and how she always told Harper, "You let people use you too much." "I won't put up with that!" Fiercely independent and self-assertive. Even abrupt. But caring--sort of the 'thundering, velvet hand' of Dan Fogleberg's song. Myrtle loved her family deeply. And you loved her and remember her. So, we come together wondering, perhaps, 'where were you Lord?' Sad, angry, hurt. Yet, we recognize that all of us will die, all of our stories, our biographies will end. Lazarus died. But Jesus called him back 'that you may come to believe', he told his disciples. Jesus added a few chapters. And changed the message. Like the disciples, we look at death as the last reality, the lost fight-of-life, the end. Even when we think in terms of the dead person's soul going to heaven, we have to face the reality that Myrtle is no longer with us--no more talking, or laughing or yelling or threats or love will come from Myrtle. We see death as the end of the story. But the story of Lazarus is a sign for us that the story is not over--'whoever believes in me will never die! That's the promise of Jesus--the one who died and who now lives. Lazarus would die again. Jesus is risen and returned to the Father--forever. I am the way, the truth and the life. No one comes to the Father except by me'. Risen. To give us hope--for life, for living. Yes, Myrtle is dead. But we are not. We remember her life, and we will tell stories about her, and we will live with hope that new chapters will yet be added by our Lord who brings life from death. We are alive--to go from here back to our world--home, school, work, play. Having faced death we can laugh--the laughter of hope and faith in the Lord of life. The laughter of the living. And I remember well that Myrtle really knew how to laugh. I am the resurrection and the life. Whoever believes in me will never die. Amen. Funeral for Myrtle Thompson, Pastor Gregory Harbaugh, John 11:1-43, May 1983

Generation 2

2. **Abel Robert Thompson** (son of Robert Bruce Thompson and Lydia Ann Goodman) was born on November 28, 1880 in Sheridan, Schuylkill Co, PA[24, 25, 26]. He died on October 15, 1918 in Tower City, Schuylkill Co, PA (Pneumonia w/influenza[24, 27]). He married **Augusta "Gussie" Mae Hensel** (daughter of Howard Andrew Carson Hensel and Clara Matilda Updegrove) on June 15, 1904 in Schuylkill Co, PA[25].

3. **Augusta "Gussie" Mae Hensel** (daughter of Howard Andrew Carson Hensel and Clara Matilda Updegrove) was born on February 16, 1885 in Wiconisco, Dauphin Co, PA[25, 28, 29, 30]. She died on March 27, 1973 in Home, Tower City, Schuylkill Co, PA (Medullary paralysis w/thrombosis w/cerebral hemorrhage & arteriosclerosis[28, 29, 31, 32]).

More About Abel Robert Thompson:
d: October 17, 1918 in Tower City, Schuylkill Co, PA[33]

Burial: October 19, 1918 in Greenwood Cemetery, Tower City, Schuylkill Co, PA[24, 33]
Census: 1900 in Porter, Schuylkill Co, PA (brother Oliver Thompson)[34]
Census: 1910 in Porter, Schuylkill Co, PA[9]
Funeral: 1918 in John F Dreisingacer, Tower City, Schuylkill Co, PA[24]
Medical Condition: ; Height Tall, Build Medium, Eyes Gray, Hair Dark[26]
Occupation: Bet. 1900-1904 ; Day laborer[25, 34]
Occupation: Bet. 1907-1908 ; Probationer
Occupation: 1910 ; Miner (Coal mines)[9]
Occupation: Abt. 1915 ; Miner (Colorado)
Occupation: 1918 ; Miner[24]
Occupation: September 15, 1918 ; Miner (PR CSJ Co, West Brookside, Tower City, Schuylkill Co, PA)[26]
Probate: Bet. February-November 1919 in Porter Tp, Schuylkill Co, PA[27]
Residence: 1900 in Wiconisco St., Sheridan, Schuylkill Co, PA[34]
Residence: 1904 in Porter Tp, Schuylkill Co, PA[25]
Residence: 1918 in Tower City, Schuylkill Co, PA[26]
Will: July 02, 1914 in Porter Tp., Schuylkill Co, PA[27, 35]

Notes for Abel Robert Thompson:
Have Photograph.

Abel Robert was named for his father, Robert Thompson [author,1995]

Born Tower City, PA [Harper Bruce Thompson birth record, #344701, #122649-07, September 1907, Schuylkill Co, PA, Department of Vital Records, New Castle, PA]

More About Augusta "Gussie" Mae Hensel:
Baptism: April 05, 1885 in Dauphin Co, PA
Burial: March 30, 1973 in Greenwood Cemetery, Tower City, Schuylkill Co, PA[28, 29, 31]
Census: 1900 in Tower City, Schuylkill Co, PA[36]
Census: 1910 in Porter, Schuylkill Co, PA
Census: 1920 in Porter, Schuylkill Co, PA[14]
Census: 1930 in Porter, Schuylkill Co, PA[37]

Census: 1940 in Porter, Schuylkill Co, PA[38]
Education: 1900 ; School[36]
Funeral: 1973 in Dean O Snyder, 304 E Grand Ave., Tower City, Schuylkill Co, PA[28, 30, 39]
Occupation: 1904 ; Domestic[25]
Occupation: 1920 ; Seamstress (at home)[14]
Occupation: 1935 ; Housewife[4]
Occupation: 1973 ; Housewife[28]
Property: 1930 in $3500[37]
Religion: 1973 ; Lykens United Methodist
Religion: 1973 ; Wesley United Methodist, Tower City, PA[30]
Residence: 1904 in Tower City, Schuylkill Co, PA[25]
Residence: 1920 in 329 Main St., Sheridan, Schuylkill Co, PA[14]
Residence: 1930 in 329 Main St., Highway Route 199, Sheridan, Schuylkill Co, PA[37]
Residence: 1973 in Schuylkill Co, PA
Residence: 1973 in 329 West Grand Ave., Tower City, Schuylkill Co, PA 17980[30, 40]
Residence: 1973 in Orwin, Porter, Reinerton, Rush, Sheridan, Tower City, all Schuylkill Co, PA[41]
Social Security Number: 1973 ; 173-46-1535[28, 41]
Will: May 27, 1950 in Sheridan, Schuylkill Co, PA[32]

Notes for Augusta "Gussie" Mae Hensel:
Member of Women's Society of Christian Service [Obituary, Pottsville Republican, Pottsville, PA, March 28, 1973]

I am sorry that I have hardly any remembrance of my grand father and grand father (Howard Andrew Carson & Clara Hensel. As you can see by their deceased dates and my birth date, I was only about six years old. I can remember their homestead in Tower City, PA. I have seen pictures of it and vaguely remember the inside of the house. I can remember a lot about my aunt gussie. Her husband died before I was born. Harper (your grand father) was a line--man for the telephone company. In going to aunt Gussie's home, Lydia was always there. Their sons by that time had left home. We were always invited into her front ram, usually going in the side entrance. I can see aunt gussie saying, "here comes junior and his family." In the front room, I can remember the "piano organ". Aunt Gussie would take our albums showing us pictures of the Hensel & Thompson family. I can still see the coal & wood stove used for not only cooking bur also heating the home. A lot of times when we went there, I would use their "out house". However Erma remembers going up stairs to use a bathroom. Talking about the second floor, I remember hearing the story about bats in the second floor. Maybe I should not have mentioned that. Thank you for everything you have given me. I surely appreciate it. As you can see, I have incorporated some of your information. I have also giving you information on my grand parents. Thought you would appreciate the above. Surely appreciated talking with you. Thanks again. --Victor D. Hensel, Manahawkin, NJ, August 1998, Letter to Marc D. Thompson

Augusta "Gussie" Mae Hensel and Abel Robert Thompson had the following children:

      i.   Virginia D Thompson (daughter of Abel Robert Thompson and Augusta "Gussie" Mae Hensel) was born in 1905 in PA. She died in 1905.

      ii.   Wilbur Clark Thompson (son of Abel Robert Thompson and Augusta "Gussie" Mae Hensel) was born in 1906 in PA. He died in 1963[42]. He married Elva May Matter. She was born in 1911. She died in 1999[42].

1.   iii.   Harper Bruce Thompson (son of Abel Robert Thompson and Augusta "Gussie" Mae Hensel) was born on September 28, 1907 in Sheridan, Schuylkill Co, PA[1, 2, 3]. He died on July 23, 1981 in Polyclinic Hospital, Harrisburg, Dauphin Co, PA (Cardiorespiratory arrest w/subdural hematoma[2, 3]). He married Myrtle Adeline Batdorf (daughter of James "Edward" Batdorf and Beulah Irene Wert) on June 15, 1935 in St. Johns (Hill) Lutheran, Lykens, Dauphin Co, PA[4, 5]. She was born on January 05, 1918 in Big Run, Dauphin Co, PA[4, 6]. She died on May 08, 1983 in Polyclinic Hospital, Harrisburg, Dauphin Co, PA (Cardiorespiratory arrest w/ASHD w/pacemaker[7, 8]).

      iv.   Abel Franklin Thompson (son of Abel Robert Thompson and Augusta "Gussie" Mae Hensel) was born on October 19, 1910 in PA. He died in June 1985 in East Petersburg, Lancaster Co, PA[43]. He married Almeda Ellen Cox in 1931. She was born in 1911. She died in 1991.

      v.   Lydia Mae Thompson (daughter of Abel Robert Thompson and Augusta "Gussie" Mae Hensel) was born on February

07, 1914 in Sheridan, Schuylkill Co, PA[44]. She died in
January 1983 in Tower City, Schuylkill Co, PA[42].

4. **Robert Bruce Thompson** (son of Alexander Thompson and Isabelle
    Stoddart Penman) was born on September 24, 1847 in York Farm
    Burial Grounds, Pottsville, Schuylkill Co, PA[45]. He died on October
    10, 1907 in Tower City, Schuylkill Co, PA (Typhoid fever
    w/contaminated water[45, 46]). He married **Lydia Ann Goodman**
    (daughter of Michael Goodman and Mary Magdalena Brown) about
    Abt. 1873 in Schuylkill Co, PA.

5. **Lydia Ann Goodman** (daughter of Michael Goodman and Mary
    Magdalena Brown) was born on February 20, 1856 in Clarks Valley,
    Dauphin Co, PA[47]. She died on October 09, 1883 in Tower City,
    Schuylkill Co, PA (Complications of pregnancy[47, 48, 49]).

More About Robert Bruce Thompson:
Burial: October 13, 1907 in Greenwood Cemetery, Tower City,
Schuylkill Co, PA[48, 50]
Census: 1850 in Norwegian, Schuylkill Co, PA[51]
Census: 1860 in Porter, Schuylkill Co, PA[52]
Census: 1870 in father; Norwegian, Schuylkill Co, PA w[53]
Census: 1880 in Rush, Dauphin Co, PA[54]
Census: 1900 in Pottsville, Schuylkill Co, PA[55]
Funeral: 1907 in John [F] Dreisingacer, Tower City, Schuylkill Co,
PA[45]
Occupation: 1870 ; Laborer[53]
Occupation: 1880 ; Coal miner[54]
Occupation: Bet. 1899-1901 ; Supervisor (Porter Tp)[48, 55]
Occupation: 1900 ; Supervisor[56]
Occupation: Abt. 1900 ; Tax collector[48]
Occupation: 1907 ; Business[45]
Residence: 1880 in ? St., Rush, Dauphin Co, PA[54]
Residence: 1900 in Pottsville Hospital, 500 Washington St, Pottsville,
Schuylkill Co, PA

Notes for Robert Bruce Thompson:
Was a writer [Heather Greene, hgreen@@hmc.psu.edu] Robert was
named for his grandfather, Robert Thompson [author,2005] Members

Sons of America, Tower City [Valley Echo, October 20, 1883]

Robert Thompson, son of Alexander Thompson, was born at York Farm, and died in 1909. During the greater part of his life he was engaged at mine work, being employed for many years at the Brookside colliery, at Tower City. He served three years as supervisor of Porter township, and was looked upon as a citizen of substantial character, deservedly respected by all who knew him. His wife, Lydia (Goodman), died in 1883, and they are buried in the Greenwood cemetery near Tower City. They were the parents of four children: Oliver C.; Laura Louise, who is the wife of Charles McGough, of Frankford, Pa.; Abel, living in Porter township; and Benjamin, who died young. [Schuylkill County, Pennsylvania: genealogy--family history ..., Volume 2 By J.H. Beers & Co]

Robert Thompson, who buried his wife and youngest child last week, is very sick. Robert Thompson of Sheridan lost a two year old boy of Diphtherotic croup. Interment took place on Thursday in Tower City Cemetery. Child by the second wife. Supervisor Robert Thompson is adding a portico to his house in Sheridan. Robert Thompson, of Sheridan, one of the Supervisors of Porter Township, met with an accident while returning home from his day's work on Tuesday, which might have cost him his life. He escaped, however, with a broken leg which will keep him confined to the house for several months to come. On the day of the accident, Mr. Thompson had a force of men at work near Keffers. It was his custom, when working any distance from home, to ride to and from work in a carriage. The horse, of which he is the owner, is kind and gentle and fearless of all things except bicycles. While coming down the State road on the evening of the accident he stopped to converse with a party whom he met. While thus engaged a bicycle and rider came along which frightened the horse who made a plunge, throwing Mr. Thompson out of the buggy to the upper side of the road. Had he fallen on the lower side, he probably would have been thrown down the embankment which might have resulted fatally. After the accident he was taken to his home where Dr. Phillips reduced the fracture which was found to be a bad one, right below the kneecap of the right leg. The injured man is unfortunate in having his legs broken. This is the third or fourth time he has had t o suffer from similar injuries. He was taken to the Pottsville hospital on Wednesday afternoon. [Records of Jim Thompson, jbthompson@@compuserve.com]

More About Lydia Ann Goodman:
Baptism: February 20, 1856 in PA
Burial: October 14, 1883 in Greenwood Cemetery, Tower City, Schuylkill Co, PA[48, 57]
Census: 1860
Census: 1870 in Rush, Dauphin Co, PA[58]
Census: 1880 in Rush, Dauphin Co, PA[59]
Occupation: 1880 ; Keeping house[54]

Notes for Lydia Ann Goodman:
Have Photograph.

Lydia & son Franklin died on same day, October 9, 1883, Tower City, PA [Valley Echo, October 20, 1883]

Last Sunday Tower City witnessed a very sad, affecting and unusual scene in the funeral of Mrs. Robert Thompson and her youngest chi ld. Mrs. Thompson was the daughter of M. and M. Goodman of Clarksvalley. She was a young-woman being but twenty-seven years, eight months and eleven days old on the day of her death. The age of her child, Franklin Henry, was eight weeks. It was the largest Sunday funeral in the history of our town, and was under the supervision of the Sons of America, of which order Mr. Thompson is a member. After a short service at the home, a very large concourse of sympathetic friends joined in the mournful procession to the church, which was crowded to the utmost capacity, hundreds being unable to gain admission. Anxious to hear, they thronged the doorway and windows, and with breathless attention, listened to a sermon by the Re v. Arthur Oakes. Subject-"Christ and the power of His resurrection;" Text-Phil. III, 10 -"To know Him and the power of His resurrection." After the sermon in the church, the services were continued in the cemetery, where, amid weeping relatives and sorrowing friends, mother and son, side by side, were lowered in the same grave. They rest in peace, waiting the resurrection morn, when -

The sainted mother shall wake and in her lap
Clasp her dear babe, partner of her grave,
And heritor with her of heaven; a flower
Washed by the blood of Jesus, from the stain
Of native guilt, even in its early bud.

Lydia Ann Goodman and Robert Bruce Thompson had the following children:

    i.   Benjamin Thompson (son of Robert Bruce Thompson and Lydia Ann Goodman) was born in 1874 in PA. He died in 1875.

    ii.   Oliver Charles Thompson (son of Robert Bruce Thompson and Lydia Ann Goodman) was born in 1875 in PA. He died in 1918. He married Blanche Charlesworth. She was born in 1883 in PA. He married <No name>.

2.   iii.   Abel Robert Thompson (son of Robert Bruce Thompson and Lydia Ann Goodman) was born on November 28, 1880 in Sheridan, Schuylkill Co, PA[24, 25, 26]. He died on October 15, 1918 in Tower City, Schuylkill Co, PA (Pneumonia w/influenza[24, 27]). He married Augusta "Gussie" Mae Hensel (daughter of Howard Andrew Carson Hensel and Clara Matilda Updegrove) on June 15, 1904 in Schuylkill Co, PA[25]. She was born on February 16, 1885 in Wiconisco, Dauphin Co, PA[25, 28, 29, 30]. She died on March 27, 1973 in Home, Tower City, Schuylkill Co, PA (Medullary paralysis w/thrombosis w/cerebral hemorrhage & arteriosclerosis[28, 29, 31, 32]).

    iv.   Blanche Thompson (daughter of Robert Bruce Thompson and Lydia Ann Goodman) was born in 1883 in PA. She died in 1915.

    v.   Living Thompson (son of Robert Bruce Thompson and Lydia Ann Goodman). He married Susan. She was born in 1882 in PA.

    vi.   Living Thompson (daughter of Robert Bruce Thompson and Lydia Ann Goodman). She married Charles John McGough. He was born in 1881 in PA.

6.   **Howard Andrew Carson Hensel** (son of Andrew Guise Hensel and Catherine Workman) was born on September 02, 1858 in Wiconisco, Dauphin Co, PA[60, 61, 62]. He died on June 06, 1927 in Tower City, Schuylkill Co, PA (Arteriosclerosis[60, 61, 62, 63]). He married **Clara**

Matilda Updegrove (daughter of Daniel Updegrove and Sarah "Salome" A Culp) on September 02, 1884 in Wiconisco, Dauphin Co, PA[60, 62].

7. **Clara Matilda Updegrove** (daughter of Daniel Updegrove and Sarah "Salome" A Culp) was born on November 30, 1866 in Lower Ranch Creek, Tremont, Schuylkill Co, PA[60, 62]. She died on March 28, 1926 in Tower City, Schuylkill Co, PA (Metastatic carcinoma of medial atrium & left chest w/carcinoma breast[60, 62, 64]).

More About Howard Andrew Carson Hensel:
Baptism: Abt. 1858 in Rev. Wm Yose, Dauphin Co, PA[65]
Burial: June 09, 1927 in Greenwood Cemetery, Tower City, Schuylkill Co, PA[60, 61, 66]
Census: 1860 in Porter, Schuylkill Co, PA[67, 68]
Census: 1870 in Wiconisco, Dauphin Co, PA[69]
Census: 1880 in Wiconisco, Dauphin Co, PA[70]
Census: 1900 in Tower City, Schuylkill Co, PA[36]
Census: 1910 in Tower City, Schuylkill Co, PA[71]
Census: 1920 in Tower City, Schuylkill Co, PA[72]
Funeral: 1927 in Duane Snyder, 304 E Grand Ave., Tower City, Schuylkill Co, PA[61]
Occupation: 1880 ; Laborer[73]
Occupation: 1900 ; Coal miner[36]
Occupation: 1910 ; Engineer (P? Mill)[71]
Occupation: Abt. 1915 ; Deacon (Methodist)[62]
Occupation: 1920 ; Fireman (Coal mine)[72]
Occupation: 1927 ; Fireman (Bestock Underwear Mills, Tower City, PA)[61]
Residence: Bet. 1910-1920 in Wiconisco Ave., Tower City, Schuylkill Co, PA[71, 74]
Residence: 1927 in Hand & Wiconisco Aves., Tower City, Schuylkill Co, PA[62, 63]
Will: January 17, 1918 in Tower City, Schuylkill Co, PA[63]

Notes for Howard Andrew Carson Hensel:
Have photograph.

Howard Andrew was named for his father Andrew G Hensel [author,1995]

Member Patriotic Order of Sons of America, Washington Camp
[Howard Andrew Carson Hensel probate file, 1927, unnumbered
original papers, 21pp, probated June 29, 1927, Schuylkill Co
Courthouse, Schuylkill, PA, Norman Nicol, Apr 2008]

More About Clara Matilda Updegrove:
d: March 30, 1926[75]
Baptism: December 1866 in Rev. Brady, Schuylkill Co, PA[62, 65]
Burial: March 31, 1926 in Greenwood Cemetery, Tower City,
Schuylkill Co, PA[60, 64, 75]
Census: 1870 in Williamstown, Dauphin Co, PA[76]
Census: 1880 in Williamstown, Dauphin Co, PA[77]
Census: 1900 in Tower City, Schuylkill Co, PA
Census: 1910 in Tower City, Schuylkill Co, PA
Census: 1920 in Tower City, Schuylkill Co, PA
Funeral: 1926 in Duane Snyder, 304 E Grand Ave., Tower City,
Schuylkill Co, PA[64]
Occupation: 1926 ; Housewife[64]

Notes for Clara Matilda Updegrove:
Have photograph.

Clara Matilda Updegrove and Howard Andrew Carson Hensel had
the following children:

3.   i.   Augusta "Gussie" Mae Hensel (daughter of Howard
Andrew Carson Hensel and Clara Matilda Updegrove) was
born on February 16, 1885 in Wiconisco, Dauphin Co,
PA[25, 28, 29, 30]. She died on March 27, 1973 in Home, Tower
City, Schuylkill Co, PA (Medullary paralysis w/thrombosis
w/cerebral hemorrhage & arteriosclerosis[28, 29, 31, 32]). She
married Abel Robert Thompson (son of Robert Bruce
Thompson and Lydia Ann Goodman) on June 15, 1904 in
Schuylkill Co, PA[25]. He was born on November 28, 1880 in
Sheridan, Schuylkill Co, PA[24, 25, 26]. He died on October 15,
1918 in Tower City, Schuylkill Co, PA (Pneumonia
w/influenza[24, 27]).

    ii.   Arthur Preston Hensel (son of Howard Andrew Carson
Hensel and Clara Matilda Updegrove) was born in 1886 in
Dayton, Dauphin Co, PA. He died in 1928. He married
Lavinia Eva White. She was born in 1890 in PA. He

married Catherine Sterner. She was born in 1890.

 iii. Helen Irene Hensel (daughter of Howard Andrew Carson Hensel and Clara Matilda Updegrove) was born in 1888 in PA. She married Edgar Isaiah Artz. He was born in 1878. He died in 1906.

 iv. Lillian "Lillie" Verna Hensel (daughter of Howard Andrew Carson Hensel and Clara Matilda Updegrove) was born in 1889 in PA. She married John F Yohe. He was born in 1887. He died in 1907.

 v. Elmer Elsworth Hensel (son of Howard Andrew Carson Hensel and Clara Matilda Updegrove) was born in 1891 in PA. He married Loretta Semrow. She was born in 1900 in Wisconsin, USA. She died in 1933[78].

 vi. Edna Boyer Hensel (daughter of Howard Andrew Carson Hensel and Clara Matilda Updegrove) was born on March 30, 1905 in PA. She died on October 14, 2001 in Allentown, Lehigh Co, PA. She married Living Knittle.

 vii. Living Hensel (daughter of Howard Andrew Carson Hensel and Clara Matilda Updegrove). She married Living Underkoffler.

 viii. Living Hensel (daughter of Howard Andrew Carson Hensel and Clara Matilda Updegrove). She married Living Houtz.

 ix. Living Hensel (daughter of Howard Andrew Carson Hensel and Clara Matilda Updegrove). She married Living Sterner.

 x. Living Hensel (son of Howard Andrew Carson Hensel and Clara Matilda Updegrove).

 xi. Living Hensel (son of Howard Andrew Carson Hensel and Clara Matilda Updegrove). He married Living Craig.

Generation 4

8. **Alexander Thompson** (son of Robert Thompson and Janet Russell) was born on October 22, 1805 in Sauchenside Farm, Cranston, Midlothian, Scotland[79, 80, 81, 82]. He died on December 04, 1873 in

Tower City, Schuylkill Co, PA[59, 83, 84]. He married **Isabelle Stoddart Penman** (daughter of David Penman and Elizabeth Stoddart) on January 01, 1835 in Pottsville, Schuylkill Co, PA[79].

9.   **Isabelle Stoddart Penman** (daughter of David Penman and Elizabeth Stoddart) was born on May 09, 1816 in Newbattle, Midlothian, Scotland[59]. She died on April 18, 1851 in Pottsville, Schuylkill Co, PA[85].

More About Alexander Thompson:
Baptism: November 03, 1805 in Cranston, Midlothian, Scotland[80]
Burial: December 1873 in Greenwood Cemetery, Tower City, Schuylkill Co, PA[83, 86]
Census: 1830
Census: 1840 in Norwegian, Schuylkill Co, PA[87]
Census: 1850 in Norwegian, Schuylkill Co, PA[51]
Census: 1860 in Porter, Schuylkill Co, PA[52]
Census: 1870 in Norwegian, Schuylkill Co, PA[53]
Immigration: July 09, 1827 in Scotland to New York, NY (ship Nimrod)[88, 89]
Naturalization: July 31, 1834 in Schuylkill Co, PA[90, 91]
Occupation: 1850 ; Farming[51]
Occupation: 1854 ; Laid out town of Sheridan, PA[83]
Occupation: 1860 ; Farmer[52]
Occupation: Abt. 1860 ; Superintendent (Potts & Co)[92]
Occupation: Bet. 1861-1873 ; Owner general store[93]
Occupation: Bet. 1865-1871 ; Contract work (Mines)[92]
Occupation: 1870 ; Laborer[53]
Occupation: ; Colliery owner[80]
Occupation: ; Teamster[80]
Political Party: Republican[94]
Probate: December 17, 1873 in Porter Tp, Schuylkill Co, PA[95]
Probate: January 25, 1912 in Porter Tp, Schuylkill Co, PA (after Mary Thompson's death)[95]
Property: 1850 in $2000[51]
Property: 1860 in $5000 + $230[52]
Residence: Abt. 1827 in Middleport, Schuylkill Co, PA[83]
Residence: Aft. 1828 in York Farm Burial Grounds, Pottsville, Schuylkill Co, PA[83]
Residence: 1854 in Porter, Schuylkill Co, PA[83]
Will: December 03, 1873 in Porter Tp, Schuylkill Co, PA[95]

Notes for Alexander Thompson:

Alexander Thompson was a native of Scotland, and came to this country during his young manhood. The rest of his life was spent in Schuylkill county, Pa., where he was widely and favorably known during his active, useful career. He first settled at Middleport, where he was engaged in hauling machinery, timber, etc., and later lived at the York Farm, near Pottsville, which he bought, cultivating that tract for many years. He also had small drifts opened on the property and sold coal to the public, this being the first coal taken from the workings later developed into the famous York Farm colliery. After a long residence there he removed to Porter Township, in 1854, being one of the early settlers in this section, where he bought a farm of no acres, from which he subsequently sold a number of building lots for the town of Sharadin [Sheridan], which was laid out in 1869. This was his home until his death, which occurred Dec. 4, 1873; he is buried in the Greenwood cemetery in Porter Township. Besides farming, Mr. Thompson also engaged in milling in Porter Township, building a gristmill upon his tract which was known in his day as Thompson's mill. It was sold to Grimm & Womer, and later to the Reading Company, the present owners of the land. Mr. Thompson was a man of intelligence and strong character, and in his day was one of the most influential men in this section. By his first marriage, to Isabella Pennman, Mr. Thompson had nine children: George was killed at York Farm; David P., deceased, was a soldier in the Civil war; Elizabeth, deceased, was the wife of Hiram Kimmel; Janette married Benjamin Houtz; William died while serving in the Civil war; Alexander is living at Lykens, Pa.; Robert is deceased; Isabella is the widow of George Powell; James is living in West Virginia. For his second wife Mr. T Thompson married Mary Bast, daughter of Isaac Bast, and by this union there was also a large family: Isaac B.; George, who is now living in Alaska; Mary, wife of Daniel Stout; John, residing at Sharadin, Pa.; Andrew, a resident of Michigan; Charles, deceased; Abraham, deceased; Winfield S., of Michigan; William U. S. G., deceased; Elmer E., of Sharadin; and Rebecca M., wife of Hoplin Evans, living on the old Thompson homestead in Porter township. [Schuylkill County, Pennsylvania, By J.H. Beers & Co, Beers (J. H.) and Company]

Thompson Homestead (Alexander), Porter Tp, Schuylkill, PA

Go to History of Schuylkill Co for more info:

More About Isabelle Stoddart Penman:
Burial: April 19, 1851 in York Farm Burial Grounds, Pottsville, Schuylkill Co, PA[96]
Census: 1830
Census: 1840 in husband; Norwegian, Schuylkill Co, PA w
Census: 1850 in Norwegian, Schuylkill Co, PA
Immigration: 1828[97]
Occupation: Abt. 1840 ; Homemaker
Occupation: ; Homemaker

Isabelle Stoddart Penman and Alexander Thompson had the following children:

    i.   George Thompson (son of Alexander Thompson and Isabelle Stoddart Penman) was born in 1835 in PA.

    ii.   Robert Thompson (son of Alexander Thompson and Isabelle Stoddart Penman) was born in 1836 in PA. He married Helen.

    iii.   David Penman Thompson (son of Alexander Thompson and Isabelle Stoddart Penman) was born in 1837 in PA. He died in 1912. He married "Cassie" Houtz. She was born in 1841 in PA. She died in 1883.

    iv.   William W Thompson (son of Alexander Thompson and Isabelle Stoddart Penman) was born in 1839 in PA. He married Mary A. She was born in 1836 in PA.

    v.   Elizabeth Thompson (daughter of Alexander Thompson and Isabelle Stoddart Penman) was born in 1841 in PA. She married Hiram Kimmel.

    vi.   Janet "Jennie" Thompson (daughter of Alexander Thompson and Isabelle Stoddart Penman) was born in 1844 in PA. She married Benjamin Houtz.

    vii.   Alexander F Thompson (son of Alexander Thompson and Isabelle Stoddart Penman) was born in 1845 in PA. He married Elizabeth Hawk. He married Mary A. She was born in 1867 in PA.

4.   viii. Robert Bruce Thompson (son of Alexander Thompson and Isabelle Stoddart Penman) was born on September 24, 1847 in York Farm Burial Grounds, Pottsville, Schuylkill Co, PA[45]. He died on October 10, 1907 in Tower City, Schuylkill Co, PA (Typhoid fever w/contaminated water[45, 46]). He married Lydia Ann Goodman (daughter of Michael Goodman and Mary Magdalena Brown) about Abt. 1873 in Schuylkill Co, PA. She was born on February 20, 1856 in Clarks Valley, Dauphin Co, PA[47]. She died on October 09, 1883 in Tower City, Schuylkill Co, PA (Complications of pregnancy[47, 48, 49]). He married Mary Margaret Moses. She was born in 1850.

           ix. Isabelle Thompson (daughter of Alexander Thompson and Isabelle Stoddart Penman) was born in 1849 in PA. She married George Powell.

           x. James C Thompson (son of Alexander Thompson and Isabelle Stoddart Penman) was born in 1851 in PA.

10. **Michael Goodman** (son of Jacob Guteman and Catherine Voller) was born on June 10, 1806 in Berks (Schuylkill), PA[98]. He died on December 27, 1900 in Rush, Dauphin Co, PA (Old age[98, 99]). He married **Mary Magdalena Brown** (daughter of Peter Brown and Anna Maria Schreckengast?) about Abt. 1832 in Schuylkill?, PA.

11. **Mary Magdalena Brown** (daughter of Peter Brown and Anna Maria Schreckengast?) was born in 1816 in Dauphin Co?, PA. She died on December 17, 1884 in Dauphin Co, PA[98].

More About Michael Goodman:
Burial: 1900 in Zion (Public Square) Lutheran Cemetery, Tower City, Schuylkill Co, PA[99]
Burial: 1900 in Orwin, Schuylkill Co, PA[100]
Census: 1810
Census: 1820
Census: 1830
Census: 1840 in Lower Mahantango, Schuylkill Co, PA[101]
Census: 1850 in Rush, Dauphin Co, PA[102]
Census: 1860 in Rush, Dauphin Co, PA[103]
Census: 1870 in Rush, Dauphin Co, PA[58]
Census: 1880 in Rush, Dauphin Co, PA[104]

Census: 1900 in Rush, Dauphin Co, PA (son William Goodman)[105]
Confirmation: July 1825 in Schuylkill Co, PA[98, 106]
Occupation: 1850 ; Carpenter[107]
Occupation: Bet. 1860-1880 ; Farmer[58, 108, 109]
Occupation: 1900 ; Retired[105]
Occupation: 1901 ; Farmer[99]
Probate: January 11, 1901 in Rush Tp, Dauphin Co, PA (listed in index only)[110]
Property: 1850 in $1000[107]
Property: 1860 in $1000 + $600[108]
Property: 1870 in $2000 + $200[111]

Notes for Michael Goodman:
Have photograph.

Married Barbara Remp [1901 Obituary, Jeff Brown, ntrprz@@dmv.com]

Michael Guteman was born June 10, 1806 and came to this valley as a young man and was confirmed in the old log church-school in July 1825, according to the old church records. He married Mary Magdalena Brown, a granddaughter of the original Peter Braun. Michael purchased the farm south of the Clark's Valley Road just east of the Dauphin County line and lived there until his death on December 27, 1900 at the grand age of ninety- four. His wife died December 17, 1884 and both are buried in the cemetery in the public square. In his later years he gave his farm to his son, William, who was b on November 20, 1835, and died January 30, 1907. He married Christina Hand, a daughter of John Hand, Jr. and they had the follow in g children: Catherine, who first married Lincoln Rhoads and on hi s death married Herman Niehenke; Ernaline, who married Elwood Showers; Mary, wife of Isaac Thompson; John; Lydia, married Nathan A. Reightler; George; Fayetta, married William Achenbach; Frank; Ellen, wife of William Novinger and David. John Goodman married Hannah Houtz and their children were Harry II, Charles E., Golda and Grace. Harry married Sadie P. Warfield and their children were Helen; Evelyn, married Frank Rosade; Lillian P.; John; stu art and Virginia, married J. Robert Hunsicker. Among the children of Ernaline Goodman Showers and her husband were Albert; Charles; Roy; Beulah, married George Schrope; Verna, married Robert Fegley. The children of Charles Showers were Lester; Helen; Anne, married Norman Unger; Violet and Lawrence. [Records of Jim Thompson, jbthompson@@compuserve.com]

A very pleasant and enjoyable affair was the reunion of the Goodman family, on Sunday, August 19th, at the residence of Mr. And Mrs. William Goodman, in Clarks Valley, which is also the birthplace of Mr. Goodman. The following were present: -- Mrs. Isaac Thompson and children, Paul, Russel and Leona, Sheridan; Mr. And Mrs. Elwood Showers and children, Charles, Beulah, Raymond, Emma, Verna and Albert, Tower City; Mr. And Mrs. David Goodman and children, Clarence and Elva, Orwin; Mrs. John Goodman and children, Harry, Charles and Golda, Orwin; Mrs. Wm. Achenbach and children, Harry, Roy and Frank of Phila.; Mrs. Catherine Rhoads and children, Charles, Oscar, Ira, Millie and Lloyd, Sheridan; Mr. And Mrs. Nathan Rightler and children, Emily and Willie, Tower City; Frank Goodman and son George, Orwin; George Goodman, Clarks Valley; Mr. an d Mrs. Wm. Novinger and daughter Hattie, Tower City.

Artist Rowland of Williamstown, photographed the group under an old cherry tree planted scores of years ago by great grandfather Michael Goodman, who was also in attendance. The family dinner was spread in bountiful manner under the ancient cherry tree, and a happy feast was enjoyed by all present, numbering 43 persons of the Goodman freund-schaft. At the planting of that cherry tree, great grandfather, Michael Goodman, who was 94 years of age in June, did not think of such a gathering under its branches, and as the venerable father offered thanks at the dinner table, he expressed the desire that they would all meet at the festal board of Heaven. May his desires be granted.

As the hour arrived for the happy parties to return to their respective homes, all seemed to realize that in the changing scenes of time, another such a gathering might never occur in this world. After 60 years of earthly pilgrimage, Mr. and Mrs. Wm. Goodman, were favored by a kind providence in the gathering of all their sons and daughters, with thirty of the grand children. It was an occasion of great joy of retrospective glances over the journey of life, and happy anticipations of a reunion in the golden world of eternal deliverance. It was such a day as expressed by the poet:

"Scattered o'er various fields by Heaven,
Through various pathways led,
What happiness in peace to meet
Around a common head!

The pleasures of the past recall,
And tell the tales again
It(s) infant dreams, and childhood joys,
And youth's delightful reign,
To plan the schemes of future bliss;
Rejoicing to confess,
That He whose love hath blessed the past
The future, too, will bless.""

[Tower City, Porter Township Centennial book, 1868-1968, Records of Jim Thompson, jbthompson@@compuserve.com]

Goodman, Gutmann: Americanized form of German Gutmann. Swiss German: literally good man, a term for the master of a household.

More About Mary Magdalena Brown:
Burial: 1884 in Zion (Public Square) Lutheran Cemetery, Tower City, Schuylkill Co, PA
Census: 1820 in Rush, Dauphin Co, PA (unlisted)[112]
Census: 1830 in father; Rush, Dauphin Co, PA w[113]
Census: 1840 in husband; Lower Mahantango, Schuylkill Co, PA w
Census: 1850 in Rush, Dauphin Co, PA
Census: 1860 in Rush, Dauphin Co, PA (Margaret)
Census: 1870 in Rush, Dauphin Co, PA[111]
Census: 1880 in Rush, Dauphin Co, PA
Occupation: 1870 ; Keeping house[111]
Occupation: 1880 ; Keeping house[104]

Notes for Mary Magdalena Brown:
Mary was named after her mother Maria [author, 2010]

Mary Magdalena Brown and Michael Goodman had the following children:

    i.   William Goodman (son of Michael Goodman and Mary Magdalena Brown) was born in 1835 in PA. He died in 1906. He married Christina "Dinah" Hand. She was born in 1835 in PA. She died in 1907.

    ii.   Susan Goodman (daughter of Michael Goodman and Mary Magdalena Brown) was born in 1837 in PA.

iii. Magdalena Goodman (daughter of Michael Goodman and Mary Magdalena Brown) was born in 1839 in PA.

iv. John Goodman (son of Michael Goodman and Mary Magdalena Brown) was born in 1841 in PA.

v. Mary Goodman (daughter of Michael Goodman and Mary Magdalena Brown) was born in 1843 in PA.

vi. Sarah "Sallie" Goodman (daughter of Michael Goodman and Mary Magdalena Brown) was born in 1844 in PA.

vii. Jane Goodman (daughter of Michael Goodman and Mary Magdalena Brown) was born in 1845 in PA.

viii. Catherine Goodman (daughter of Michael Goodman and Mary Magdalena Brown) was born in 1846 in PA.

ix. Anna Maria Goodman (daughter of Michael Goodman and Mary Magdalena Brown) was born in 1848 in PA.

x. Jacob Goodman (son of Michael Goodman and Mary Magdalena Brown) was born in 1849 in PA.

xi. George H Goodman (son of Michael Goodman and Mary Magdalena Brown) was born in 1853 in PA.

5. xii. Lydia Ann Goodman (daughter of Michael Goodman and Mary Magdalena Brown) was born on February 20, 1856 in Clarks Valley, Dauphin Co, PA[47]. She died on October 09, 1883 in Tower City, Schuylkill Co, PA (Complications of pregnancy[47, 48, 49]). She married Robert Bruce Thompson (son of Alexander Thompson and Isabelle Stoddart Penman) about Abt. 1873 in Schuylkill Co, PA. He was born on September 24, 1847 in York Farm Burial Grounds, Pottsville, Schuylkill Co, PA[45]. He died on October 10, 1907 in Tower City, Schuylkill Co, PA (Typhoid fever w/contaminated water[45, 46]).

12. **Andrew Guise Hensel** (son of Andrew W Hensel and Mary A Guise) was born on February 18, 1831 in Home, New Bloomfield, Perry Co, PA[60, 114, 115, 116]. He died on December 14, 1908 in Wiconisco, Dauphin Co, PA (Bright's disease (ie, Chronic inflammation of

kidneys) w/old age[60, 117]). He married **Catherine Workman** (daughter of Joseph Workman and Susan Romberger) on May 17, 1853 in Halifax, Dauphin Co, PA[114, 115].

13.   **Catherine Workman** (daughter of Joseph Workman and Susan Romberger) was born on May 17, 1838 in Old Lincoln, Dauphin Co, PA[60]. She died on February 10, 1877 in Joliett, Schuylkill Co, PA[60].

More About Andrew Guise Hensel:
b: February 20, 1832 in PA[118]
Burial: December 16, 1908 in Calvary United Methodist, Wiconisco, Dauphin Co, PA[60]
Census: 1840 in Perry Co, PA; Centre, Perry Co, PA w/father[119]
Census: 1850 in Centre, Perry Co, PA[120]
Census: 1860 in Porter, Schuylkill Co, PA (Hentzel)[68, 121]
Census: 1870 in Wiconisco, Dauphin Co, PA[69, 122]
Census: 1880 in Wiconisco, Dauphin Co, PA[123]
Census: 1900 in Wiconisco, Dauphin Co, PA (Weist-Heheel)[124]
Funeral: 1908 in John Reiff, Lykens, Dauphin Co, PA[117]
Military Service: August 28, 1864 in Pittsburgh); Civil War, Private, 155th Reg PA Inf, Co F (Harrisburg[125, 126]
Military Service: June 02, 1865 ; Civil War, Private, 191st Reg PA Inf, Co G (organized in fields)
Occupation: Bet. 1850-1900 ; Plasterer[73, 120, 127, 128, 129]
Occupation: Abt. 1850 ; Servant
Occupation: 1853 ; Plasterer[114, 115]
Occupation: 1900 ; Boarder[130]
Occupation: 1908 ; Mason & School teacher[117]
Property: 1860 in $250 + $123[127]
Property: 1870 in $340[131]
Religion: 1853 ; Methodist Episcopal[114]

Notes for Andrew Guise Hensel:
Have photograph.

Andrew was named after his father Andrew Hensel [author, 2010]

Andrew Hensel, Private, 47th Reg, Co F, NY Inf [Civil War to 1900 Pension index, footnote.com]

Andrew Henson [Union Inf, 107th Reg, PA. from Hbg, Civil War Soldiers & Sailors, www.itd.nps.gov/cwss/]

More About Catherine Workman:
Burial: 1877 in Calvary United Methodist, Wiconisco, Dauphin Co, PA[60]
Census: 1840 in family; Not listed w[132]
Census: 1850 in Wiconisco, Dauphin Co, PA[133]
Census: 1860 in Porter, Schuylkill Co, PA
Census: 1870 in Wiconisco, Dauphin Co, PA
Occupation: 1870 ; Keeping house[69]
Probate: May 24, 1878

Notes for Catherine Workman:
Have photograph.

Catherine Workman and Andrew Guise Hensel had the following children:

i. John Henry William Hensel (son of Andrew Guise Hensel and Catherine Workman) was born in 1853 in PA. He died about Abt. 1854.

ii. Joseph Franklin Hensel (son of Andrew Guise Hensel and Catherine Workman) was born in 1854 in PA. He died in 1909. He married Agnes A Faust. She was born in 1855 in PA. She died in 1932.

iii. Ira Sylvester Hensel (son of Andrew Guise Hensel and Catherine Workman) was born in 1856 in PA. He died in 1916. He married Sarah Elizabeth Day. She was born in 1859 in PA. She died in 1922.

6. iv. Howard Andrew Carson Hensel (son of Andrew Guise Hensel and Catherine Workman) was born on September 02, 1858 in Wiconisco, Dauphin Co, PA[60, 61, 62]. He died on June 06, 1927 in Tower City, Schuylkill Co, PA (Arteriosclerosis[60, 61, 62, 63]). He married Clara Matilda Updegrove (daughter of Daniel Updegrove and Sarah "Salome" A Culp) on September 02, 1884 in Wiconisco, Dauphin Co, PA[60, 62]. She was born on November 30, 1866 in Lower Ranch Creek, Tremont, Schuylkill Co, PA[60, 62].

She died on March 28, 1926 in Tower City, Schuylkill Co, PA (Metastatic carcinoma of medial atrium & left chest w/carcinoma breast[60, 62, 64]).

    v. Anna Catherine Hensel (daughter of Andrew Guise Hensel and Catherine Workman) was born about Abt. 1862 in PA.

    vi. Lillian "Lillie" Emma Susan Hensel (daughter of Andrew Guise Hensel and Catherine Workman) was born in 1864 in PA. She married David Alfred Boyer. He was born in 1860. He died in 1940.

    vii. Emma Hensel (daughter of Andrew Guise Hensel and Catherine Workman) was born in 1866 in PA.

    viii. Anne "Annie" Clarissa Workman Hensel (daughter of Andrew Guise Hensel and Catherine Workman) was born in 1866 in PA. She married Edward Beedle. He was born in 1863 in PA.

14. **Daniel Updegrove** (son of John M Updegrove and Elizabeth Trovinger) was born on June 28, 1839 in Wiconisco, Dauphin Co, PA[134, 135]. He died on March 25, 1899 in Williamstown, Dauphin Co, PA[135]. He married **Sarah "Salome" A Culp** (daughter of Jacob Kulp and Elizabeth Schneck) on October 09, 1862 in Dauphin Co, PA.

15. **Sarah "Salome" A Culp** (daughter of Jacob Kulp and Elizabeth Schneck) was born on June 30, 1844 in Union Co, PA[136]. She died on July 03, 1923 in Williamstown, Dauphin Co, PA (? due to carcinoma of shoulder (recurrent) w/secondary ?[136]).

More About Daniel Updegrove:
d: 1899 in Williamstown, Dauphin Co, PA; Suffocated by mine gas[137]
Burial: March 28, 1899 in Seyberts (Old) Lutheran, Williamstown, Dauphin Co, PA[134, 138]
Census: 1840 in father; Wiconisco, Dauphin Co, PA w
Census: 1850 in Wiconisco, Dauphin Co, PA[139, 140]
Census: 1860 in Brady, Lycoming Co, PA (Hullsizer)[141]
Census: 1870 in Williamstown, Dauphin Co, PA[76, 135, 142]
Census: 1880 in Williamstown, Dauphin Co, PA[77]
Education: 1850 ; School[143]
Height: ; 5 ft. 5 in.

Medical Condition: ; Hair sandy, Complexion Light, Eyes gray, Daniel Updegrove, Civil War Veterans Card File, 1861-1866, PA State Archives, www.digitalarchives.state.pa.us
Military Service: July 01, 1863 ; Civil War, Private
Military Service: August 16, 1864 ; Civil War, Private, 9th Reg PA Cav, Co B, 92nd Volunteers (Harrisburg, Capt. Edward Savage)[138, 144, 145, 146, 147]

Occupation: 1860 ; Blksmith App.[141]
Occupation: Bet. 1864-1865 ; Miner[148]
Occupation: 1870 ; Laborer in mine[76]
Occupation: 1880 ; Laborer[77]
Occupation: 1899 ; Miner (Brookside Colliery)[134]
Property: 1870 in $100[76]
Residence: Bet. 1864-1865 in Dauphin Co, PA[148]
Residence: 1890 in Tower City, Schuylkill Co, PA[146]

Notes for Daniel Updegrove:
1889May16, Pension App [Daniel Updegrave, Co B, 9 Reg, PA Cav, App #7-05327 Cert #737767 & App #530812, Cert #326251, footnote.com]

1890July10, Pension App [Daniel Updegrove, Co K, PA Militia, Inf, App #823939 & App #703246, footnote.com]

POW, 21 days, Libby Prison, Richmond, VA [Schuylkill Countians captured in the Civil War, rootsweb.com]

More About Sarah "Salome" A Culp:
Burial: July 06, 1923 in Seyberts (Old) Lutheran, Williamstown, Dauphin Co, PA[136]
Census: 1850 in West Buffalo, Union Co, PA[149]
Census: 1860 in Buffalo, Union Co, PA[150]
Census: 1870 in Williamstown, Dauphin Co, PA[76]
Census: 1880 in Williamstown, Dauphin Co, PA
Census: 1900[151]
Census: 1910 in Williamstown, Dauphin Co, PA (Shadel)[152]
Census: 1920 in Tower City, Schuylkill Co, PA (Weist)[153]
Education: 1850 ; School[154]
Funeral: 1923 in Aaron Ralphsson, Williamstown, Dauphin Co, PA[136]
Occupation: Bet. 1870-1880 ; Keeping house[76, 77]

Occupation: 1923 ; Domestic[136]
Pension: May 1899 in PA[155]
Probate: Bet. April 02-08 1927 in Harrisburg, Dauphin Co, PA[156]
Residence: 1910 in Pottsville St., Williams, Dauphin Co, PA[152]
Residence: 1920 in 25 West Grand Ave., Tower City, Schuylkill Co, PA[153]

Notes for Sarah "Salome" A Culp:
Have photograph.

Nee Hoffman [Updegrove family information, Updegrove Genealogy, PA State library]

Sarah "Salome" A Culp and Daniel Updegrove had the following children:

    i.   Anna M Updegrove (daughter of Daniel Updegrove and Sarah "Salome" A Culp) was born in 1864 in PA.

7.   ii.   Clara Matilda Updegrove (daughter of Daniel Updegrove and Sarah "Salome" A Culp) was born on November 30, 1866 in Lower Ranch Creek, Tremont, Schuylkill Co, PA[60, 62]. She died on March 28, 1926 in Tower City, Schuylkill Co, PA (Metastatic carcinoma of medial atrium & left chest w/carcinoma breast[60, 62, 64]). She married Howard Andrew Carson Hensel (son of Andrew Guise Hensel and Catherine Workman) on September 02, 1884 in Wiconisco, Dauphin Co, PA[60, 62]. He was born on September 02, 1858 in Wiconisco, Dauphin Co, PA[60, 61, 62]. He died on June 06, 1927 in Tower City, Schuylkill Co, PA (Arteriosclerosis[60, 61, 62, 63]).

    iii.   William Henry Updegrove (son of Daniel Updegrove and Sarah "Salome" A Culp) was born in 1870 in PA. He died in 1871. He married <No name>.

    iv.   Nora Jane Updegrove (daughter of Daniel Updegrove and Sarah "Salome" A Culp) was born in 1874 in PA. She married Henry L Shadel. He was born in 1865 in PA.

Generation 5

16. **Robert Thompson** (son of Robert Thomson and Mary Black) was born on June 27, 1771 in Edgehead, Cranston, Midlothian,

Scotland[79]. He died after Aft. 1811 in Scotland. He married **Janet Russell** (daughter of William Russell and Christina Moffatt) on April 22, 1791 in Borthwick, Newbattle, Midlothian, Scotland[47, 59, 79, 157].

17. **Janet Russell** (daughter of William Russell and Christina Moffatt) was born on December 21, 1766 in Newbattle, Midlothian, Scotland[47, 79]. She died after Aft. 1811 in Scotland.

More About Robert Thompson:
Occupation: Abt. 1810 ; Coalier (Earl of Stair)[79]
Occupation: ; Coal Overseer[80]

Notes for Robert Thompson:
Born Borthwick, Midlothian, Scotland, Thompson History, Jim Thompson, jbthompson@@compuserve.com, pp 4-11.
Born 1766, Thompson family information, John B. Linden, Lynden@@comcast.net.

Janet Russell and Robert Thompson had the following children:
- i. Christina Thompson (daughter of Robert Thompson and Janet Russell) was born in 1792 in Scotland. She married John King.

- ii. Robert Thompson (son of Robert Thompson and Janet Russell) was born in 1795 in Scotland. He married Elizabeth Wilson.

- iii. William Thompson (son of Robert Thompson and Janet Russell) was born in 1797 in Scotland. He married Anna Penman.

- iv. Mary Thompson (daughter of Robert Thompson and Janet Russell) was born in 1800 in Scotland. She married James Wilson.

- v. George W Thompson (son of Robert Thompson and Janet Russell) was born in 1802 in Scotland. He married Catherine Penman. She was born on July 12, 1802 in Newbattle, Midlothian, Scotland. He married Margaret McLeran. She was born in 1816.

vi. John Thompson (son of Robert Thompson and Janet Russell) was born in 1804 in Scotland.

8. vii. Alexander Thompson (son of Robert Thompson and Janet Russell) was born on October 22, 1805 in Sauchenside Farm, Cranston, Midlothian, Scotland[79, 80, 81, 82]. He died on December 04, 1873 in Tower City, Schuylkill Co, PA[59, 83, 84]. He married Isabelle Stoddart Penman (daughter of David Penman and Elizabeth Stoddart) on January 01, 1835 in Pottsville, Schuylkill Co, PA[79]. She was born on May 09, 1816 in Newbattle, Midlothian, Scotland[59]. She died on April 18, 1851 in Pottsville, Schuylkill Co, PA[85]. He married Mary A Bast in 1853. She was born in 1833 in PA. She died in 1910.

viii. John Thompson (son of Robert Thompson and Janet Russell) was born in 1808 in Scotland.

ix. James Smith Thompson (son of Robert Thompson and Janet Russell) was born in 1811 in Scotland.

18. **David Penman** (son of John Penman and Catherine Brown) was born on December 31, 1775 in Gladsmuir, East Lothian or, Newbattle, Midlothian, Scotland[97, 158]. He died about Abt. 1826 in Scotland[97]. He married **Elizabeth Stoddart** (daughter of David Stoddart and Margaret Muckle) about Abt. 1800 in Scotland.

19. **Elizabeth Stoddart** (daughter of David Stoddart and Margaret Muckle) was born on January 05, 1779 in Stobgreen Temple, Edinburgh, Midlothian, Scotland[97, 158]. She died on December 25, 1849 in Pottsville, Schuylkill Co, PA[97, 158].

Notes for David Penman:
Born 12/14/1775, Penman family information, John Penman, PenmanJC@@aol.com

More About Elizabeth Stoddart:
Burial: 1849 in Presbyterian Burial Grounds, Pottsville, Schuylkill Co, PA[159]
Census: 1830
Census: 1840 in Norwegian, Schuylkill Co, PA[160]

Census: 1841 in Liberton, Midlothian, Scotland[161]
Immigration: Bet. 1816-1830
Occupation: 1841 ; Pauper sup by children[161]

Notes for Elizabeth Stoddart:
Clear up Census discrepancy, 1840 PA, 1841 SCO [author, 2001]

Elizabeth Stoddart and David Penman had the following children:
  i.   John Penman (son of David Penman and Elizabeth
       Stoddart) was born on April 18, 1798 in Newbattle,
       Midlothian, Scotland[162].

  ii. Margaret Penman (daughter of David Penman and
       Elizabeth Stoddart) was born on July 20, 1800 in
       Newbattle, Midlothian, Scotland.

  iii. Catherine Penman (daughter of David Penman and
       Elizabeth Stoddart) was born on July 12, 1802 in
       Newbattle, Midlothian, Scotland. She married George W
       Thompson. He was born in 1802 in Scotland.

  iv. Elizabeth Penman (daughter of David Penman and
       Elizabeth Stoddart) was born on February 22, 1807 in
       Newbattle, Midlothian, Scotland.

  v.   Anne Penman (daughter of David Penman and Elizabeth
       Stoddart) was born on June 13, 1809 in Inveresk,
       Midlothian, Scotland.

  vi. James Penman (son of David Penman and Elizabeth
       Stoddart) was born on October 12, 1811 in Newbattle,
       Midlothian, Scotland.

9. vii. Isabelle Stoddart Penman (daughter of David Penman and
         Elizabeth Stoddart) was born on May 09, 1816 in
         Newbattle, Midlothian, Scotland[59]. She died on April 18,
         1851 in Pottsville, Schuylkill Co, PA[85]. She married
         Alexander Thompson (son of Robert Thompson and Janet
         Russell) on January 01, 1835 in Pottsville, Schuylkill Co,
         PA[79]. He was born on October 22, 1805 in Sauchenside
         Farm, Cranston, Midlothian, Scotland[79, 80, 81, 82]. He died on
         December 04, 1873 in Tower City, Schuylkill Co, PA[59, 83,]

    viii. Alexander Penman (son of David Penman and Elizabeth Stoddart) was born on October 24, 1820 in Newbattle, Midlothian, Scotland.

    ix. Robert Penman (son of David Penman and Elizabeth Stoddart) was born on December 11, 1824 in Newbattle, Midlothian, Scotland.

    x. Miriam Penman (daughter of David Penman and Elizabeth Stoddart) was born in Scotland.

20. **Jacob Guteman** was born in 1780 in PA[163]. He died on November 21, 1844 in PA[163]. He married **Catherine Voller** on April 26, 1801 in Exerter, Berks Co, PA[164].

21. **Catherine Voller** was born in 1780 in PA. She died in 1806 in PA.

More About Jacob Guteman:
b: Abt. 1775

More About Catherine Voller:
b: Abt. 1775 in PA

Notes for Catherine Voller:
Also Catherine Voller

Catherine Voller and Jacob Guteman had the following children:

    i. George? Goodman (son of Jacob Guteman and Catherine Voller) was born about Abt. 1800 in PA. He married Catherine. She was born in 1820 in PA.

    ii. John? Goodman (son of Jacob Guteman and Catherine Voller) was born about Abt. 1805.

10.   iii. Michael Goodman (son of Jacob Guteman and Catherine Voller) was born on June 10, 1806 in Berks (Schuylkill), PA[98]. He died on December 27, 1900 in Rush, Dauphin Co, PA (Old age[98, 99]). He married Mary Magdalena Brown (daughter of Peter Brown and Anna Maria

Schreckengast?) about Abt. 1832 in Schuylkill?, PA. She was born in 1816 in Dauphin Co?, PA. She died on December 17, 1884 in Dauphin Co, PA[98]. He married Barbara Remp.

22. **Peter Brown** (son of Peter Braun and Catherine) was born in 1775 in Berks (Schuylkill) Co, PA[165]. He died in 1861 in Rush, Dauphin Co, PA[165]. He married **Anna Maria Schreckengast?** about Abt. 1812 in Dauphin Co?, PA.

23. **Anna Maria Schreckengast?** was born on June 15, 1795 in Dauphin Co, PA[166]. She died on April 10, 1879 in Rush, Dauphin Co, PA[166].

More About Peter Brown:
Census: 1790[167]
Census: 1800[168]
Census: 1810 in father; Lower Mahantango, Berks Co, PA w[169]
Census: 1820 in Rush, Dauphin Co, PA[170]
Census: 1830 in Rush, Dauphin Co, PA[171]
Census: 1840 in Rush, Dauphin Co, PA[172]
Census: 1850 in Rush, Dauphin Co, PA[173, 174]
Occupation: Abt. 1835 ; Laborer
Occupation: 1850 ; Weaver[173]
Property: 1850 in $100[175]
Residence: 1916 in Clarks Valley, PA, now Charles Kessler farm[176]

Notes for Peter Brown:
Born DEU, Brown household, 1850 United States Census, Dauphin Co, PA, p 336, Kathleen M. Fagnani, katfagn@@erols.com

More About Anna Maria Schreckengast?:
Burial: April 1879 in McCallister's Methodist Cemetery, Rush, Dauphin Co, PA[177]
Census: 1810
Census: 1820 in husband; Rush, Dauphin Co, PA w
Census: 1830 in husband; Rush, Dauphin Co, PA w
Census: 1840 in husband; Rush, Dauphin Co, PA w
Census: 1850 in Rush, Dauphin Co, PA
Census: 1860 in Rush, Dauphin Co, PA (son John Brown)[178]
Census: 1870

Immigration: Bet. 1797-1820

Notes for Anna Maria Schreckengast?:
Maiden name maybe Lewis.

Born PA, 1860 Census.

Note: Burial listed prior to death

Anna Maria Schreckengast? and Peter Brown had the following children:

    i.   John Brown (son of Peter Brown and Anna Maria Schreckengast?) was born in 1812 in PA. He married Catherine Hautz?.

    ii.   Peter Brown (son of Peter Brown and Anna Maria Schreckengast?) was born in 1814 in PA. He married Anna Maria. She was born in 1810 in PA.

    iii. Anna Maria Brown (daughter of Peter Brown and Anna Maria Schreckengast?) was born on February 17, 1815 in Clarks Valley, Dauphin Co, PA[166]. She died on September 07, 1891 in Dauphin, PA[166]. She married William Miller. He was born in 1813 in PA.

11. iv.   Mary Magdalena Brown (daughter of Peter Brown and Anna Maria Schreckengast?) was born in 1816 in Dauphin Co?, PA. She died on December 17, 1884 in Dauphin Co, PA[98]. She married Michael Goodman (son of Jacob Guteman and Catherine Voller) about Abt. 1832 in Schuylkill?, PA. He was born on June 10, 1806 in Berks (Schuylkill), PA[98]. He died on December 27, 1900 in Rush, Dauphin Co, PA (Old age[98, 99]).

    v.   William Brown (son of Peter Brown and Anna Maria Schreckengast?) was born in 1818 in PA. He married Ellen Updegrove. She was born about Abt. 1812 in PA.

    vi.   Philip Brown (son of Peter Brown and Anna Maria Schreckengast?) was born in 1821 in PA.

    vii. Elizabeth Brown (daughter of Peter Brown and Anna Maria Schreckengast?) was born in 1830 in PA.

24. **Andrew W Hensel** (son of John Casper Hensel and Maria Eva) was born on June 28, 1793 in Littlestown, York (Adams) Co, PA[179, 180]. He died on July 07, 1875 in Home, New Bloomfield, Perry Co, PA[181, 182]. He married **Mary A Guise** (daughter of John Adam Guise and Maria?) about Abt. 1814 in Adams, PA[116].

25. **Mary A Guise** (daughter of John Adam Guise and Maria?) was born on December 16, 1791 in Northampton Co, PA. She died on January 16, 1877 in Perry Co, PA[183, 184].

More About Andrew W Hensel:
Baptism: August 11, 1793 in Christ Reformed, Littlestown, York (Adams) Co, PA[179, 180]
Burial: July 1875 in St. Peters (Christ, Old Union) Cemetery, New Bloomfield, Perry Co, PA[116, 185]
Census: 1800 in father; Maheim, York Co, PA w[186]
Census: 1810 in parents; w
Census: 1820 in Mount Joy, Adams Co, PA (Hensle)[187]
Census: 1830 in Juniata, Perry Co, PA[188]
Census: 1840 in Centre, Perry Co, PA (Hensley)[189]
Census: 1850 in Centre, Perry Co, PA[120]
Census: 1860 in Centre, Perry Co, PA (Miller)[190]
Census: 1870 in Centre, Perry Co, PA (Hentzelle)[191]
Military Service: February 1814 ; War of 1812, Private, 5th Reg PA Militia (Fentons), detachment (Adams, Capt. John McMillan)[116, 181, 192]
Occupation: 1850 ; Laborer[120]
Occupation: Bet. 1850-1855 ; Deacon (Christ's Church, Bloomfield, Perry Co, PA)[193]
Occupation: 1860 ; Farmer[190]
Occupation: Abt. 1865 ; Hostler
Occupation: 1870 ; Laborer[191]
Probate: August 13, 1875 in Perry Co, PA[194]
Probate: May 24, 1878 in Dauphin Co, PA[195]
Property: 1850 in $450[196]
Property: 1860 in $800 + $300[197]
Property: 1870 in $500 + $120[191]
Religion: 1875 ; Lutheran & German Reformed Church[116, 181]
Residence: 1823 in near Gettysburg, Adams Co, PA[198]
Will: Bet. March-December 1864 in Centre, Perry Co, PA[194]

Notes for Andrew W Hensel:
Democrat, Andrew Hensel, Death of an Old Soldier, Obituary, New Bloomfield newspaper, July 1875.

More About Mary A Guise:
Burial: January 1877 in St. Peters (Christ, Old Union) Cemetery, New Bloomfield, Perry Co, PA[116, 199]
Census: 1800 in parents; w[200]
Census: 1810 in parents; w[201]
Census: 1820 in husband; Mount Joy, Adams Co, PA w[202]
Census: 1830 in husband; Juniata, Perry Co, PA w
Census: 1840 in husband; Centre, Perry Co, PA w
Census: 1850 in Centre, Perry Co, PA
Census: 1860 in Centre, Perry Co, PA
Census: 1870 in Centre, Perry Co, PA
Occupation: 1870 ; Invalid[191]

Notes for Mary A Guise:
Youngest of 12 children, Hensel Family information, History of Michael Hensel (Hentzel) Sr. & His Related Families, R. Longtin-Thompson.

Mary A Guise and Andrew W Hensel had the following children:

    i.   John Adam Hensel (son of Andrew W Hensel and Mary A Guise) was born in 1814 in PA. He married Anna Maria Haverstick.

    ii.   Anna Maria Barbara Hensel (daughter of Andrew W Hensel and Mary A Guise) was born in 1820 in PA. She died about Abt. 1890. She married David Swartz. He was born in 1816 in PA.

    iii.   John Hensel (son of Andrew W Hensel and Mary A Guise) was born in 1824 in Perry Co, PA. He died in Lykens, Dauphin Co, PA. He married Susan Moyer. She was born in 1833 in PA.

    iv.   George Hensel (son of Andrew W Hensel and Mary A Guise) was born in 1825 in Perry Co, PA. He died in IL.

12.   v.   Andrew Guise Hensel (son of Andrew W Hensel and Mary

A Guise) was born on February 18, 1831 in Home, New Bloomfield, Perry Co, PA[60, 114, 115, 116]. He died on December 14, 1908 in Wiconisco, Dauphin Co, PA (Bright's disease (ie, Chronic inflammation of kidneys) w/old age[60, 117]). He married Catherine Workman (daughter of Joseph Workman and Susan Romberger) on May 17, 1853 in Halifax, Dauphin Co, PA[114, 115]. She was born on May 17, 1838 in Old Lincoln, Dauphin Co, PA[60]. She died on February 10, 1877 in Joliett, Schuylkill Co, PA[60]. He married Grace Arrison. She was born in 1823. She died in 1893[78].

vi. Michael Hensel (son of Andrew W Hensel and Mary A Guise) was born in 1834 in Perry Co, PA. He married Elizabeth. She was born in 1837 in PA.

Notes for Michael Hensel:
Reverend

26. **Joseph Workman** (son of <No name>) was born on December 03, 1795 in Lykens, Dauphin Co, PA[60, 203]. He died on May 23, 1857 in Dauphin Co, PA[60, 203, 204]. He married **Susan Romberger** (daughter of Balthasar Romberger and Susan Lehman) about Abt. 1818 in Dauphin Co, PA.

27. **Susan Romberger** (daughter of Balthasar Romberger and Susan Lehman) was born on April 16, 1799 in Lykens, Dauphin Co, PA[60, 203, 205, 206]. She died on February 23, 1857 in Dauphin Co, PA[60, 205].

More About Joseph Workman:
Burial: 1857 in Calvary United Methodist, Wiconisco, Dauphin Co, PA[60, 203, 204]
Census: 1800
Census: 1810
Census: 1820 in Lykens, Dauphin Co, PA[207]
Census: 1830 in Lykens, Dauphin Co, PA (James)[208]
Census: 1840 in Wiconisco, Dauphin Co, PA[132]
Census: 1850 in Wiconisco, Dauphin Co, PA[133, 209]
Confirmation: 1827 in Zion Union, Tower City, Schuylkill Co, PA
Military Service: Bet. September 01, 1814-March 05, 1825 ; War of 1812, Private, 2nd Reg PA Militia (Ritschers), 1st Brig (York, Capt.

Jacob District)
Occupation: 1820 ; Agriculture[207]
Occupation: 1850 ; Farmer[133]
Occupation: Abt. 1850 ; School director
Probate: June 18, 1857 in Dauphin Co, PA (listed in index only)[210]
Property: 1850 in $294[133]
Religion: 1819 ; St. Johns (Hill) Lutheran, Lykens, Dauphin Co, PA[211]

More About Susan Romberger:
Baptism: July 07, 1799 in St. Johns (Hill) Lutheran, Berrysburg, Dauphin Co, PA[65]
Burial: 1857 in Calvary United Methodist, Wiconisco, Dauphin Co, PA[60]
Census: 1800 in father; Upper Paxton, Dauphin Co, PA w[212]
Census: 1810 in father; Upper Paxton, Dauphin Co, PA w[213]
Census: 1820 in husband; Lykens, Dauphin Co, PA w
Census: 1830
Census: 1840 in husband; Wiconisco, Dauphin Co, PA w
Census: 1850 in Wiconisco, Dauphin Co, PA
Confirmation: 1827 in Zion Union, Tower City, Schuylkill Co, PA
Religion: ; Upper Paxton, Dauphin Co, PA[205]

Notes for Susan Romberger:
Nee Myers, Hensel family information, Dauphin Co Marriages, 1852-1855, CAGS.
Baptism April 16, 1799 Balthaser & Elizabeth, St. Johns (Hill) Church, Lykens, Dauphin Co, PA, PA Births, Dauphin County, J. Humphrey.

Susan Romberger and Joseph Workman had the following children:

    i.   Jacob Workman (son of Joseph Workman and Susan Romberger) was born in 1819 in Dauphin Co, PA. He married Mary. She was born in 1826 in PA.

    ii.   Susan Workman (daughter of Joseph Workman and Susan Romberger) was born in 1821 in Dauphin Co, PA. She married David S Doebler. He was born in 1816. He died in 1869. She married Louis A Greshammer. He was born in 1835. He died in 1870.

    iii.   John Workman (son of Joseph Workman and Susan Romberger) was born in 1823 in PA. He died in 1858. He married Sidnam. She was born in 1824 in PA.

    iv. Nancy Workman (daughter of Joseph Workman and Susan Romberger) was born in 1826 in PA. She married Emmanuel Sassaman. He was born in 1827 in PA. She married Henry Singer. He was born in 1825.

    v. Elizabeth Workman (daughter of Joseph Workman and Susan Romberger) was born in 1829 in Dauphin Co, PA. She married Isaac Smink. He was born in 1828 in PA.

    vi. Carolina Workman (daughter of Joseph Workman and Susan Romberger) was born in 1831 in PA.

    vii. Joseph R Workman (son of Joseph Workman and Susan Romberger) was born in 1836 in PA. He died in 1916. He married Susan. She was born in 1838 in PA. She died in 1899.

13.   viii. Catherine Workman (daughter of Joseph Workman and Susan Romberger) was born on May 17, 1838 in Old Lincoln, Dauphin Co, PA[60]. She died on February 10, 1877 in Joliett, Schuylkill Co, PA[60]. She married Andrew Guise Hensel (son of Andrew W Hensel and Mary A Guise) on May 17, 1853 in Halifax, Dauphin Co, PA[114, 115]. He was born on February 18, 1831 in Home, New Bloomfield, Perry Co, PA[60, 114, 115, 116]. He died on December 14, 1908 in Wiconisco, Dauphin Co, PA (Bright's disease (ie, Chronic inflammation of kidneys) w/old age[60, 117]).

    ix. ? Workman (son of Joseph Workman and Susan Romberger). He married Juliana. She was born in 1841 in Ireland (PA).

28. **John M Updegrove** (son of Conrad Updegrove and Maria Elizabeth Angst) was born on March 23, 1805 in Pine Grove, Berks (Schylkill) Co, PA[214, 215]. He died in 1864 in Somerset County, PA[215]. He married **Elizabeth Trovinger** in 1823 in Dauphin Co, PA[216].

29. **Elizabeth Trovinger** was born about Abt. 1798 in Somerset County, PA[216]. She died between 1860-1870 in Berks Co, PA (Apoplexy (ie, Paralysis due to stroke)[216]).

More About John M Updegrove:
Baptism: April 14, 1805 in St. Jacobs Lutheran, Pine Grove, Berks (Schuylkill) Co, PA[214]
Census: 1810 in father; Jonestown, Dauphin (Lebanon) Co, PA w[217]
Census: 1820 in father; Lykens, Dauphin Co, PA w[218]
Census: 1830[219]
Census: 1840 in Wiconisco, Dauphin Co, PA[220]
Census: 1850 in Wiconisco, Dauphin Co, PA[140, 143]
Census: 1860 in Clinton, Lycoming Co, PA[221]
Occupation: 1850 ; Labor[143]
Occupation: 1860 ; Laborer[221]
Property: 1850 in $500[143]

More About Elizabeth Trovinger:
Census: 1810
Census: 1820
Census: 1830 in husband; w
Census: 1840 in husband; Wiconisco, Dauphin Co, PA w
Census: 1850 in Wiconisco, Dauphin Co, PA
Census: 1860 in Clinton, Lycoming Co, PA

Elizabeth Trovinger and John M Updegrove had the following children:

    i.   Jacob Updegrove (son of John M Updegrove and Elizabeth Trovinger) was born in 1827 in PA. He married Sophia. She was born in 1835 in PA.

    ii.   Catherine Updegrove (daughter of John M Updegrove and Elizabeth Trovinger) was born in 1833 in PA.

    iii.   John J Updegrove (son of John M Updegrove and Elizabeth Trovinger) was born in 1835 in PA. He died in 1901. He married Elizabeth. She was born in 1839 in OH.

    iv.   Nancy Updegrove (daughter of John M Updegrove and Elizabeth Trovinger) was born in 1838 in PA.

14.   v.   Daniel Updegrove (son of John M Updegrove and Elizabeth Trovinger) was born on June 28, 1839 in Wiconisco, Dauphin Co, PA[134, 135]. He died on March 25, 1899 in Williamstown, Dauphin Co, PA[135]. He married Sarah "Salome" A Culp (daughter of Jacob Kulp and

Elizabeth Schneck) on October 09, 1862 in Dauphin Co, PA. She was born on June 30, 1844 in Union Co, PA[136]. She died on July 03, 1923 in Williamstown, Dauphin Co, PA (? due to carcinoma of shoulder (recurrent) w/secondary ?[136]).

    vi. Solomon Updegrove (son of John M Updegrove and Elizabeth Trovinger) was born in 1845 in PA. He died in 1864.

    vii. Rebecca Updegrove (daughter of John M Updegrove and Elizabeth Trovinger) was born in 1847 in PA.

30. **Jacob Kulp** (son of <No name> and <No name>) was born about Abt. 1802 in PA. He died about Abt. 1865 in Union Co, PA. He married **Elizabeth Schneck** (daughter of Peter Schneck and Mary) about Abt. 1835 in Union Co, PA.

31. **Elizabeth Schneck** (daughter of Peter Schneck and Mary) was born on August 13, 1805 in Northumberland (Union) Co, PA[222]. She died on June 02, 1861 in Union Co, PA[222].

More About Jacob Kulp:
Census: 1810
Census: 1820
Census: 1830 in parents; w
Census: 1840
Census: 1850 in West Buffalo, Union Co, PA[149, 222, 223]
Census: 1860 in Buffalo, Union Co, PA[150]
Occupation: 1850 ; Carpenter[149, 223]
Occupation: 1860 ; Laborer[224]
Property: 1850 in $120[154]
Property: 1860 in $100[224]

Notes for Jacob Kulp:
Kulp, Kolb: Variant of German Kolb or Kalb. German: habitational name from Kulpin in Mecklenburg. German: from Middle High German kolbe in various meanings. The main sense is 'mace' or 'cudgel', which was both a weapon and part of an official's insignia, in some cases the insignia of a jester. It may also be a house name: there is also record of a house named 'zum Kolben' in Strasbourg. In

Silesia the term denoted a shock of hair or a shorn head. Any of these senses could have given rise to the surname.

More About Elizabeth Schneck:
Burial: 1861
Census: 1810 in father; Centre, Northumberland (Union) Co, PA w[225]
Census: 1820 in parents; w[226]
Census: 1830 in parents; w
Census: 1840
Census: 1850 in West Buffalo, Union Co, PA
Census: 1860 in Buffalo, Union Co, PA
Occupation: Abt. 1840 ; Homemaker

Elizabeth Schneck and Jacob Kulp had the following children:

     i.   Jonas Culp (son of Jacob Kulp and Elizabeth Schneck) was born in 1839 in PA.

    ii.   Elizabeth Culp (daughter of Jacob Kulp and Elizabeth Schneck) was born in 1842 in PA.

15.   iii.   Sarah "Salome" A Culp (daughter of Jacob Kulp and Elizabeth Schneck) was born on June 30, 1844 in Union Co, PA[136]. She died on July 03, 1923 in Williamstown, Dauphin Co, PA (? due to carcinoma of shoulder (recurrent) w/secondary ?[136]). She married Daniel Updegrove (son of John M Updegrove and Elizabeth Trovinger) on October 09, 1862 in Dauphin Co, PA. He was born on June 28, 1839 in Wiconisco, Dauphin Co, PA[134, 135]. He died on March 25, 1899 in Williamstown, Dauphin Co, PA[135].

    iv.   Fielta Culp (daughter of Jacob Kulp and Elizabeth Schneck) was born in 1848 in PA.

    v.   Living Culp (daughter of Jacob Kulp and Elizabeth Schneck).

    vi.   Living Culp (daughter of Jacob Kulp and Elizabeth Schneck).

Generation 6

32. Robert Thomson (son of Robert Thomson and Isabelle Cochran)

---

was born on September 13, 1734[79, 80] in Cranston, Midlothian, Scotland. He died after Aft. 1779 in Scotland. He married **Mary Black** (daughter of George Black and Mary Helen Smith) about Abt. 1760 in Scotland[79].

33. **Mary Black** (daughter of George Black and Mary Helen Smith) was born in 1737 in Prestonpans, East Lothian, Scotland[79]. She died after Aft. 1779 in Scotland.

More About Robert Thomson:
Baptism: September 15, 1734 in Cranston, Midlothian, Scotland[80, 227]
Occupation: Abt. 1760 in Collier; Coal miner[79]
Occupation: 1767 ; Overseer (Coal mine)[79]
Residence: Abt. 1750 in Lasswade, Duddingston, Borthwick, Midlothian, Scotland[79]

Notes for Mary Black:
Born 1760, Thompson family information, John L. linden, jllinden@@comcast.net.

Mary Black and Robert Thomson had the following children:
  i. Helen Thompson (daughter of Robert Thomson and Mary Black) was born in 1761 in Scotland.

  ii. Isabelle Thompson (daughter of Robert Thomson and Mary Black) was born in 1761 in Scotland.

  iii. Elizabeth Thompson (daughter of Robert Thomson and Mary Black) was born in 1763 in Scotland.

  iv. Mary Thompson (daughter of Robert Thomson and Mary Black) was born in 1764 in Scotland.

  v. Helen Thompson (daughter of Robert Thomson and Mary Black) was born in 1767 in Scotland.

16. vi. Robert Thompson (son of Robert Thomson and Mary Black) was born on June 27, 1771 in Edgehead, Cranston, Midlothian, Scotland[79]. He died after Aft. 1811 in Scotland. He married Janet Russell (daughter of William Russell and Christina Moffatt) on April 22, 1791 in Borthwick,

Newbattle, Midlothian, Scotland[47, 59, 79, 157]. She was born on December 21, 1766 in Newbattle, Midlothian, Scotland[47, 79]. She died after Aft. 1811 in Scotland.

    vii. George Thompson (son of Robert Thomson and Mary Black) was born in 1773 in Scotland. He married Mary Russell.

    viii. Mary Thompson (daughter of Robert Thomson and Mary Black) was born in 1775 in Scotland.

    ix. Nicole Thompson (daughter of Robert Thomson and Mary Black) was born in 1777 in Scotland.

    x. Anna Thompson (daughter of Robert Thomson and Mary Black) was born in 1779 in Scotland. She married William Russell.

34. **William Russell** (son of John Russell and Janet Malcolm) was born on September 28, 1725 in Midlothian, Scotland[228]. He died in 1792 in Newbattle, Scotland[228]. He married **Christina Moffatt** (daughter of David Moffatt and Agnes Keitchen) on January 13, 1750 in Edinburgh, Midlothian, Scotland[97, 229].

35. **Christina Moffatt** (daughter of David Moffatt and Agnes Keitchen) was born on December 11, 1731 in Dalkeith, Midlothian, Scotland[79, 97, 228, 229]. She died after Aft. 1766 in Scotland.

More About Christina Moffatt:
Baptism: December 19, 1731 in Dalkeith, Midlothian, Scotland[229]

Notes for Christina Moffatt:
Born Newcastle, Thompson History, Jim Thompson, jbthompson@@compuserve.com, pp 4-11.

Christina Moffatt and William Russell had the following children:

    i. Mary Russell (daughter of William Russell and Christina Moffatt) was born about Abt. 1755 in Scotland.

    ii. William Russell (son of William Russell and Christina Moffatt) was born about Abt. 1755 in Scotland.

17.   iii.   Janet Russell (daughter of William Russell and Christina Moffatt) was born on December 21, 1766 in Newbattle, Midlothian, Scotland[47, 79]. She died after Aft. 1811 in Scotland. She married Robert Thompson (son of Robert Thomson and Mary Black) on April 22, 1791 in Borthwick, Newbattle, Midlothian, Scotland[47, 59, 79, 157]. He was born on June 27, 1771 in Edgehead, Cranston, Midlothian, Scotland[79]. He died after Aft. 1811 in Scotland.

       iv.   Living Russell (daughter of William Russell and Christina Moffatt).

36.   **John Penman** (son of James Penman and Jean Hamilton) was born on April 08, 1747 in Lassware, Midlothian, Scotland[230]. He died after Aft. 1775 in Scotland. He married **Catherine Brown** (daughter of Robert Brown and Isabelle Wilson) on October 28, 1763 in Lassware, Midlothian, Scotland[231, 232].

37.   **Catherine Brown** (daughter of Robert Brown and Isabelle Wilson) was born about Abt. 1747 in Liberton, Midlothian, Scotland[233]. She died after Aft. 1775 in Scotland.

Catherine Brown and John Penman had the following child:

18.   i.   David Penman (son of John Penman and Catherine Brown) was born on December 31, 1775 in Gladsmuir, East Lothian or, Newbattle, Midlothian, Scotland[97, 158]. He died about Abt. 1826 in Scotland[97]. He married Elizabeth Stoddart (daughter of David Stoddart and Margaret Muckle) about Abt. 1800 in Scotland. She was born on January 05, 1779 in Stobgreen Temple, Edinburgh, Midlothian, Scotland[97, 158]. She died on December 25, 1849 in Pottsville, Schuylkill Co, PA[97, 158].

38.   **David Stoddart** (son of John Stoddart and Margaret Bowman) was born on May 19, 1754 in Newbattle, Midlothian, Scotland[234]. He died after Aft. 1779 in Scotland. He married **Margaret Muckle** (daughter of Thomas Muckle and Elizabeth Mason) on February 16, 1778 in Cockpen, Midlothian, Scotland[235].

39.   **Margaret Muckle** (daughter of Thomas Muckle and Elizabeth Mason) was born on November 05, 1756 in Cockpen, Midlothian, Scotland. She died after Aft. 1779 in Scotland.

More About David Stoddart:
Baptism: May 25, 1755 in Newbattle, Midlothian, Scotland[236]

Notes for Margaret Muckle:
Muckle: English (Northumberland) Co: nickname for a big man, from Middle English muchel 'big' (Old English mycel).

Margaret Muckle and David Stoddart had the following child:

19.   i.   Elizabeth Stoddart (daughter of David Stoddart and Margaret Muckle) was born on January 05, 1779 in Stobgreen Temple, Edinburgh, Midlothian, Scotland[97, 158]. She died on December 25, 1849 in Pottsville, Schuylkill Co, PA[97, 158]. She married David Penman (son of John Penman and Catherine Brown) about Abt. 1800 in Scotland. He was born on December 31, 1775 in Gladsmuir, East Lothian or, Newbattle, Midlothian, Scotland[97, 158]. He died about Abt. 1826 in Scotland[97].

44.   **Peter Braun** (son of John Philip Braun and Elisabeth Magdalena Losch) was born about Abt. 1745 in Rhineland-Palatinate, Germany. He died in 1835 in Son Philip's home, Tower City, Schuylkill Co, PA. He married **Catherine** about Abt. 1775.

45.   **Catherine** was born about Abt. 1760. She died between 1820-1830 in Dauphin Co, PA.

More About Peter Braun:
Census: 1800
Census: 1810 in Lower Mahantango, Berks Co, PA[169]
Census: 1820 in Rush, Dauphin Co, PA[237]
Census: 1830 in Lower Mahantango, Schuylkill Co, PA (son Philip Brown)[171]
Immigration: 1770 in his 2 brothers); Germany to VA (w
Military Service: ; 1775 American Revolution, Private Co B (British Army)[176, 238]
Occupation: ; Servant (General George Washington, Mt. Vernon)
Occupation: ; Teamster (Philadelphia to Pittsburgh)
Religion: ; Lutheran, Host Church (Yohst), Berks Co, PA
Residence: 1765 in Alsace, France[239]
Residence: Bet. 1775-1800 in VA

More About Catherine:
Census: 1810 in husband; Lower Mahantango, Berks Co, PA w
Census: 1820 in husband; Rush, Dauphin Co, PA w

Catherine and Peter Braun had the following children:

22.   i.   Peter Brown (son of Peter Braun and Catherine) was born in 1775 in Berks (Schuylkill) Co, PA[165]. He died in 1861 in Rush, Dauphin Co, PA[165]. He married Anna Maria Schreckengast? about Abt. 1812 in Dauphin Co?, PA. She was born on June 15, 1795 in Dauphin Co, PA[166]. She died on April 10, 1879 in Rush, Dauphin Co, PA[166].

        ii.   Philip Brown (son of Peter Braun and Catherine) was born about Abt. 1788 in PA. He married Catherine "Kate" Swab. She was born in 1788 in PA. She died in Dauphin Co, PA.

        iii.   Jonas Brown (son of Peter Braun and Catherine) was born about Abt. 1790 in PA.

        iv.   Brown (daughter of Peter Braun and Catherine) was born in PA. She married U Reedy. He was born about Abt. 1780.

        v.   Brown (daughter of Peter Braun and Catherine) was born in PA. She married Snoke. He was born about Abt. 1780.

48.   **John Casper Hensel** (son of Casper Hensel and Maria Salome Walter) was born on September 30, 1764 in Richmond, York Co, PA[240]. He died in January 1804 in Manheim Tp, Adams Co, PA[116, 241, 242, 243]. He married **Maria Eva** about Abt. 1789 in York Co, PA.

49.   **Maria Eva** was born about Abt. 1765 in PA[244]. She died between 1800-1802 in Adams Co, PA[245].

More About John Casper Hensel:
Baptism: September 30, 1764 in St. Peters Reformed, Richmond, York Co, PA[240]
Burial: 1804
Census: 1790
Census: 1800 in Manheim, York Co, PA[244]
Confirmation: April 21, 1776 in Christ Church, Littlestown, York (Adams) Co, PA[246, 247]

Military Service: Abt. 1780 ; American Revolution, Private PA Reg, 4th Co, ? class (York, Capt. Martin Will)[248, 249]
Occupation: Bet. 1799-1800 ; Weaver[250, 251]
Probate: January 03, 1805 in Manheim, York Co, PA[252, 253, 254]
Residence: Bet. 1778-1795 in York Co, PA[255]
Residence: Bet. 1798-1799 in Mt. Pleasant, York Co, PA[250]
Will: April 28, 1800 in Manheim, York Co, PA[251]

Notes for John Casper Hensel:
also Bp Richmond Tp, BERKS Co, PA [Hensel Family Information, H Andrew Brown, Los Angeles, CA, habraun2@@netscape.net, Jan 2009]

More About Maria Eva:
Census: 1790 in husband; w
Census: 1800 in husband; Manheim, York Co, PA w

Notes for Maria Eva:
Born DEU, Hensel household, 1850 United States Census, Adams Co, PA, www.ancestry.com

Maria Eva and John Casper Hensel had the following children:
  i.   Casper Hensel (son of John Casper Hensel and Maria Eva) was born about Abt. 1790 in PA. He died about Abt. 1831 in Adams Co, PA.

  ii. Lawrence Hensel (son of John Casper Hensel and Maria Eva) was born about Abt. 1791 in PA.

  iii. Maria Eva Hensel (daughter of John Casper Hensel and Maria Eva) was born in 1792 in York (Adams) Co, PA.

  iv. Catherine Hensel (daughter of John Casper Hensel and Maria Eva) was born in 1792 in York (Adams) Co, PA.

24. v.   Andrew W Hensel (son of John Casper Hensel and Maria Eva) was born on June 28, 1793 in Littlestown, York (Adams) Co, PA[179, 180]. He died on July 07, 1875 in Home, New Bloomfield, Perry Co, PA[181, 182]. He married Mary A Guise (daughter of John Adam Guise and Maria?) about

Abt. 1814 in Adams, PA[116]. She was born on December 16, 1791 in Northampton Co, PA. She died on January 16, 1877 in Perry Co, PA[183, 184].

vi.   Jacob Hensel (son of John Casper Hensel and Maria Eva) was born in 1795 in PA.

vii. George Hensel (son of John Casper Hensel and Maria Eva) was born in 1796 in PA. He died in VA (OH).

viii. Philip Hensel (son of John Casper Hensel and Maria Eva) was born about Abt. 1800 in PA.

50. **John Adam Guise** (son of <No name>) was born between 1756-1766 in Germany[256]. He died after Aft. 1800 in Adams Co, PA. He married **Maria?** about Abt. 1784 in Northampton Co, PA.

51. **Maria?** was born about Abt. 1765. She died after Aft. 1801 in Adams Co, PA.

More About John Adam Guise:
Census: 1790[257]
Census: 1800 in Menallan, Adams Co, PA[258]
Immigration: Bef. 1780[259]
Military Service: 1780 ; American Revolution, Private 6th PA Reg, 4th Co, 6th class (Northampton, Capt. Andrew Dapper)[260]
Occupation: 1799 ; Weaver[261]
Residence: 1799 in Butler (Menallen), Adams Co, PA[261]
Residence: 1813 in near Gettysburg, Adams Co, PA[262]
Residence: 1824 in near Gettysburg, Adams Co, PA[262]
Will: 1834 in Adams Co, PA[263]

Notes for John Adam Guise:
Grandmother died in voyage to America, Hensel family information, History of Michael Hensel (Hentzel) Sr. & His Related Families, R. Longtin-Thompson.
May be buried Bender's Lutheran church cemetery, Biglerville, Butler Tp., Adams Co, PA, Adams Co County Historical Society.

The House of Guise was a French ducal family, partly responsible for the French Wars of Religion. The Guises were Catholic, and Henry

Guise wanted to end growing Calvinist influence. The assassination of Guise heightened passions and inspired Catholic attacks on Huguenots and their culture. The House of Guise was founded as a cadet branch of the House of Lorraine by Claude de Lorraine, first Duke of Guise (1496-1550), who entered French service and was made a duke by King François I. Claude's daughter, Mary of Guise (1515-1560), married King James V of Scotland and was mother of Mary Queen of Scots. Claude's eldest son, François, became a military hero thanks to his capture of Calais from the English in 1558. [http://en.wikipedia.org/wiki/House_of_Guise]

de Guise: French and the Coat of Arms contains a gold shield with three silver eagles displayed on a red bend. Spelling variations include: Deguise, Dguise and others. First found in Isle of France. Some of the first settlers of this name or some of its variants were: Guillaume Deguise dit Flamand of St-loi, Flanders, who married Marie-Anne Morin in Quebec, in 1691; Catherine Deguise, who was recorded in Quebec in 1727.

Giese, Geis: German: variant of Geis 1. From the personal name Giso, a short form of any of the various personal names with the initial element Gis- such as Giselbrecht, Giselher. Probably a respelling of Geiss, Gies, Giese.

More About Maria?:
Census: 1800 in Manallen, Adams Co, PA[258]

Maria? and John Adam Guise had the following children:

25.   i.   Mary A Guise (daughter of John Adam Guise and Maria?) was born on December 16, 1791 in Northampton Co, PA. She died on January 16, 1877 in Perry Co, PA[183, 184]. She married Andrew W Hensel (son of John Casper Hensel and Maria Eva) about Abt. 1814 in Adams, PA[116]. He was born on June 28, 1793 in Littlestown, York (Adams) Co, PA[179, 180]. He died on July 07, 1875 in Home, New Bloomfield, Perry Co, PA[181, 182].

     ii.   Living Guise (son of John Adam Guise and Maria?). He married <No name>. She was born in 1786 in PA.

     iii.   Peter? Guise (son of John Adam Guise and Maria?) was born in 1795 in PA. He married Anna. She was born in

1793 in PA.

52. **<No name>**.

<No name> had the following children:
- i. Benjamin Workman (son of <No name>) was born in 1787 in PA. He married Susan. She was born in 1790 in PA.

26. ii. Joseph Workman (son of <No name>) was born on December 03, 1795 in Lykens, Dauphin Co, PA[60, 203]. He died on May 23, 1857 in Dauphin Co, PA[60, 203, 204]. He married Susan Romberger (daughter of Balthasar Romberger and Susan Lehman) about Abt. 1818 in Dauphin Co, PA. She was born on April 16, 1799 in Lykens, Dauphin Co, PA[60, 203, 205, 206]. She died on February 23, 1857 in Dauphin Co, PA[60, 205].

- iii. John Workman (son of <No name>).

- iv. Jacob Workman (son of <No name>).

- v. James Workman (son of <No name>).

54. **Balthasar Romberger** (son of John Balthaser Romberger and Anna Maria Brucker) was born on July 05, 1747 in Ingolstadt, Bavaria, Germany[264, 265, 266]. He died about Abt. 1825 in Mifflin, Dauphin Co, PA[60, 266, 267, 268]. He married **Susan Lehman** (daughter of Jacob Lehman and Martha Pennypacker) on June 15, 1798 in Zion Lutheran, Harrisburg, Dauphin Co, PA[205, 265, 267, 269, 270].

55. **Susan Lehman** (daughter of Jacob Lehman and Martha Pennypacker) was born on February 19, 1771 in Trappe, Philadelphia (Montgomery) Co, PA[60, 205]. She died after Aft. 1821 in Dauphin Co, PA.

More About Balthasar Romberger:
Burial: Abt. 1839 in St. Johns (Hill) Lutheran, Berrysburg, Dauphin Co, PA[60]
Census: 1790 in parents; w
Census: 1800 in parents; Upper Paxton, Dauphin Co, PA w[271]
Census: 1810 in Upper Paxton, Dauphin Co, PA age 44[272]
Census: 1820 in Lykens, Dauphin Co, PA (Rimberger)[273]
Census: 1830 in Mifflin, Dauphin Co, PA (Blthase)[274]

Occupation: Abt. 1785 ; Laborer[275]
Occupation: Bet. 1806-1809 ; Deacon[206, 276]
Occupation: Bet. 1813-1815 ; Elder[206]
Occupation: 1820 ; Manufacturing[273]
Probate: September 02, 1839 in Dauphin Co, PA (listed in index only)[277]
Residence: Bet. 1764-1783 in Lancaster Co, PA
Residence: Bet. 1798-1811 in Dauphin Co, PA
Residence: Abt. 1800 in Mifflin, Dauphin Co, PA[205]

Notes for Balthasar Romberger:
Buried Zion Church, Harrisburg, Dauphin Co, PA, Descendants of Johann Pfannabecker, Pfennebaker History & John A. Romberger manuscript, 1997.

More About Susan Lehman:
Baptism: Abt. 1771 in St. Lukes Reformed, Trappe, Philadelphia (Montgomery) Co, PA
Census: 1790 in father; Dauphin Co, PA w
Census: 1800 in husband; Upper Paxton, Dauphin Co, PA w
Census: 1810 in husband age 25; Upper Paxton, Dauphin Co, PA w
Census: 1820 in husband; Lykens, Dauphin Co, PA w
Residence: Abt. 1800 in Harrisburg, Dauphin Co, PA[205]

Notes for Susan Lehman:
Maybe Zion Lutheran, Tower City, Schuylkill Co, PA

Susan Lehman and Balthasar Romberger had the following children:
27.   i.   Susan Romberger (daughter of Balthasar Romberger and Susan Lehman) was born on April 16, 1799 in Lykens, Dauphin Co, PA[60, 203, 205, 206]. She died on February 23, 1857 in Dauphin Co, PA[60, 205]. She married Joseph Workman (son of <No name>) about Abt. 1818 in Dauphin Co, PA. He was born on December 03, 1795 in Lykens, Dauphin Co, PA[60, 203]. He died on May 23, 1857 in Dauphin Co, PA[60, 203, 204].

     ii.   Samuel Romberger (son of Balthasar Romberger and Susan Lehman) was born in 1803 in Dauphin Co, PA. He married Mary Elizabeth Brown.

More About Samuel Romberger:
b: 1803

    iii. Jacob Romberger (son of Balthasar Romberger and Susan Lehman) was born in 1806 in Dauphin Co, PA. He died in 1864. He married Margaret Rebecca Ferree. She was born in 1810 in PA.

    iv. Salome Romberger (daughter of Balthasar Romberger and Susan Lehman) was born in 1808 in Dauphin Co, PA. She died in 1890. She married Peter Bellis. He was born in 1800.

    v. Joseph Romberger (son of Balthasar Romberger and Susan Lehman) was born in 1811 in PA. He died in 1890. He married Rosanna Coleman. She was born in 1814 in PA.

56. **Conrad Updegrove** (son of John William Updegroff and Anna Maria Elizabeth Benfield) was born on November 27, 1771 in Oley, Berks Co, PA[278, 279]. He died in April 1865 in Williamstown, Dauphin Co, PA[216, 278, 279]. He married **Maria Elizabeth Angst** (daughter of John Daniel Angst and Maria Elizabeth Harman) in 1803 in Oley, Berks Co, PA[216].

57. **Maria Elizabeth Angst** (daughter of John Daniel Angst and Maria Elizabeth Harman) was born on November 11, 1776[280] in Rockland, Berks Co, PA. She died about Abt. 1850 in Somerset Co, PA.

More About Conrad Updegrove:
Baptism: December 29, 1771 in St. Josephs Union (Oley Hill), Church, Berks Co, PA[281]
Baptism: 1778 in St. Josephs Union (Oley Hill), Church, Berks Co, PA
Burial: 1865 in Dressler Cemetery, Susquehanna, Juniata, PA[215]
Census: 1790 in parents; w
Census: 1800
Census: 1810 in Upper Paxton, Dauphin Co, PA[282]
Census: 1820 in Lykens, Dauphin Co, PA[283, 284]
Census: 1830 in Lykens, Dauphin Co, PA[285]
Census: 1840 in Wiconisco, Dauphin Co, PA[220, 286]

Census: 1850 in Wiconisco, Dauphin Co, PA[143, 287]
Census: 1860 in Susquehanna, Juniata, PA (son Solomon Updegrove)[288]
Confirmation: October 09, 1803 in St Jacobs Lutheran, Pine Grove, Berks (Schuylkill) Co, PA[216, 289]
Occupation: 1820 ; Agriculture[283]
Occupation: 1850 ; Laborer[143, 216]
Occupation: Abt. 1850 ; Great hunter[216, 289]
Occupation: ; Millwright[290]
Property: 1850 in $1500
Religion: ; St. Johns Lutheran, Mifflin, Dauphin Co, PA[216]
Residence: 1817 in Williams Valley, Dauphin Co, PA[289]

Notes for Conrad Updegrove:
Conrad Updegrove, who was one of the earliest and best known among the pioneers of the Williams Valley, in Dauphin county, Pa., was a great hunter, and many stories are still told of his skill and prowess in this direction. During the days when game of all kinds was plentiful, he had many experiences, with bears, and at one time would have been killed by one of these beasts had it not been for his faithful dogs. As it was he bore the marks of this encounter up to the day of his death. He was one of the sturdy, energetic, industrious men of his day who laid broad and deep the foundation for advancement and progress, and lived a long, active and useful life, passing away at the advanced age of ninety-four years, three months, fifteen days. His home at that time was on the present site of Williamstown, Dauphin county.[Schuylkill County, Pennsylvania: genealogy--family history ..., Volume 2 By J.H. Beers & Co]

Conrad Updergove-Listed in 1850 Pennsylvania census as a laborer, living in Wiconisco Township, Dauphin County. Value of property is $1500 and neither he nor his wife could read or write. Conrad married Elizabeth prior to 1803. His birth date is also recorded in 1778. He was confirmed October 9, 1803 at Jacobs Lutheran Church in Pine Grove. Conrad had a twin brother named Edward (or possibly Isaac). He was a laborer, a farmer, and a mill operator. He attended St. Johns Lutheran Church, Mifflin Township. He resided in many counties, but mostly in Dauphin County. In 1840, he was the head of the household, living with his wife and three children. He was living next door to his son, John. In 1850, he lived next door to his sons, John and Solomon, and their families. In 1860, he lived with his grandson, Solomon. He owned 120 acres of land in Williams Valley. His date of death has been recorded from 1865-1873, but regardless of the date he lived a very long and prosperous life. He passed at about the age of 94 and is remembered as "one of the sturdy, energetic, industrious men who laid the foundations for progress in Williams Valley." "Conrad Updegrove was one of the earliest and best known pioneers of Williams Valley. Many stories are told of his skill and prowess as a hunter. During the days when game of all kinds was plentiful he had many experiences with bears. One time (he) was almost killed by one of these beasts, had it not been for his dogs. Having crippled a bear with his first shot, the bear attacked him. Not having time to reload his breech loader with bullets, he quickly poured gun powder into the barrel of his gun while the dogs kept the bear busy. He set the cap, pulled the trigger, and burned out the eyes of the bear, and in this way saved his life." [From Rutzel Family Genealogy, David Rutzel, leztur@@hotmail.com, December 2003]

Born 1/1/1778, Updegrove genealogy, Father Peter Obtigrav [Updegrove genealogy, vol 10, PA State library]

Died March 15, 1863, Juniata, PA [Updegrove Family information, Rosie Byard, rbyard@@bigfoot.com]

More About Maria Elizabeth Angst:
Burial: Abt. 1850 in Seyberts (Old) Lutheran, Williamstown, Dauphin Co, PA
Census: 1790 in father; Pine Grove, Berks (Schuylkill) Co, PA w
Census: 1800 in husband; w
Census: 1810 in husband; Jonestown, Dauphin (Lebanon) Co, PA w
Census: 1820 in husband; Lykens, Dauphin Co, PA w
Census: 1830 in husband; Lykens, Dauphin Co, PA w
Census: 1840 in husband; Wiconisco, Dauphin Co, PA w
Census: 1850 in Wiconisco, Dauphin Co, PA
Confirmation: October 09, 1803 in St. Jacobs Lutheran, Pine Grove, Berks (Schuylkill) Co, PA
Medical Condition: ; Deaf[143]

Notes for Maria Elizabeth Angst:
Died 1872, aged 94-3-15

Maria Elizabeth Angst and Conrad Updegrove had the following children:

  i.   Updegrove (son of Conrad Updegrove and Maria Elizabeth Angst) was born about Abt. 1802 in PA.

  ii. Elizabeth Updegrove (daughter of Conrad Updegrove and Maria Elizabeth Angst) was born in 1803 in PA. She married Peter Zimmerman. He was born in 1808 in PA.

28. iii. John M Updegrove (son of Conrad Updegrove and Maria Elizabeth Angst) was born on March 23, 1805 in Pine Grove, Berks (Schylkill) Co, PA[214, 215]. He died in 1864 in Somerset County, PA[215]. He married Elizabeth Trovinger in 1823 in Dauphin Co, PA[216]. She was born about Abt. 1798 in Somerset County, PA[216]. She died between 1860-1870 in Berks Co, PA (Apoplexy (ie, Paralysis due to stroke)[216]). He married Sarah M. She was born in 1810.

  iv. Anna Updegrove (daughter of Conrad Updegrove and Maria Elizabeth Angst) was born in 1807 in PA.

  v.   Sarah Updegrove (daughter of Conrad Updegrove and Maria Elizabeth Angst) was born in 1809 in PA.

  vi. Solomon Updegrove (son of Conrad Updegrove and Maria Elizabeth Angst) was born in 1809 in Dauphin Co, PA. He married Barbara Ellen Rickert. She was born in 1807 in PA.

  vii. Nellie Updegrove (daughter of Conrad Updegrove and Maria Elizabeth Angst) was born in 1811 in PA. She married William Brown. He was born in 1815.

60. **<No name>**. He married **<No name>**.

61. **<No name>**.

<No name> and <No name> had the following children:

30. i. Jacob Kulp (son of <No name> and <No name>) was born about Abt. 1802 in PA. He died about Abt. 1865 in Union Co, PA. He married Elizabeth Schneck (daughter of Peter Schneck and Mary) about Abt. 1835 in Union Co, PA. She was born on August 13, 1805 in Northumberland (Union) Co, PA[222]. She died on June 02, 1861 in Union Co, PA[222].

ii. Living Culp (son of <No name> and <No name>). He married Esther. She was born in 1814 in PA.

62. **Peter Schneck** was born about Abt. 1765. He died between 1830-1840 in Northumberland Co, PA. He married **Mary** about Abt. 1790.

63. **Mary** was born about Abt. 1765. She died after Aft. 1820 in Union Co, PA.

More About Peter Schneck:
Census: 1790 in parents; w
Census: 1800 in parents; w
Census: 1810 in Centre, Northumberland (Union) Co, PA[291]
Census: 1820 in Buffalo, Union Co, PA (Snook)[292]
Census: 1830 in Centre, Northumberland (Centre) Co, PA[293]
Occupation: 1810 ; Farmer[291]
Occupation: 1830 ; Farmer[293]

More About Mary:
Census: 1800 in husband; w
Census: 1810 in husband; Centre, Northumberland (Union) Co, PA w
Census: 1820 in husband; Centre, Union Co, PA w

Mary and Peter Schneck had the following children:
31. i. Elizabeth Schneck (daughter of Peter Schneck and Mary) was born on August 13, 1805 in Northumberland (Union) Co, PA[222]. She died on June 02, 1861 in Union Co, PA[222]. She married Jacob Kulp (son of <No name> and <No name>) about Abt. 1835 in Union Co, PA. He was born about Abt. 1802 in PA. He died about Abt. 1865 in Union Co, PA.

ii. Living Schneck (son of Peter Schneck and Mary).

iii. Schneck (son of Peter Schneck and Mary).

iv. Schneck (son of Peter Schneck and Mary).

Generation 7

64. **Robert Thomson** was born on October 25, 1695 in Cochran,

Scotland[80]. He died about Abt. 1744 in Scotland. He married **Isabelle Cochran** on November 21, 1718 in Ormiston, East Lothian, Scotland[294].

65. **Isabelle Cochran** was born on February 07, 1699 in Scotland[79, 80]. She died after Aft. 1744 in Scotland.

More About Robert Thomson:
Baptism: November 19, 1695 in Haddington, Scotland[80]
Occupation: Abt. 1730 ; Cap maker[79]

Notes for Robert Thomson:
s/o Robert Thomson b c1660 & Margaret Cochran of Haddington, Scotland

More About Isabelle Cochran:
Baptism: February 19, 1699 in Haddington, Scotland[80]
Residence: Abt. 1720 in Haddington, East Lothian, Scotland[79]

Notes for Isabelle Cochran:
prob. d/o James Cochran & Isabelle Edminston b1664 of Haddington, Scotland
d/o John Edminston & Bessie Cathie of Haddington, Scotland

Cochran: Scottish: habitational name from lands in the parish of Paisley, near Glasgow. The place name is of uncertain derivation, perhaps from Welsh coch 'red', although this etymology is not supported by the early spelling Coueran.

Isabelle Cochran and Robert Thomson had the following children:

 i. Isabelle Thompson (daughter of Robert Thomson and Isabelle Cochran) was born in 1719 in Scotland.

 ii. Margaret Thompson (daughter of Robert Thomson and Isabelle Cochran) was born in 1721 in Scotland.

 iii. James Thompson (son of Robert Thomson and Isabelle Cochran) was born in 1725 in Scotland.

iv. John Thompson (son of Robert Thomson and Isabelle Cochran) was born in 1728 in Scotland.

32. v. Robert Thomson (son of Robert Thomson and Isabelle Cochran) was born on September 13, 1734[79, 80] in Cranston, Midlothian, Scotland. He died after Aft. 1779 in Scotland. He married Mary Black (daughter of George Black and Mary Helen Smith) about Abt. 1760 in Scotland[79]. She was born in 1737 in Prestonpans, East Lothian, Scotland[79]. She died after Aft. 1779 in Scotland.

vi. Grissel Thompson (daughter of Robert Thomson and Isabelle Cochran) was born in 1737 in Scotland.

vii. Mary Thompson (daughter of Robert Thomson and Isabelle Cochran) was born in 1741 in Scotland.

viii. Jacobina Thompson (daughter of Robert Thomson and Isabelle Cochran) was born in 1744 in Scotland.

66. **George Black** was born about Abt. 1697 in Scotland. He died after Aft. 1739 in Scotland. He married **Mary Helen Smith** on August 04, 1732 in Inversek, Scotland[80].

67. **Mary Helen Smith** was born about Abt. 1707 in Scotland. She died after Aft. 1739 in Scotland.

More About George Black:
Occupation: Abt. 1730 ; Coal miner[295]

Notes for George Black:
prob. s/o William Black & Isabelle Ramage

Black: Scottish and English: from Middle English blak(e) 'black' (Old English blæc, blaca), a nickname given from the earliest times to a swarthy or dark-haired man. Scottish and English: from Old English blac 'pale', 'fair', i.e. precisely the opposite meaning to 1, and a variant of Blake 2. Blake and Black are found more or less interchangeably in several surnames and place names.

Notes for Mary Helen Smith:
prob. d/o John Smith & Mary Wylie of Prestonpans, Scotland

Mary Helen Smith and George Black had the following children:

       i.   Mary Black (daughter of George Black and Mary Helen Smith) was born in 1733 in Scotland. She died in 1733.

      ii.   John Black (son of George Black and Mary Helen Smith) was born in 1735 in Scotland.

33.   iii. Mary Black (daughter of George Black and Mary Helen Smith) was born in 1737 in Prestonpans, East Lothian, Scotland[79]. She died after Aft. 1779 in Scotland. She married Robert Thomson (son of Robert Thomson and Isabelle Cochran) about Abt. 1760 in Scotland[79]. He was born on September 13, 1734[79, 80] in Cranston, Midlothian, Scotland. He died after Aft. 1779 in Scotland.

     iv.   William Black (son of George Black and Mary Helen Smith) was born in 1739 in Scotland.

68. **John Russell** was born about Abt. 1690. He died on April 16, 1750 in Scotland[228]. He married **Janet Malcolm** on May 10, 1712 in Scotland[228].

69. **Janet Malcolm** was born about Abt. 1690. She died on February 25, 1760 in Scotland[228].

Janet Malcolm and John Russell had the following children:

34.   i.   William Russell (son of John Russell and Janet Malcolm) was born on September 28, 1725 in Midlothian, Scotland[228]. He died in 1792 in Newbattle, Scotland[228]. He married Christina Moffatt (daughter of David Moffatt and Agnes Keitchen) on January 13, 1750 in Edinburgh, Midlothian, Scotland[97, 229]. She was born on December 11, 1731 in Dalkeith, Midlothian, Scotland[79, 97, 228, 229]. She died after Aft. 1766 in Scotland.

     ii.   James Russell (son of John Russell and Janet Malcolm) was born about Abt. 1730. He married Helen Moffatt. She was born in 1729 in Scotland.

70. **David Moffatt** was born on September 14, 1700 in Inveresk, Scotland[229]. He died after Aft. 1745 in Scotland. He married **Agnes**

Keitchen on October 06, 1727 in Dalkeith Parish, Midlothian Scotland[229].

71. **Agnes Keitchen** was born in August 1701 in Midlothian, Scotland[228]. She died after Aft. 1745 in Scotland.

More About David Moffatt:
Occupation: 1734 ; Collier[229]

Notes for David Moffatt:
s/o Andrew Moffatt b1671 Inveresk, Scotland & Christiana Lumbsdaill
d/o John Keatchie & Helen Blair
s/o Patrick Moffatt 1640 Scotland & Barbara Kelso
s/o John Moffatt b c1610

Moffatt: Scottish and northern Irish: habitational name from Moffat in Dumfriesshire, named in Gaelic as 'the long plain', from magh 'plain' + fada 'long'.

Agnes Keitchen and David Moffatt had the following children:

    i.   Andrew Moffatt (son of David Moffatt and Agnes Keitchen) was born in 1728 in Scotland.

    ii.   Helen Moffatt (daughter of David Moffatt and Agnes Keitchen) was born in 1729 in Scotland. She married James Russell. He was born about Abt. 1730.

35.   iii.   Christina Moffatt (daughter of David Moffatt and Agnes Keitchen) was born on December 11, 1731 in Dalkeith, Midlothian, Scotland[79, 97, 228, 229]. She died after Aft. 1766 in Scotland. She married William Russell (son of John Russell and Janet Malcolm) on January 13, 1750 in Edinburgh, Midlothian, Scotland[97, 229]. He was born on September 28, 1725 in Midlothian, Scotland[228]. He died in 1792 in Newbattle, Scotland[228].

    iv.   Henry Moffatt (son of David Moffatt and Agnes Keitchen) was born in 1734 in Scotland.

    v.   John Moffatt (son of David Moffatt and Agnes Keitchen) was born in 1736 in Scotland.

vi. Allison Moffatt (daughter of David Moffatt and Agnes Keitchen) was born in 1738 in Scotland.

vii. Agnes Moffatt (daughter of David Moffatt and Agnes Keitchen) was born in 1740 in Scotland.

viii. Agnes Moffatt (daughter of David Moffatt and Agnes Keitchen) was born in 1745 in Scotland.

72. **James Penman** was born about Abt. 1719. He married **Jean Hamilton**.

73. **Jean Hamilton**.

Jean Hamilton and James Penman had the following child:

36.   i.   John Penman (son of James Penman and Jean Hamilton) was born on April 08, 1747 in Lassware, Midlothian, Scotland[230]. He died after Aft. 1775 in Scotland. He married Catherine Brown (daughter of Robert Brown and Isabelle Wilson) on October 28, 1763 in Lassware, Midlothian, Scotland[231, 232]. She was born about Abt. 1747 in Liberton, Midlothian, Scotland[233]. She died after Aft. 1775 in Scotland.

74. **Robert Brown** was born about Abt. 1720 in Scotland. He died after Aft. 1748 in Scotland. He married **Isabelle Wilson** on July 12, 1747 in Scotland.

75. **Isabelle Wilson** was born about Abt. 1720 in Libertan, Midloathian, Scotland. She died after Aft. 1748 in Scotland.

Notes for Robert Brown:
maybe s/o John Brown & Elizabeth Williamson
s/o James Brown 7 Helen Douglas

Brown: English, Scottish, and Irish: generally a nickname referring to the color of the hair or complexion, Middle English br(o)un, from Old English brun or Old French brun. This word is occasionally found in Old English and Old Norse as a personal name or byname. Brun- was also a Germanic name-forming element. Some instances of Old English Brun as a personal name may therefore be short forms of compound names such as Brungar, Brunwine, etc. As a Scottish and

Irish name, it sometimes represents a translation of Gaelic Donn. As an American family name, it has absorbed numerous surnames from other languages with the same meaning.

Isabelle Wilson and Robert Brown had the following child:

37.   i.   Catherine Brown (daughter of Robert Brown and Isabelle Wilson) was born about Abt. 1747 in Liberton, Midlothian, Scotland[233]. She died after Aft. 1775 in Scotland. She married John Penman (son of James Penman and Jean Hamilton) on October 28, 1763 in Lassware, Midlothian, Scotland[231, 232]. He was born on April 08, 1747 in Lassware, Midlothian, Scotland[230]. He died after Aft. 1775 in Scotland.

76.   **John Stoddart** was born on December 25, 1728 in Newbattle, Midlothian, Scotland[296]. He died after Aft. 1767 in Scotland. He married **Margaret Bowman** on June 08, 1754 in Newbattle, Midlothian, Scotland[296].

77.   **Margaret Bowman** was born on August 20, 1732 in Gladsmuir, East Lothian, Scotland[296]. She died after Aft. 1767 in Scotland.

More About John Stoddart:
Baptism: January 05, 1729 in Newbattle, Midlothian, Scotland[236]

Notes for John Stoddart:
s/o William Stoddart b1683 Liberton, Midlothian, Scotland & Margaret Gilmer
s/o David Stoddart b1642 Liberton, Midlothian, Scotland & Catherine Fair
d/o William Gilmer bc1661 & Isabelle Lyle
s/o Walter Stoddart b1614 Liberton, Midlothian, Scotland & Magaret Arnat
d/o George Fare b1620 & Marion Davie
d/o John Lyle bc1826 Newton, Midlothian, Scotland & Elizabeth Ballenie

Notes for Margaret Bowman:
d/o David Bowman b1705 Gladsmuir, East Lothian, Scotland & Isabelle Hog b1703 Gladsmuir, East Lothian, Scotland

s/o David Bowman bc1677 Gladsmuir, East Lothian, Scotland & Margaret Cornwall

d/o John Hog bc1777 Gladsmuir, East Lothian, Scotland & Elizabeth Johnston

Bowman: English and Scottish: occupational name for an archer, Middle English bow(e)man, bouman (from Old English boga 'bow' + mann 'man'). This word was distinguished from Bowyer, which denoted a maker or seller of the articles. It is possible that in some cases the surname referred originally to someone who untangled wool with a bow. This process, which originated in Italy, became quite common in England in the 13th century. The vibrating string of a bow was worked into a pile of tangled wool, where its rapid vibrations separated the fibers, while still leaving them sufficiently entwined to produce a fine, soft yarn when spun.

Margaret Bowman and John Stoddart had the following children:

38.   i.   David Stoddart (son of John Stoddart and Margaret Bowman) was born on May 19, 1754 in Newbattle, Midlothian, Scotland[234]. He died after Aft. 1779 in Scotland. He married Margaret Muckle (daughter of Thomas Muckle and Elizabeth Mason) on February 16, 1778 in Cockpen, Midlothian, Scotland[235]. She was born on November 05, 1756 in Cockpen, Midlothian, Scotland. She died after Aft. 1779 in Scotland.

      ii.   James Stoddart (son of John Stoddart and Margaret Bowman) was born in 1767 in Scotland. He married Martha Miller.

78.   **Thomas Muckle** was born on February 15, 1718/19 in Lasswade, Midlothian, Scotland. He married **Elizabeth Mason**.

79.   **Elizabeth Mason** was born on May 15, 1709 in Dalkeith, Midlothian, Scotland.

Elizabeth Mason and Thomas Muckle had the following child:

39.   i.   Margaret Muckle (daughter of Thomas Muckle and Elizabeth Mason) was born on November 05, 1756 in Cockpen, Midlothian, Scotland. She died after Aft. 1779 in Scotland. She married David Stoddart (son of John Stoddart and Margaret Bowman) on February 16, 1778 in Cockpen, Midlothian, Scotland[235]. He was born on May 19, 1754 in Newbattle, Midlothian, Scotland[234]. He died after

Aft. 1779 in Scotland.

88. **John Philip Braun** was born on August 17, 1697 in Thuringa, Germany. He died on August 16, 1767 in Tulpehocken, Berks, Pennsylvania, United States. He married **Elisabeth Magdalena Losch**.

89. **Elisabeth Magdalena Losch** was born in 1699 in Germany. She died in 1763 in PA.

Elisabeth Magdalena Losch and John Philip Braun had the following child:

44.   i.   Peter Braun (son of John Philip Braun and Elisabeth Magdalena Losch) was born about Abt. 1745 in Rhineland-Palatinate, Germany. He died in 1835 in Son Philip's home, Tower City, Schuylkill Co, PA. He married Catherine about Abt. 1775. She was born about Abt. 1760. She died between 1820-1830 in Dauphin Co, PA.

96. **Casper Hensel** was born about Abt. 1735 in Palatinate, Germany. He died about Abt. 1789 in York Co, PA. He married **Maria Salome Walter** about Abt. 1755 in VA (PA).

97. **Maria Salome Walter** was born about Abt. 1730 in VA. She died after Aft. 1777 in York Co, PA[297].

More About Casper Hensel:
Immigration: 1739 in father); Germany to VA (w
Naturalization: September 15, 1765 in Windsor, Berks Co, PA[298]
Religion: April 21, 1776 ; Christ Church (Conewago), Littlestown, York (Adams) Co, PA[299]
Residence: Abt. 1750 in VA
Residence: 1764 in PA[240]
Residence: 1767 in Windsor Tp, PA[240, 300]
Residence: 1776 in Littlestown, York (Adams) Co, PA[301]
Residence: 1779 in Germany, York Co, PA[302]

Notes for Casper Hensel:
s/o Casper Hansel b 1691 of Southern Germany
s/o Casper Hansel b 1647 Altorf, Saxony, Germany
s/o Casper Hansel b 1622 Trangnitz/Leipzig, Saxony, Germany & Barbara Premier

s/o Casper Hansel b 1589 Leipzig, Saxony, Germany & Barbara Profrandt
s/o Johann La Hentzelle b 1549 of Lorraine, France d Leipzig, Saxony, Germany

s/o John Lorentz Hentzel b c 1701 So. Germany & Catherine Elizabeth ?
s/o Johann Lorentz Hentzel b c 1680

Hansel, Hensel: German from a pet form of the personal name Hans. German (also Hänsel): from a pet form of the personal name Hans. La Hansel: German and the Coat of Arms contains a shield divided per pale blue and silver with two fleur de lys counterchanged. Spelling variations include: Hanselman, Hansemann, Hansel, Hanson, Hansen, Hensen, Hansing, Hansson, Hansenman, Hansenman, Hanssoman and many more. First found in Hamburg, where the name contributed greatly to the development of an emerging nation which would later play a large role in the tribal and national conflicts of the area. Some of the first settlers of this name or some of its variants were: Philip Hanselman, who settled in Germantown, Pennsylvania in 1684; George Hanselman, who emigrated from Württemberg to Pennsylvania in 1749; Catharine Hanselmann, who came to Mississippi in 1820.

Maria Salome Walter and Casper Hensel had the following children:
    i.   John Hensel (son of Casper Hensel and Maria Salome Walter) was born in 1762.

48.   ii.   John Casper Hensel (son of Casper Hensel and Maria Salome Walter) was born on September 30, 1764 in Richmond, York Co, PA[240]. He died in January 1804 in Manheim Tp, Adams Co, PA[116, 241, 242, 243]. He married Maria Eva about Abt. 1789 in York Co, PA. She was born about Abt. 1765 in PA[244]. She died between 1800-1802 in Adams Co, PA[245]. He married Anna Magdelena. She was born about Abt. 1760.

    iii.   Lawrence Hensel (son of Casper Hensel and Maria Salome Walter) was born in 1766.

    iv.   Catherine Hensel (daughter of Casper Hensel and Maria Salome Walter) was born in 1768.

     v.   Michael Hensel (son of Casper Hensel and Maria Salome Walter) was born about Abt. 1770.

     vi.   Peter Hensel (son of Casper Hensel and Maria Salome Walter) was born about Abt. 1770.

     vii.   Philip Hensel (son of Casper Hensel and Maria Salome Walter) was born about Abt. 1770.

     viii.   Jacob Hensel (son of Casper Hensel and Maria Salome Walter) was born about Abt. 1773.

     ix.   George Hensel (son of Casper Hensel and Maria Salome Walter) was born in 1777.

100. **<No name>**.

    <No name> had the following children:

  50.   i.   John Adam Guise (son of <No name>) was born between 1756-1766 in Germany[256]. He died after Aft. 1800 in Adams Co, PA. He married Maria? about Abt. 1784 in Northampton Co, PA. She was born about Abt. 1765. She died after Aft. 1801 in Adams Co, PA.

     ii.   John? Guise (son of <No name>).

     iii.   Abraham? Guise (son of <No name>) was born about Abt. 1740.

     iv.   Peter? Guise (son of <No name>).

108. **John Balthaser Romberger** was born on May 04, 1716 in Theilheim, Schweinfurt, Bavaria, Germany[264, 266, 303, 304]. He died on September 25, 1800 in Annville, Lebanon Co., PA[264, 265, 266]. He married **Anna Maria Brucker** in 1765 in Lancaster Co, PA[305].

109. **Anna Maria Brucker** was born about Abt. 1723 in Theilheim, Bavaria, Germany. She died between 1778-1798 in Mifflin, Lancaster (Dauphin) Co, PA[306, 307].

More About John Balthaser Romberger:
Census: 1790
Census: 1800 in Upper Paxton, Dauphin Co, PA[308]

Census: 1810 in Upper Paxton, Dauphin Co, PA[309]
Census: 1820
Census: 1830
Immigration: September 24, 1753 in Germany to USA (ship Neptune)[205, 265, 276, 310]
Military Service: Abt. 1775 ; American Revolution, Private 1st PA Reg, 5th Co, 3rd class (Lancaster)[311]
Residence: 1754 in Philadelphia, PA[312]
Residence: 1758 in Leacock, Lancaster Co, PA[276]
Residence: Bet. 1780-1790 in Lancaster Co, PA
Residence: Bet. 1790-1800 in Annville, Dauphin (Lebanon) Co, PA[205, 276]

Notes for John Balthaser Romberger:
s/o John Bartolomus Romberger 1716 Franken, Bavaria, Germany
s/o John Casper Rauchenberger & Catherine ? of Theilheim, Bavaria, Germany

Ancestor of Dwight David "Ike" Eisenhower (October 14, 1890 - March 28, 1969) was the 34th President of the United States from 1953 until 1961 and a five-star general in the United States Army. During the Second World War, he served as Supreme Commander of the Allied forces in Europe, with responsibility for planning and supervising the successful invasion of France and Germany in 1944-45. In 1951, he became the first supreme commander of NATO. As President, he oversaw the cease-fire of the Korean War, kept up the pressure on the Soviet Union during the Cold War, made nuclear weapons a higher defense priority, launched the Space Race, enlarged the Social Security program, and began the Interstate Highway System. He was the last World War I veteran to serve as U.S. president.[http://en.wikipedia.org/wiki/Dwight_D._Eisenhower]

1 John Balthaser Romberger b: 1736 in Franken, Bavaria, Germany d: 1831
.. +Anna Maria Brucker b: about 1743 in Bavaria, Germany d: Bet. 1778 - 1798
..... 2 Anna Maria Romberger b: 1771 in PA
.... +John Michael Matter
.... 3 Henry Matter b: 1796
.... +Anna Maria Deitrich
.... 4 Margaret Matter b: 1825

.... +Jacob Frederick Eisenhower
.... 5 David Eisenhower b: 1863
.... +Ida Stover
.... 6 Dwight D Eisenhower b: 1890 (US
President)

More About Anna Maria Brucker:
Immigration: Abt. 1760
Religion: ; Protestant[313]

Notes for Anna Maria Brucker:
Also Anna Maria Bruckner
Trying to find validity of born in ENG, married in DEU, immigrated to
PA.

Anna Maria Brucker and John Balthaser Romberger had the following
children:

54.   i.   Balthasar Romberger (son of John Balthaser Romberger
and Anna Maria Brucker) was born on July 05, 1747 in
Ingolstadt, Bavaria, Germany[264, 265, 266]. He died about Abt.
1825 in Mifflin, Dauphin Co, PA[60, 266, 267, 268]. He married
Susan Lehman (daughter of Jacob Lehman and Martha
Pennypacker) on June 15, 1798 in Zion Lutheran,
Harrisburg, Dauphin Co, PA[205, 265, 267, 269, 270]. She was born
on February 19, 1771 in Trappe, Philadelphia
(Montgomery) Co, PA[60, 205]. She died after Aft. 1821 in
Dauphin Co, PA.

ii.   Anna Maria Romberger (daughter of John Balthaser
Romberger and Anna Maria Brucker) was born in 1771 in
PA. She married John Michael Matter.

iii.   Henry Romberger (son of John Balthaser Romberger and
Anna Maria Brucker) was born in 1773 in Lancaster Co,
PA. He married Elizabeth Hoffman.

iv.   Adam Romberger (son of John Balthaser Romberger and
Anna Maria Brucker) was born in 1775 in Lancaster Co,
PA.

v.   Anna Catherine Romberger (daughter of John Balthaser

Romberger and Anna Maria Brucker) was born in 1777 in Lancaster Co, PA.

110. **Jacob Lehman** was born in 1744[267, 314]. He died on October 20, 1805 in Hanover, Dauphin (Lebanon) Co, PA[267, 314]. He married **Martha Pennypacker** about Abt. 1763 in PA.

111. **Martha Pennypacker** was born in 1746 in Philadelphia (Montgomery) Co, PA[315]. She died after Aft. 1805 in Dauphin Co, PA.

More About Jacob Lehman:
Burial: 1805 in Bindagles Lutheran, Palmyra, Dauphin (Lebanon) Co, PA[314]
Census: 1790 in Dauphin Co, PA[316]
Census: 1800 in Bethel, Dauphin Co, PA (Lehmey)[317]
Military Service: Bet. 1775-1781 ; American Revolution, Ensign, 2nd PA Reg, 8th Co (Lancaster)[314]
Probate: Bet. October 30-November 02, 1805 in Hanover, Dauphin Co, PA[318]
Will: December 13, 1800 in Hanover, Dauphin Co, PA[318, 319]

Notes for Jacob Lehman:
s/o Christian Lehman c1696 & Anna Maria margaret ?

Layman, Lehman, Lehmann: Americanized spelling of German Lehmann. German: variant of Lay 3. German: see Lehmann. German: status name for a feudal tenant or vassal, Middle High German leheman, lenman (from lehen 'to hold land as a feudal tenant' + man 'man'). The tenant held land on loan for the duration of his life in return for rent or service, but was not free to transfer or divide it.

More About Martha Pennypacker:
Census: 1790 in husband; Dauphin Co, PA w
Census: 1800 in husband; w

Notes for Martha Pennypacker:
d/o Adolph Pennebecker b1717 Skippack, Mont. Co, PA & Agnes Miller

s/o Henry Pennebecker b1674 Flomborn, Rhineland-Palatinate, Germany & Eva Umstadt 1673 Krefeld, Rhineland-Palatinate, Germany

s/o John Pfannebecker b 1645 & Sybilla ? of Holland

s/o John Peter Umstat b1640 Krefeld, Rhineland-Palatinate, Germany & Barbara ?

s/o Nicholas Umstat of Germany

Related to:

Marlon Brando II (1924-2004), a.k.a. Marlon Brando was an Academy Award-winning American actor whose body of work spanned over half a century. He is widely regarded as one of the most influential actors of all time. Brando is best known for his roles in A Streetcar Named Desire and On the Waterfront, both directed by Elia Kazan in the early 1950s, as well as his Academy-Award winning performance as Vito Corleone in The Godfather and as Colonel Walter E. Kurtz in Apocalypse Now, the latter two directed by Francis Ford Coppola in the 1970s. Brando also garnered worldwide attention by playing Jor-El in Superman: The Movie (1978), directed by Richard Donner. Brando was also an activist, lending his presence to many issues, including the American Civil Rights and American Indian Movements. He was named the fourth Greatest Male Star of All Time by the American Film Institute.
[http://genealogy.wikia.com/wiki/Marlon_Brando_II_(1924-2004)]

Samuel Whitaker Pennypacker, Governor of PA, was described as "the perfect Victorian," and "the ideal first governor of the twentieth century." Pennypacker was born in Phoenixville, Chester County, on April 9, 1843. He descended from Hendrick Pannebakker (Dutch for "maker of tiles"), an émigré from Crefeld, Germany, of Dutch origin, who was a surveyor for William Penn. His grandfather, Mathias Pennypacker, a member of the General Assembly and president of the Philadelphia and Reading Railroad, helped write the state Constitution of 1837. His mother, Anna Maria Whitaker, came from a family that owned a local ironworks. His father, Isaac Pennypacker, was the first burgess (similar to mayor) of Phoenixville and held a professorship at the Philadelphia Medical College. Young Pennypacker, after attending Northwest Grammar School, Philadelphia, was given a scholarship at Saunders Institute, West Philadelphia, but before completing his studies, his father died of typhoid fever. The young scholar returned to live with his mother and maternal grandfather, Joseph Whitaker, and completed his education at nearby Grovemont Seminary. [PA Governors Past to Present, Governor Samuel Whitaker Pennypacker (1843-1916), http://www.phmc.state.pa.us/]

Galusha Pennypacker (June 1, 1844 - October 1, 1916) was a Union general during the American Civil War. He is to this day the youngest person to hold the rank of brigadier general in the U.S. Army, at the age of 20, the only general who was ineligible by age to vote for the president who appointed him. [http://en.wikipedia.org/wiki/Galusha_Pennypacker]

1) John Pfannebecker b 1645 & Sybilla ? of Holland
...2) Henry Pennebecker b1674 Flomborn, Alzey, Germany & Eva Umstadt 1673
...... 3) Jacob Pennebacker
.........4) Matthias Pennebacker b1742
............5) Matthias Pennebacker b1786 & Sarah Anderson
..............6) Isaac Pennybaker bc1815 & Anna Maria Whitaker
.................7) Samuel W Pennypacker b1843 (PA Governor)
.............6) Joseph Pennypacker & Elizabeth Funk
.................7) Joseph Pennypacker & Tamson Workizer
....................8) Galusha Pennypacker b1844 (Civil War General)
...2) Johann Friedrich Pfannebecker b1675
......3) Weiant Pennebaker b1716
.........4) Wyand Pennebaker b1763 & Precious Ruby
............5) Samuel W Pennebaker b1796 & Sarah Findley
..............6) William Pennybaker c1828 & Sarah Solman
.................7) William J Pennybaker b1868 & Bessie Gahan
....................8) Dorothy Pennybaker b1897 & Marlon Brando
.....................9) Marlon Brando b 1924 (US actor)

Martha Pennypacker and Jacob Lehman had the following children:

55. i. Susan Lehman (daughter of Jacob Lehman and Martha Pennypacker) was born on February 19, 1771 in Trappe, Philadelphia (Montgomery) Co, PA[60, 205]. She died after Aft. 1821 in Dauphin Co, PA. She married Balthasar Romberger (son of John Balthaser Romberger and Anna Maria Brucker) on June 15, 1798 in Zion Lutheran, Harrisburg, Dauphin Co, PA[205, 265, 267, 269, 270]. He was born on July 05, 1747 in Ingolstadt, Bavaria, Germany[264, 265, 266]. He died about Abt. 1825 in Mifflin, Dauphin Co, PA[60, 266, 267, 268].

ii. Elizabeth Layman (daughter of Jacob Lehman and Martha Pennypacker).

iii. Rebecca Layman (daughter of Jacob Lehman and Martha Pennypacker) was born in PA.

iv. Henry Layman (son of Jacob Lehman and Martha Pennypacker) was born in PA.

v. Joseph Layman (son of Jacob Lehman and Martha Pennypacker) was born in PA.

vi. Mary Layman (daughter of Jacob Lehman and Martha Pennypacker) was born in PA.

vii. Jacob Layman (son of Jacob Lehman and Martha Pennypacker) was born in PA.

viii. John Layman (son of Jacob Lehman and Martha Pennypacker) was born in PA.

ix. Martha Layman (daughter of Jacob Lehman and Martha Pennypacker) was born in PA.

x. Samuel Layman (son of Jacob Lehman and Martha Pennypacker).

112. **John William Updegroff** was born on February 24, 1732 in Kirchberg Hunsruck, Rhineland-Palatinate, Germany[278, 320, 321, 322, 323]. He died between 1800-1804 in Berks Co, PA[216]. He married **Anna Maria Elizabeth Benfield** about Abt. 1755 in Berks Co, PA.

113. **Anna Maria Elizabeth Benfield** was born on April 01, 1729 in Oley, Philadelphia (Berks) Co, PA[321, 324, 325, 326]. She died on February 23, 1804 in Exeter, Berks Co, PA[216, 278, 320, 321, 323, 326].

More About John William Updegroff:
b: April 24, 1732 in Kirchberg Hunsruck, Rhineland-Palatinate, Germany[327]
Census: 1790
Census: 1800
Immigration: 1753[216, 328]

Occupation: Abt. 1760 ; Mechanic
Occupation: Abt. 1770 ; Locksmith, Gunsmith[216]
Residence: 1753 in Germantown, Philadelphia, PA[328]
Residence: Abt. 1770 in Reading, Berks Co, PA[328]
Residence: Bet. 1772-1775 in Western Dt, Berks Co, PA[215, 328]

Notes for John William Updegroff:
s/o Frederick Opdengraff b1702 Germany & Elizabeth Miller
s/o Adolph Opdengraeff b1654 Muir, Rhineland-Palatinate, Germany
s/o Herman Isaac Opdengraeff b1616 Krefeld, Rhineland-Palatinate,
Prussia (Germany) & Maria Grietje Pletjes (Mary Margaret Peters)
d/o Drissen Plejtes (Andrew Peters)
s/o Herman Isaac Opdengraef b1585 Aldekerk, Muir,
Rhineland-Palatinate, Prussia (Germany) & Grietje Pletjes (Margaret
Peters)
s/o Isaac Opdengraef b c 1550
d/o Driessen Pletjes & Alet Gobels
s/o Abraham Opdengraef b1490 Dusseldorf, Rhineland-Palatinate,
Germany

Possible relation to
John William of Mark b1562 & Anna Van Aldekerk
s/o William of Cleves V b1516516 & Mary of Habsburg b1530

OpDenGraef: German and the Coat of Arms contains a blue shield
consisting of a demi-lion rampant holding a silver anchor. The Crest is
A demi-lion rampant holding an anchor. Spelling variations include:
Graf, Grafe,Graef, Graff, Graffen, Graffin, Grafen, Grafin, Grav, Graaf
and many more. First found in Switzerland, where the family
contributed to the development of the region. Some of the first settlers
of this name or some of its variants were: Philip Leonhardt Graf, who,
with his wife and five children, came to America in 1709. He was
bearers of the name Graf to emigrate to the New World. Georg Graf
arrived in Pennsylvania between 1743-1746.

More About Anna Maria Elizabeth Benfield:
Burial: 1804
Census: 1790 in husband; w
Census: 1800 in husband; w
Probate: March 21, 1804 in Exeter, Berks Co, PA[215, 329]

Notes for Anna Maria Elizabeth Benfield:
The family historian of the Benfields has traced his name back to the time of William the Conqueror in his conquest of England, 1066. In his army was General John Benfield, from Normandy, who after the conquest moved his family to England and became a man of prominence in the circles of the court of William the Conqueror, then ruler of England. After his death he was buried in Westminster Abbey, where there is a tablet to his memory. The family in the course of time spread into Scotland and Ireland, and from the Scotland family, so far as the historian is able to discover, came two brothers, which no doubt is correct. These two brothers were Thomas Benfield and John Benfield. The former is the head of the Benfields of this section as well as those of the Central and Western States. The latter is the head of the Benfield family in North and South Carolina as well as Georgia, whither he emigrated from Union Township, Berks county, about 1760, with the Boone family. These two persons came to America about 1712, so far as can be learned from records. The said brothers then located west of Pottstown several miles, in Union township, where both owned tracts of land. In 1728 Thomas Benfield bought a tract of land in Oley township, Berks county, but sold it to Abijah Sands in 1733, he having lived there all that time. The next year he received a patent for land (100 acres) in District township, Berks Co., Pa. This tract is now owned by Israel Weller and his brother. In 1744 another patent was granted to him for a tract of fifty-two acres, adjoining the 100-acre tract. This then for years became the home of the family, and there he raised a family of two sons and four daughters. This same Thomas Benfield while he lived here purchased several other tracts in Union and Amity townships. Two tracts were sold by him in 1762 to John Wanger, of the same township; these two tracts are located near Port Union and still in the Wanger family name. From the tax lists in the possession of the Berks County Historical Society we find that he paid taxes at different dates, showing that he either lived in these townships or at least owned property and paid tax. In 1759 he paid 8 tax in District township. And from 1761 to 1769 he paid tax in that township, where he died and where his son Samuel was executor of his will and filed his statement in 1771. [The Historical and Biographical Annals of Berks County Pennsylvania, compiled by Morton L. Montgomery and published by J. H. Beers & Company of Chicago in 1909]

d/o Thomas Benfield b1720 Harefield, London, Middlesex, England &

Mary Hill
s/o John Benfield & Mary ?
d/o John Hill & Rachel ?

Benfield Homestead (Thomas), Berks, PA

d/o John Swartz, Burials 1782-19807, Rev. John William Boos, Ind.
reformed Minister, Central Berks Co, BCGS, Berks Co, PA

Born January 1, Selvage & Peterson Families & More, Charles J
Peterson, PetersonC@@missouri.edu, awt.ancestry.com

Benfield, Benefield: English: variant of Benefield. Variant of Banfield
or Bonfield. Topographic name from Middle English bent 'bent-grass'
+ feld 'open country' or 'land converted to arable use', or a
habitational name from a place named with these elements (Old
English beonet + feld), such as Binfield in Berkshire.

Anna Maria Elizabeth Benfield and John William Updegroff had the
following children:

   i.   Frances Updegrove (daughter of John William Updegroff
        and Anna Maria Elizabeth Benfield) was born on
        September 10, 1756 in PA.

   ii. Anna Magdalena Updegrove (daughter of John William
        Updegroff and Anna Maria Elizabeth Benfield) was born on
        March 09, 1759 in PA.

   iii. John Adam Updegrove (son of John William Updegroff and
        Anna Maria Elizabeth Benfield) was born in 1761 in PA.

   iv. Peter Updegrove (son of John William Updegroff and Anna
        Maria Elizabeth Benfield) was born on May 01, 1766 in PA.
        He married Catherine. She was born about Abt. 1760.

56.   v. Conrad Updegrove (son of John William Updegroff and
          Anna Maria Elizabeth Benfield) was born on November 27,
          1771 in Oley, Berks Co, PA[278, 279]. He died in April 1865 in
          Williamstown, Dauphin Co, PA[216, 278, 279]. He married Maria
          Elizabeth Angst (daughter of John Daniel Angst and Maria
          Elizabeth Harman) in 1803 in Oley, Berks Co, PA[216]. She
          was born on November 11, 1776[280] in Rockland, Berks
          Co, PA. She died about Abt. 1850 in Somerset Co, PA.

     vi. Edward Isaac Updegrove (son of John William Updegroff and Anna Maria Elizabeth Benfield) was born on November 27, 1771 in Berks Co, PA. He married Elizabeth Miller. She was born about Abt. 1775.

114. **John Daniel Angst** was born on December 14, 1749 in East Hanover, Lancaster (Lebanon) Co, PA[280]. He died on June 11, 1815 in Pine Grove, Schuylkill Co, PA. He married **Maria Elizabeth Harman** in 1774 in Berks?, PA.

115. **Maria Elizabeth Harman** was born about Abt. 1749 in NY. She died about Abt. 1810 in Berks (Schuylkill) Co, PA.

More About John Daniel Angst:
Baptism: January 02, 1751 in St John Hill (Quittaphilla) Lutheran, Cleona, Lancaster (Lebanon) Co, PA
Burial: 1815 in St. Jacobs Lutheran, Pine Grove, Schuylkill Co, PA
Census: 1790 in Pine Grove, Berks (Schuylkill) Co, PA[330]
Census: 1800 in Pine Grove, Berks (Schuylkill) Co, PA[331]
Census: 1810 in Pine Grove, Berks (Schuylkill) Co, PA[332]
Military Service: Bet. 1777-1779 ; American Revolution, Private 6th PA Reg, 5th Co, ? class (Berks, Capt. Michael Bretz)[333, 334]
Occupation: Abt. 1770 ; Farmer
Occupation: Abt. 1790 ; Miller
Residence: Bet. 1773-1777 in Pine Grove, Berks (Schuylkill) Co PA[335]
Residence: Bet. 1779-1786 in Pine Grove, Berks (Schuylkill) Co PA[335]

Notes for John Daniel Angst:
s/o John Daniel Angst b1723 Enkirch, Rhineland-Palatinate, Germany & Maria Elizabeth Stroeher
s/o John Daniel Angst b1686 Enkirch, Rhineland-Palatinate, Germany & Maria Dorothy Junker
d/o John Nicholas Stroeher of Irmenach, Rhineland-Palatinate, Germany & Eva Maria ?
s/o John Daniel Angst b1650 Germany & Eva Catherine Christina Kramp
d/o John Conrad Juncker & Maria Margaret Matthes
s/o Joes Burkhart Angst b1612 Enkirch, Rhineland-Palatinate,

Germany & Catherine Mueller
s/o Simon Angst b 1585 in Enkirch, Germany & Margaret ?

Angst: South German and Swiss German: topographic name from Middle High German angest 'narrowness', i.e. 'narrow place' (whence the modern vocabulary word Angst 'anxiety', 'fear'). Bahlow cites an early example, 'Bertschi an der angist' (1382), which is clearly topographical, but in other cases Angst may equally well be a nickname for a timid person.

More About Maria Elizabeth Harman:
Census: 1790 in husband; Pine Grove, Berks (Schuylkill) Co, PA w
Census: 1800 in husband; Pine Grove, Berks (Schuylkill) Co, PA w
Census: 1810 in husband; Pine Grove, Berks (Schuylkill) Co, PA w

Notes for Maria Elizabeth Harman:
d/o Daniel Harman (aka Daniel Hamma)

Harman: English (mainly southeast), French, German (Harmann) and Dutch: from a Germanic personal name composed of the elements heri, hari 'army' + man 'man' (see Hermann). In England this name was introduced by the Normans.

Maria Elizabeth Harman and John Daniel Angst had the following children:

     i.   Juliana Angst (daughter of John Daniel Angst and Maria Elizabeth Harman) was born in 1775 in PA.

57. ii. Maria Elizabeth Angst (daughter of John Daniel Angst and Maria Elizabeth Harman) was born on November 11, 1776[280] in Rockland, Berks Co, PA. She died about Abt. 1850 in Somerset Co, PA. She married Conrad Updegrove (son of John William Updegroff and Anna Maria Elizabeth Benfield) in 1803 in Oley, Berks Co, PA[216]. He was born on November 27, 1771 in Oley, Berks Co, PA[278, 279]. He died in April 1865 in Williamstown, Dauphin Co, PA[216, 278, 279]. She married Jacob Albert. He was born about Abt. 1770.

    iii. Daniel Angst (son of John Daniel Angst and Maria Elizabeth Harman) was born in 1786 in Pine Grove, Berks (Schuylkill) Co, PA.

iv. Jacob Angst (son of John Daniel Angst and Maria Elizabeth Harman) was born about Abt. 1790 in PA.

v. John Angst (son of John Daniel Angst and Maria Elizabeth Harman) was born in 1792 in Pine Grove, Berks (Schuylkill) Co, PA.

vi. William Angst (son of John Daniel Angst and Maria Elizabeth Harman) was born in 1794 in PA.

Sources

1 Harper Bruce Thompson birth record, #344701, #122649-07, September 1907, Schuylkill Co, PA, Department of Vital Records, New Castle, PA.

2 Harper B Thompson, Obituary, Harrisburg Patriot Newspaper, July 1981.

3 Harper B Thompson death certificate, #2501265, Department of Vital Records, New Castle, PA.

4 Thompson-Batdorf marriage record, Register of Wills, Clerk of Orphans Court, Dauphin Co, PA, 1935.

5 Samuel Peters, Descendants of John Peters, Evelyn S. Hartman.

6 Myrtle A. Batdorf birth certificate, January 1918, Department of Vital records, New Castle, PA.

7 Myrtle A Thompson death certificate, #3455802, Department of Vital records, New Castle, PA.

8 Myrtle Thompson, Obituary, Harrisburg Patriot newspaper, 1983.

9 Thompson household, 1910 United States Census, Schuylkill Co, PA, www.ancestry.com and 1910 United States Census, Schuylkill Co, PA, ED 62, Sheet 32A, PA State Library.

10 Thompson household, 1920 United States Census, Schuylkill Co, PA, PA State library, microfilm image.

11 Thompson household, 1920 United States Census, Schuylkill Co, PA, Roll T625 1651, ED 84, Image 0280, ancestry.com & Microfilm, PA State Library, Hbg, PA.

12 Knittle household, 1930 United States Census, Lehigh Co, PA, ancestry.com & Microfilm, PA State Library, Hbg, PA.

13 Thompson household, 1940 US Federal census, Bruce Thompson, Snyder, PA, www.ancestry.com.

14 Thompson household, 1920 United States Census, Schuylkill Co, PA, Roll T625 1651, ED 84, Image 0280, www.ancestry.com and 1920 United States Census, Schuylkill Co, PA, PA State library, microfilm image.

15 Harper B Thompson, Social Seurity numident record, application for SS-5, SSA, Nov 2006, Baltimore, MD.

16 Harper Thompson, July 1981, PA, Social Security Death Index, www.familysearch,org.

17 Batdorf household, 1920 United States Census, Dauphin Co, PA, Roll T625 1559, p 3A, ED 148, Image 1081, ancestry.com & Microfilm, PA State Library, Hbg, PA.

18 Batdorf household, 1930 United States Census, Dauphin Co, PA, Roll T626 2027, p 19A, ED 76, Image 0959, ancestry.com & Microfilm, PA State Library, Hbg, PA.

19 Batdorf household, 1930 United States Census, Dauphin Co, PA, Roll T626 2027, p 19A, ED 76, Image 0959, ancestry.com & Microfilm, PA State Library, Hbg, PA.

20 Myrtle A Thompson, Obituary, Harrisburg Patriot newspaper, 1983.

21 Myrtle A Thompson, Probate files, 1983, File 424-1983, Dauphin County Courthouse, Reg of Wills, Deborah Hershey, Elizabethtown, PA, Mar 2008.

22 Myrtle Thompson, Gerald G Thompson.

23 Myrtle Thompson, May 1983, PA, Social Security Death Index, www.familysearch.org.

24 Abel Thompson death certificate, #0506211, #133775-93, January 1918, Department of Vital Records, New castle, PC.

25 Thompson-Hensel Marriage, Office of the Register of Wills, Schuylkill County, PA, June 1904.

26 Abel Robert Thompson, WW I Draft Reg Cards, 1917-1918 Record, www.ancestry.com.

27 Abel R Thompson, Probate file, 1918, unnumbered original papers, 34pp, Schuylkill Co Courthouse, Schuylkill, PA, Norman Nicol, Apr 2008.

28 Gussie May Thompson death certificate, #0506187, #31982, March 1973, Department of Vital Records, New Castle, PA.

29 Gussie May Hensel, Funeral obituary, March 1973.

30 Gussie Mae Thompson, Obituary, Pottsville Republbican, Pottsville, PA, March 28, 1973.

31 Gussie M. Thompson, Greenwood Cemetery, Tower City, Schuylkill Co, PA, John Barket, Tower City, PA, B-3-1.

32 Gussie M. Thompson, Reg of Will book, Book 145, pp578-82, May 27, 1950, probated Sept 11, 1973, Schuylkill Co Courthouse, Schuylkill, PA, Norman Nicol, Apr 2008.

33 Abel Thompson, Greenwood Cemetery, Tower City, Schuylkill Co, PA, John Barket, Tower City, PA, B-3-1.

34 Thompson household, 1900 United States Census, Schuylkill Co, PA www.ancestry.com, Liz McKinnon.

35 Abel R Thompson, 1918, Schuylkill County Register of Wills, Schuylkill Co, PA, #284.

36 Hensel household, 1900 United States Census, Schuylkill Co, PA, ww.ancestry.com and 1900 United States Census, Schuylkill Co, PA, PA State library microfilm image.

37 Thompson household, 1930 United States Census, Schuylkill Co, PA, Roll T626 2146, p 3A, ED 84, Image 0462, ancestry.com & Microfilm, PA State Library, Hbg, PA.

38 Thompson household, 1940 US Federal census, Guusie M Thompson, Snyder, PA, www.ancestry.com.

39 Gussie May Thompson, Funeral obituary, March 1973.

40 Gussie May Thompson, #0506187, #31982, March 1973, Department of Vital Records, New Castle, PA.

41 Gussie Thompson, March 1973, PA, Social Security Death Index, www.familysearch.org.

42 Michael Goodman, Descendants of Michael Goodman, Evelyn S Hartman, deanh@@voicenet.com.

43 Abel F Thompson, Bob Averell Family Tree, Entries: 7956, Updated: 2004-08-01 00:29:03 UTC (Sun), Contact: Bob Averell.

44 Lydia Mae Thompson, Obituary, Pottsville Repulbican, Pottsville, PA, Jan 18, 1983.

45 Robert B Thompson death certificate, #0042512, #102079, Reg # 102, October 1907, Department of Vital records, New Castle, PA.

46 Robert B Thompson, Greenwood Cemetery, Tower City, Schuylkill Co, PA, John Barket, Tower City, PA, B-1-1.

47 Thompson family information, John L linden, jllinden@@comcast.net.

48 Alexander Thompson, Schuylkill County, PA, p 1054.

49 Lydia B. Thompson, Greenwood Cemetery, Tower City, Schuylkill Co, PA, John Barket, Tower City, PA, B-1-1.

50 Robert B. Thomspon, Greenwood Cemetery, Tower City, Schuylkill Co, PA, John Barket, Tower City, PA, B-3-1.

51 Thompson household, 1850 United States Census, Schuylkill Co, PA, ancestry.com & Microfilm, PA State Library, Hbg, PA.

52 Thompson household, 1860 United States Census, Schuylkill Co, PA, PA State library microfilm.

53 Thompson household, 1870 United States Census, Schuylkill Co, PA, ancestry.com & Microfilm, PA State Library, Hbg, PA.

54 Thompson household, 1880 United States Census, Dauphin Co, PA, FHL 1255124, Film T9-1124, p 432B, www.familysearch.org.

55 Pottsville Hospital, 1900 United States Census, Schuylkill Co, PA, T623, Roll 1485, p 189, www.ancestry.com and 1900 United States Census, Schuylkill Co, PA, PA State library microfilm image.

56 Thompson household, 1900 United States Census, Schuylkill Co, PA, T623, Roll 1485, p 189, www.ancestry.com and 1900 United States Census, Schuylkill Co, PA, PA State library microfilm image.

57 Lydia B. Thompson, Greenwood Cemetery, Tower City, Schuylkill Co, PA, John Barket, Tower City, PA, B-3-1.

58 Goodman household, 1870 United States Census, Dauphin Co, PA, ancestry.com & Microfilm, PA State Library, Hbg, PA.

59 Thompson family information, Irene C. Stearns, DeKalb, IL.

60 Bob Averell Family Tree, Bob Averell, raverell@@carolina.rr.com, awt.ancestry.com.

61 Howard A.C. Hensel, #0036895, #63360, Reg # 66, June 1927, Department of Vital records, New Castle, PA.

62 Hensel family information, Victor Hensel, NJ.

63 Howard Andrew Carson Hensel, Howard Andrew Carson Hensel probate file, 1927, unnumbered orginal papers, 21pp, probated June 29, 1927, Schuylkill Co Courthouse, Schuylkill, PA, Norman Nicol, Apr 2008.

64 Clara M Hensel death certificate, #0042528, #37124, Reg # 29, March 1926, Department of Vital records, New Castle, PA.

65 Joseph Workman, Descendants of Joseph Workman, Evelyn S. Hartman.

66 Howard A.C. Hensel, Greenwood Cemetery, Tower City, Schuylkill Co, PA, John Barket, Tower City, PA, B-3-1.

67 Hentzel household, 1860 United States Census, Schuylkill Co, PA, ancestry.com & Microfilm, PA State Library, Hbg, PA.

68 Hentzel household, 1860 United States Census, Schuylkill Co, PA, PA State library microfilm.

69 Hensel household, 1870 United States Census, Dauphin Co, PA, PA State library microfilm.

70 Hensel household, 1880 United States Census, Dauphin Co, PA, FHL 1255124, Film T9-1124, p 270D, www.familysearch.org.

71 Hensel household, 1910 United States Census, Schuylkill Co, PA, www.ancestry.com and 1910 United States Census, Schuylkill Co, PA, ED 102, Sheet 4, PA State Library.

72 Hensel household, 1920 United States Census, Schuylkill Co, PA, T625 1652, p 17A, ED 143, Image 0877, www.ancestry.com and 1920 United States Census, Schuylkill Co, PA, PA State Libraray, microfilm image.

73 Hensel household, 1880 United States Census, Dauphin Co, PA, FHL 1255124, Film T9-1124, p 270D, www.familysearch.org.

74 Hensel household, 1920 United States Census, Schuylkill Co, PA, T625 1652, p 17A, ED 143, Image 0877, www.ancestry.com and 1920 United States Census, Schuylkill Co, PA, PA State Libraray, microfilm image.

75 Clara Hensel, Greenwood Cemetery, Tower City, Schuylkill Co, PA, John Barket, Tower City, PA, B-3-1.

76 Updegrove household, 1870 United States Census, Dauphin Co, PA, PA State library microfilm.

77 Updegrove household, 1880 United States Census, Dauphin Co, PA, www.ancestry.com and 1880 United States Census, Dauphin Co, PA, FHL 1255125, Film T9-1125, p 312B, www.familysearch.org.

78 Casper Hansel, Descendants of Casper (LaHentzelle) Hensel, Evelyn S Hartman, deanh@@voicenet.com.

79 Thompson family information, Jim Thompson, jbthompson@@compuserve.com, pp 4-11.

80 Thompson family information, Films from 1993, Jane L Fouraker, Lancaster Co, PA.

81 Thompson family information, Jim Thompson, jbthompson@@compuserve.com, pp 4-11 & Thompson family information, Irene C. Stearns, DeKalb, IL.

82 Isabel Penman, Vital records Index, British Isles, Intellectual Reserve Inc, 8/5/2010.

83 Alexander Thompson, Schuylkill County, PA, p 668-669.

84 Alexander Thompson, Miners Journal, December 5, 1873.

85 Mrs. Thompson, Burial record, Miners Journal deaths, 1851.

86 Alexander Thompson, Greenwood Cemetery, Tower City, Schuylkill Co, PA, John Barket, Tower City, PA, A-4-2.

87 Thompson household, 1840 United States Census, Schuylkill Co, PA, ancestry.com & Microfilm, PA State Library, Hbg, PA.

88 Thompson family information, Jennifer Bachman.

89 Thompson family information, James Thompson, jbthompson@@compuserve.com.

90 Thompson family information, Signed November 1, 1836, Jim Thompson, jbthompson@@compuserve.com, pp 4-11.

91 Alexander Thompson, November 1836, Court of Common Pleas, Schuylkill Co, PA.

92 Alexander Thompson, Dauphin Co Biograhpical Encyclopedia.

93 Tower City Centennial.

94 Alexander Thompson, Sheridan, Pottsville & Schuylkill Co, PA, J.H. Zerbey, pp 1131-1132.

95 Alexander Thompson, Reg of Wills, Bk 4, pp 142-3; probate file, 1873, unnumbered original papers, 10pp, Schuylkill Co Courthouse, Schuylkill, PA, Norman Nicol, Apr 2008.

96 Mrs. Thompson, Burial record, Miners Journal deaths, April 1851.

97 Penman family information, Jim Thompson, jbthompson@@compuserve.com.

98 Michael Goodman, Tower City, Porter Centennial, 1868-1968, p 188.

99 Michael Goodman death certificate, #1252, May 1901, Dauphin County Register of Wills, Harrisburg, PA.

100 Michael Goodman death certificate, #1252, May 1901, Dauphin County Register of Wills, Harrisburg, PA.

101 Goodman household, 1840 United States Census, Schuylkill Co, PA, Roll M704 492, p 79, Image 159, ancestry.com & Microfilm, PA State Library, Hbg, PA.

102 Goodman household, 1850 United States Census, Dauphin Co, PA, 338, ancestry.com & Microfilm, PA State Library, Hbg, PA.

103 Goodman household, 1860 United States Census, Dauphin Co, PA, ancestry.com & Microfilm, PA State Library, Hbg, PA.

104 Goodman household, 1880 United States Census, Dauphin Co, PA, www.ancestry.com and 1880 United States Census, Dauphin Co, PA, FHL 1255124, Film T9-1124, p 432B, www.familysearch.org.

105 Goodman household, 1900 United States Census, Dauphin Co, PA, www.ancestry.com and 1900 United States Census, Dauphin Co, PA, Pa State Library microfilm image.

106 Michael Gutman, St. Peter's Evangelical Lutheran Church, Reinertown, PA, Pastor Arthur Sonnenberg, July 6, 2005.

107 Goodman household, 1850 United States Census, Dauphin Co, PA, 338, ancestry.com & Microfilm, PA State Library, Hbg, PA.

108 Goodman household, 1860 United States Census, Dauphin Co, PA, ancestry.com & Microfilm, PA State Library, Hbg, PA.

109 Goodman household, 1880 United States Census, Dauphin Co, PA, www.ancestry.com and 1880 United States Census, Dauphin Co, PA, FHL 1255124, Film T9-1124, p 432B, www.familysearch.org.

110 Michael Goodman, Probate files, 1901, Inventory, 3-173, Aff. of Death, Bk D, p434, Dauphin County Courthouse, Reg of Wills, Deborah Hershey, Elizabethtown, PA, Mar 2008.

111 Goodman household, 1870 United States Census, Dauphin Co, PA, ancestry.com & Microfilm, PA State Library, Hbg, PA.

112 Brown household, 1820 United States Census, Schuylkill Co, PA, ancestry.com & Microfilm, PA State Library, Hbg, PA.

113 Brown household, 1830 United States Census, Dauphin Co, PA, ancestry.com & Microfilm, PA State Library, Hbg, PA.

114 Hensel-Workman marriage record, 1853, Register of Wills, Dauphin Co, PA.

115 Hensel family information, Dauphin Co Marriages, 1852-1855, CAGS.

116 Hensel family information, History of Michael Hensel (Hentzel) Sr. & His Related Families, R. Longtin-Thompson.

117 Andrew Gise Hensel death certificate, #0036891, #115081, Reg # 84, December 1908, Department of Vital records, New Castle, PA.

118 Andrew Gise Hensel, #0036891, #115081, Reg # 84, December 1908, Department of Vital records, New Castle, PA.

119 Hensel household, 1840 United States Census, Perry Co, PA, ancestry.com & Microfilm, PA State Library, Hbg, PA.

120 Hensil household, 1850 United States Census, Perry Co, PA, Roll M432-805, p 433, Image 283, ancestry.com & Microfilm, PA State Library, Hbg, PA.

121 Hentzel household, 1860 United States Census, Schuylkill Co, PA, M653-1181, 628-9, ancestry.com & Microfilm, PA State Library, Hbg, PA.

122 Hensel household, 1870 United States Census, Dauphin Co, PA, M593-1335, 997-566, ancestry.com & Microfilm, PA State Library, Hbg, PA.

123 Hensel household, 1880 United States Census, Dauphin Co, PA, FHL 1255124, Film T9-1124, p 270D, 71-76, www.familysearch.org.

124 Weist household, 1900 United States Census, Dauphin Co, PA, Roll T623 1404, p 2A, ED 190, ancestry.com & Microfilm, PA State Library, Hbg, PA.

125 Andrew Henzel, Anton Hentschel, Civil war Soldier & Sailor System, M554, Roll 53, http://www.itd.nps.gov/cwss/soldiers.cfm.

126 Andrew Henzel, US Civil War Soldiers, 1861-1865, M554 roll 53, www.ancestry.com.

127 Hentzel household, 1860 United States Census, Schuylkill Co, PA, PA State library microfilm.

128 Hensel household, 1870 United States Census, Dauphin Co, PA, PA State library microfilm.

129 Weist household, 1900 United States Census, Dauphin Co, PA, Roll T623 1404, p 2A, ED 190, ancestry.com & Microfilm, PA State Library, Hbg, PA.

130 Heheel household, 1900 United States Census, Dauphin Co, PA, Roll T623 1404, p 2A, ED 190, ancestry.com & Microfilm, PA State Library, Hbg, PA.

131 Hensel household, 1870 United States Census, Dauphin Co, PA, M593-1335, 997-566, ancestry.com & Microfilm, PA State Library, Hbg, PA.

132 Workman household, 1840 United States Census, Dauphin Co, PA, ancestry.com & Microfilm, PA State Library, Hbg, PA.

133 Workman household, 1850 United States Census, Dauphin Co, PA, PA State library microfilm.

134 Daniel Updegrove death certificate, #1071, March 1899, Dauphin County Register of Wills, Harrisburg, PA.

135 Updegrove Family information, Updegrove Genealogy, PA State library.

136 Mrs Sarah Updegrove death certificate, #0042525, #81494, File 42, Reg 2193, July 1923, Department of Vital Records, New Castle, PA.

137 Daniel Updegrove, Vital records, Dauphin County, p 26.

138 Daniel Updegrove, Vital records, Dauphin County, p 26.

139 Bastoe household, 1850 United States Census, Dauphin Co, PA ancestry.com & Microfilm, PA State Library, Hbg, PA.

140 Updegrove household, 1850 United States Census, Dauphin Co, PA, PA State library microfilm.

141 Hullsizer household, 1860 United States Census, Lycoming Co, PA, ancestry.com & Microfilm, PA State Library, Hbg, PA.

142 Updegrove household, 1870 United States Census, Dauphin Co, PA, Roll 1335, p 792, Jan.

143 Updegrove household, 1850 United States Census, Dauphin Co, PA ancestry.com & Microfilm, PA State Library, Hbg, PA.

144 Daniel Updegrove, Civil War Pension Index, www.ancestry.com.

145 Daniel Updegrove, Schuylkill Countians captured in the Civil War, rootsweb.com.

146 Daniel Updegrave, 1864-5 service, 1890 Veterans Schedule, private, Tower City, Schuylkill Co, PA, Roll 83, p 3, ED 215, www.ancestry.com.

147 Daniel Updegrove, Civil War Pension Index, K 39 PA infantry, filed 1899, www.ancestry.com.

148 Daniel Updegrove, Civil War Veterans Card File, 1861-1866, PA State Archives, www.digitalarchives.state.pa.us.

149 Culp household, 1850 United States Census, Union Co, PA, ancestry.com & Microfilm, PA State Library, Hbg, PA.

150 Culp household, 1860 United States Census, Union Co, PA, ancestry.com & Microfilm, PA State Library, Hbg, PA.

151 Updegrove household, 1900 United States Census, Juniata, PA, ancestry.com & Microfilm, PA State Library, Hbg, PA.

152 Shadel household, 1910 United States Census, Dauphin Co, PA, ED 0133, Visit 0014, www.ancestry.com and 1910 United States Census, Dauphin Co, PA, ED 133, Sheet 1, PA State Library microfilm image.

153 Weist household, 1920 United States Census, Schuylkill Co, PA, ED 143, sheet A, PA State Library, microfilm image.

154 Culp household, 1850 United States Census, Union Co, PA, ancestry.com & Microfilm, PA State Library, Hbg, PA.

155 Daniel Updegrove, Civil War Pension Index: General Index to Pension Files, 1861-1934, www.ancestry.com.

156 Sarah Salome Updegrove, Probate files, Roll 43, U4, Dauphin County Courthouse, Reg of Wills, Harrisburg, PA, Deborah Hershey, Elizabethtown, PA, Mar 2008.

Sources (con't)

157 Thompson family information, Jane Fouraker,
    mjfour@@mindpsring.com.

158 David Penman, FHL, Pedigree chart, www.ancestry.com.

159 Penman family information, John Penman,
    JCPenman@@aol.com.

160 Pennman household, 1840 United States Census, Schuylkill Co,
    PA, ancestry.com & Microfilm, PA State Library, Hbg, PA.

161 Elizabeth Penman, 1841 Scotland Census Record, Midlothian,
    SCO, www.ancestry.com.

162 John Penman, Vital records Index, British Isles, Intellectual
    Reserve Inc, 8/5/2010.

163 Ancestry Public Tree, Goodman Family Tree, Robert Goodman,
    Phila, PA, ancestry,com.

164 Schofield Family Tree, jenn 13146, ancestry pubic trees,
    ancestry.com.

165 Public Family Tree, Ancestry Famnily Tree, carolcaroll115, Carol
    Weanfeb, CA, ancestry.com.

166 Brown family information, Peter Brown descedants, Deb
    Kandybowksi, debkandy@@epix.net.

167 Brown household, 1790 United States Census, Berks Co, PA,
    ancestry.com & Microfilm, PA State Library, Hbg, PA.

168 Brown household, 1820 United States Census, York Co, PA,
    ancestry.com.

169 Brown household, 1810 United States Census, Berks Co, PA
    ancestry.com & Microfilm, PA State Library, Hbg, PA.

170 Brown household, 1820 United States Census, Dauphin Co, PA,
    ancestry.com & Microfilm, PA State Library, Hbg, PA.

171 Brown household, 1830 United States Census, Dauphin Co, PA
    ancestry.com & Microfilm, PA State Library, Hbg, PA.

172 Brown household, 1840 United States Census, Dauphin Co, PA
    ancestry.com & Microfilm, PA State Library, Hbg, PA.

173 Brown household, 1850 United States Census, Dauphin Co, PA, p
    336, Kathleen M Fagnani, katfagn@@erols.com.

174 Brown household, 1850 United States Census, Dauphin Co, PA,
    338, ancestry.com & Microfilm, PA State Library, Hbg, PA.

175 Brown household, 1850 United States Census, Dauphin Co, PA,
    338, ancestry.com & Microfilm, PA State Library, Hbg, PA.

176 Peter Braun, Schuylkill County, PA, Chicago, JH Beers & Co,
    1916, vol II, p 1071, Historical Society of Schuykill County.

177 Maria Brown, McCallister's Methodist Cemetery, Barbara, Homelybin@@aol.com.

178 Brown household, 1860 United States Census, Dauphin Co, PA, ancestry.com & Microfilm, PA State Library, Hbg, PA.

179 Andreas Hansel, Baptism, York Co, PA library, cards on file.

180 Andrew Hensel, Christ Church, Littlestown, PA, Adams Co County 18th records lookup, Virginia, vperry1@@shawneelink.net.

181 Andrew Hensel, Death of an Old Soldier, Obituary, New Bloomfield newspaper, July 1875.

182 Andrew Hensel, Source 146, index card, Perry County Historians.

183 Mrs Hensel, Source 140 & 146, index cards, Perry County Historians.

184 Mrs Mary Hensel, New Bloomfield Times, January 20, 1877.

185 Andrew Hensel, Union Lutheran Cemetery, New Bloomfield, Perry Co, PA, 30 Perry Co PA Cemetery Records, Closson Press, Apollo, PA, 1992.

186 Hensel household, 1800 United States Census, York Co, PA, ancestry.com & Microfilm, PA State Library, Hbg, PA.

187 Hinsle household, 1820 United States Census, Adams Co, PA, ancestry.com & Microfilm, PA State Library, Hbg, PA.

188 Henzell household, 1830 United States Census, Perry Co, PA, ancestry.com & Microfilm, PA State Library, Hbg, PA.

189 Hensley household, 1840 United States Census, Perry Co, PA, ancestry.com & Microfilm, PA State Library, Hbg, PA.

190 Miller household, 1860 United States Census, Perry Co, PA, PA State library microfilm.

191 Hentzelle household, 1870 United States Census, Perry Co, PA, PA State library microfilm.

192 Andrew Hensel, War of 1812 Records, DDC, 1999-, www.ancestry.com.

193 Churches Between the Mountains, A History of the Lutheran Congregatioons in Perry County, PA,. D.H. Focht.

194 Andrew Hensel, Probate files, 1875, rep 49, Perry County Historicans, Newport, PA, Deborah Hershey, Elizabethtown, PA, Jan 2009.

195 Andrew Hensel, 1878, August 02, 1875, Dauphin County Register of Wills, Harrisburg, PA.

196 Hensil household, 1850 United States Census, Perry Co, PA, Roll M432-805, p 433, Image 283, ancestry.com & Microfilm, PA State Library, Hbg, PA.

197 Miller household, 1860 United States Census, Perry Co, PA, PA State library microfilm.

198 Andrew Hentzell, Adams Co Centinel, Gettysburg, PA, October 8, 1823.

199 Mary Hensel, Union Lutheran Cemetery, New Bloomfield, Perry Co, PA, 30 Perry Co PA Cemetery Records, Closson Press, Apollo, PA, 1992.

200 Guise household, 1800 United States Census, Adams Co, PA, ancestry.com & Microfilm, PA State Library, Hbg, PA.

201 Guise household, 1810 United States Census, Adams Co, PA, ancestry.com & Microfilm, PA State Library, Hbg, PA.

202 Guise household, 1820 United States Census, Adams Co, PA, ancestry.com & Microfilm, PA State Library, Hbg, PA.

203 Workman family information, Evelyn Hartman, Evelyn S Hartman, deanh@@voicenet.com.

204 Joseph Workman, Wiconisco Calvary Cemetery, Rhonda, yeahbaby@@penn.com, Row 4.

205 The Romberger Line, Ancestors of Richard Alan Lebo.

206 Romberger Family, St. John's Lutheran Church, p 10, John Romberger.

207 Workman household, 1820 United States Census, Dauphin Co, PA, ancestry.com & Microfilm, PA State Library, Hbg, PA.

208 Workman household, 1830 United States Census, Dauphin Co, PA, ancestry.com & Microfilm, PA State Library, Hbg, PA.

209 Workman household, 1850 United States Census, Union Co, PA, FTM CD 305, Disk 4, film 775.

210 Joseph Workman Sr, Probate files, 1857, Letter of Admin, A-35, Dauphin County Courthouse, Reg of Wills, Deborah Hershey, Elizabethtown, PA, Mar 2008.

211 Workman, PA Births, Dauphin County, J. Humphrey.

212 Romberger household, 1800 United States Census, Dauphin Co, PA, ancestry.com & Microfilm, PA State Library, Hbg, PA.

213 Romberger household, 1810 United States Census, Dauphin Co, PA, ancestry.com & Microfilm, PA State Library, Hbg, PA.

214 Johann Uptegrav, 1805, Jacobs Church, Pine Grove, Swedberg, SCUR III, p 240.

215 Updegrove Family information, Rosie Byard, rbyard@@bigfoot.com.

216 Rutzel Family Genealogy, David Rutzel, leztur@@hotmail.com, awt.ancestry.com.

217 Updegrove household, 1810 United States Census, Dauphin Co, PA, ancestry.com & Microfilm, PA State Library, Hbg, PA.

218 Updegrove household, 1820 United States Census, Dauphin Co, PA, ancestry.com & Microfilm, PA State Library, Hbg, PA.

219 Updagrove household, 1830 United States Census, Berks Co, PA, ancestry.com & Microfilm, PA State Library, Hbg, PA.

220 Updegraf household, 1840 United States Census, Dauphin Co, PA, ancestry.com & Microfilm, PA State Library, Hbg, PA.

221 Updegrove household, 1860 United States Census, Lycoming Co, PA, ancestry.com & Microfilm, PA State Library, Hbg, PA.

222 Kulp family information, J. Wagner, Union County.

223 Culp household, 1850 United States Census, Union Co, PA, FTM CD 305, Disk 10, film 831.

224 Culp household, 1860 United States Census, Union Co, PA, ancestry.com & Microfilm, PA State Library, Hbg, PA.

225 Schneck household, 1810 United States Census, Northumberland Co, PA, ancestry.com & Microfilm, PA State Library, Hbg, PA.

226 Schneck household, 1820 United States Census, Union Co, PA, ancestry.com & Microfilm, PA State Library, Hbg, PA.

227 Tax lists.

228 Ancestors of John Wedgewood White, Ancestors of John Wedgewood White, jwcotton, Russellville, Arkansas ancestry Tree, ancestry.com.

229 Our Coal Mining Ancestors, Lindsay Reeks, pp 161-172, c/o Tammy Tarbet, Bennington, ID.

230 John Penman, FHL, IGI Individual record, www.familysearch.org.

231 John Penman, FHL, IGI Individual record, www.familysearch.com.

232 Penman family information, Penman family information, John Penman, PenmanJC@@aol.com.

233 Katherine Brown, FHL, IGI Individual record, www.familysearch.com and FHL, IGi Individual record, CD 54, Pin 16549, www.ancestry.com.

234 David Stoddart, FHL, IGI Individual record, www.familysearch.org.

235 David Stoddard, FHL, Individual record, AFN 148J-5NB, www.familysearch.com.

236 Penman family information, John Penman, PenmanJC@@aol.com.

237 Brown household, 1820 United States Census, Berks Co, PA, Roll, ancestry.com & Microfilm, PA State Library, Hbg, PA.

238 Peter Braun, Brown/Braun Family Line, Gayle T. Clews, gclews@@aessuccess.org.

239 Brown family information, Schuylkill County, USgenweb.com, p 156.

240 Berks County Early Church Records, Volume 2, Diana Quinones, audianaq@@msn.com.

241 Casper Hensel, Descendants of Casper (LaHentzelle) Hensel, Evelyn S. Hartman.

242 Casper Hentzel, Abstract of York County, PA Wills, 1749-1819, F.E. Wright, Family llne Productions, 1995, Gene Smith, GSmithan@@aol.com.

243 Hensel family information, H Andrew Brown, habraun2@@netscape.net, Los Angeles, CA, 2007.

244 Caspar Haenssel, FGS, York PA library.

245 Capser Hensel, Descendants of Casper (LaHentzelle) Hensel, Evelyn S. Hartman.

246 Casper Hensel, H.J. Young, Christ Reformed Church 1747-1871, Littlestown, Adams Co, PA.

247 Capser Hensel, Adams Co Church Records, PA of the 18th Century, Family Line Prod., NY, c/o Gene Smith, GSmithsan@@aolom.

248 Hensel family information, York Co, History of Michael Hensel (Hentzel) Sr. & His Related Families, R. Longtin-Thompson.

249 Casper Hensel, Muster Roll of the 4th Company York County, 1785, Capt.M Will, Lt H Shilt, footnote.com.

250 Warner, Beers & Co, History of Adams Co County, 1886, p 316.

251 Casper Hentzel, Probate files, 1800, Rep 37, York County Archives, York, PA, Deborah Hershey, Elizabethtown, PA, Dec 2008.

252 Casper Hentzel, April 28, 1800, January 3, 1805, York County Will Abstracts, York County, PA.

253 Casper Hentzel, April 28, 1800, 1805, OCI 257, L25, 7-5, York PA library.

254 Casper Hentzel, Probate files, 1805, Rep 37, York County Archives, York, PA, Deborah Hershey, Elizabethtown, PA, Dec 2008.

255 Tax lists, Germany & Mt. Pleasant Townships, Adams Co County Historical Society.

256 Mary A Guise, Family pedigree, www.rootsweb.com, tiana.geo@@yahoo.com.

257 Gise household, 1790 United States Census, Northampton Co, PA, ancestry.com & Microfilm, PA State Library, Hbg, PA.

258 Gise household, 1800 United States Census, Adams Co, PA, ancestry.com & Microfilm, PA State Library, Hbg, PA.

259 Adam Gise, Revolutionary War Military Abstract Card File, PA State Archives, www.digitalarchives.state.pu.us/archive.

260 Adam Gise, PA State Archives, Rev War Index, http://www.digitalarchives.state.pa.us/archive.asp?view=ArchiveIte ms&ArchiveID=13&FID=478075&LID=478174&FL=&p=4.

261 Adam Gise, 1799 Menallan Twp. Tax List, Histopry of Adams Co County, Donna Zinn, djzinnn@@pa.net.

262 Adam Gice, Adams Co Centinel, Gettysburg, PA, October 8, 1823.

263 Adam Gise, 1834, A1784, Index to Wills and Administration Bonds of Adams Co, PA 1800-1864, SCPGS, York, PA 1997, c/o Gene Smith, GSmithsan@@aolom.

264 Romberger Family information, Family Group sheet, Corethel J. Vinup, Shaomkin, PA.

265 Direct Descendants of John Bartholomus Romberger, Weiss, Shreffler & Romberg, Roger Cramer, members.aol.com/roghistory.

266 Romberger All-Family History Site, http://freepages.genealogy.rootsweb.ancestry.com/~rombergerfa mily/, Dr John Romberger, Jan 2010.

267 Descendants of Johann Pfannebecker, Pfennebaker History & John A. Romberger manuscript, 1997.

268 Romberger Family, Gratz History, p 207.

269 Baltzer Romberger, Tax list, 1798, Dauphin Co, PA, John Romberger.

270 Romberger Family information, Ron Mitchell, ronnie@@itol.com.

271 Rumberger household, 1800 United States Census, Dauphin Co, PA, ancestry.com & Microfilm, PA State Library, Hbg, PA.

272 Rumberger household, 1810 United States Census, Dauphin Co, PA, ancestry.com & Microfilm, PA State Library, Hbg, PA.

273 Romberger household, 1820 United States Census, Dauphin Co, PA, ancestry.com & Microfilm, PA State Library, Hbg, PA.

274 Romberger household, 1830 United States Census, Dauphin Co, PA, ancestry.com & Microfilm, PA State Library, Hbg, PA.

275 Romberger Family, p 261.

276 Romberger Family information, John A Romberger, Elizabethville, PA.

277 Balthaser Romberger, Probate files, 1839, Letter of Admin, Dauphin County Courthouse, Reg of Wills, Deborah Hershey, Elizabethtown, PA, Mar 2008.

278 Selvage & Peterson Families & More, Charles J Peterson, PetersonC@@missouri.edu, awt.ancestry.com.

279 Conrad Updegrove, Church records, St. Pauls Church, Tower City, PA, Marie Rodichok, Church Secretary.

280 Strayer & Other Families, Glenda S. Strayer, oolong@@dragonbbs.com, awt.ancestry.com.

281 Uptegraff Family Genalogy Forum, Rosie Byard, rbyard@@bigfoot.com.

282 Updegrove Family information, p 58, Ed Froeschle, Salem, OR, shared@@teleport.com.

283 Updegrove household, 1820 United States Census, Dauphin Co, PA, Roll M33 102, p 256, Image 104, ancestry.com & Microfilm, PA State Library, Hbg, PA.

284 Updegrove Family information, p 115, Ed Froeschle, Salem, OR, shared@@teleport.com.

285 Updegrove Family information, p 164, Ed Froeschle, Salem, OR, shared@@teleport.com.

286 Updegrove Family information, p 358, Ed Froeschle, Salem, OR, shared@@teleport.com.

287 Updegrove Family information, p 371, Ed Froeschle, Salem, OR, shared@@teleport.com.

288 Updegrove household (Updigrove), 1860 United States Census, Juniata, PA, PA State library microfilm.

289 Updegrove genealogy, Vol 10, PA State library.

290 Rutzel Family Genealogy, Rosie Byard, rbyard@@bigfoot.com.

291 Schnuke household, 1710 United States Census, Northumberland Co, PA, ancestry.com & Microfilm, PA State Library, Hbg, PA.

292 Snook household, 1820 United States Census, Union Co, PA ancestry.com & Microfilm, PA State Library, Hbg, PA.

293 Schnuke household, 1830 United States Census, Northumberland Co, PA ancestry.com & Microfilm, PA State Library, Hbg, PA.

294 Thompson History, Jim Thompson, jbthompson@@compuserve.com, pp 4-11.

295 Thompson family information.

296 Margaret Bowman, One tree, from WFT collection, trees.ancestry.com/owt, www.ancestry.com.

297 Casper Hensel, Hensels of Adams Co County, Adams Co County Historical Society.

298 Caspar Hentsell, September 1765,. Naturalizations, PA, p 113.

299 Casper Hensel, Christ Church commnuicants, Littlestown, Adams Co, PA, 1776, p 86, Victoria Cawood Thompson, thompst7@@yahoo.com.

300 Casper Hensel, 1767 Pennsylvania Tax Lists, http://freepages.genealogy.rootsweb.com/~genbel/sept/patowshp 1767.htm.

301 Casper Hensel, Christ Church, Littlestown, PA, Adams Co County 18th records lookup, Virginia, vperry1@@shawneelink.net.

302 Casper Hansel, Tax List of York County 1779, PA Archives 3rd Ed., Family Line Production, 1989, Gene Smith, GSmithan@@aol.com.

303 Romberger Family information, Carol Mallory, wamcam@@cjnetworks.com.

304 Direct Descendants of John Bartholomus Romberger to Roger Cramer, Roger Cramer, October 10, 2004.

305 Balthaser Romberger, & Anna Marie Bricker, Bob Salzman, Beavertown, OR, www.e-familytree.net/f2850.htm.

306 John Romberger, Romberger family, Onetree, ancestry.com.

307 Balthaser Romberger, Debbie Ferguson's Family Tree, 2006, debbief56@@myfamily.com, worldconnect.genealogy.rootsweb.com.

308 Rumberger household, 1800 United States cenus, Dauphin Co, PA, ancestry.com & Microfilm, PA State Library, Hbg, PA.

309 Rumberger household, 1810 United States cenus, Dauphin Co, PA, ancestry.com & Microfilm, PA State Library, Hbg, PA.

310 Bartel Raumberger, Passenger and Immigration Lists Index, 1500-1900, myfamily.com, P. William Filby, ancestry.com.

311 Balser Ramberger, PA State Archives, Rev War Index, http://www.digitalarchives.state.pa.us/archive.asp?view=ArchiveIte ms&ArchiveID=13&FID=478075&LID=478174&FL=&p=4.

312 Bartel Raumberger, PA Census, 1772-1890, Philadelphia, PA, www.ancestry.com.

313 Romberger Family information, John Romberger, email 7/31/2005.

314 Jacob Leyman, Revolutonary War Soldiers buried at Bindnagles Cemetery, Vaughn Hostettler, Palmyra, PA.

315 Lehman family information, Sherry L Johnson, sherrjo@@tenet.edu.

316 Leman household, 1790 United States Census, Dauphin Co, PA ancestry.com & Microfilm, PA State Library, Hbg, PA.

317 Lehmey household, 1800 United States Census, Dauphin Co, PA, ancestry.com & Microfilm, PA State Library, Hbg, PA.

318 Jacob Leman, Probate files, 1805, Bk B, p291, File 1, Dauphin County Courthouse, Reg of Wills, Deborah Hershey, Elizabethtown, PA, Mar 2008.

319 Jacob Leman, December 13, 1800, November 2, 1805, Abstracts of Wills, PA, p 290.

320 Benfield Family information, MihnBu@@aol.com.

321 Updegrove Family information, Robin Kornides, kornides@@usaor.net.

322 Updegrove Family information, GED imported October 1999, Robin Kornides.

323 John William Op Den Graeff, Descendants of Herman Op den Graef, www.kevin-sholder.net.

324 Rutzel Family, David Rutzel, leztur@@hotmail.com, awt.ancestry.com.

325 John William Op Den Graeff, Descendants of Herman Op den Graef, www.kevin-sholder.net.

326 Burials 1782-1807, Rev. John William Boos, Ind. reformed Minister, Central Berks Co, BCGS, Berks Co, PA.

327 John William Op Den Graeff, Updegrove History, Kevin L Sholder, Dayton, OH, www.scholderer.org, June 2010.

328 Descedants of Herman OpDenGraeff, Cathy Berger, Bedford, PA.

329 Elizabeth Updegroff, Probate file, 1804, unnumbered original papers, 4pp, Berks Co Courthouse, Berks, PA, Norman Nicol, Apr 2008.

330 Angst household, 1790 United States Census, Berks Co, PA, Roll M637 8, p 38, Image 0201, ancestry.com & Microfilm, PA State Library, Hbg, PA.

331 Angst household, 1800 United States Census, Berks Co, PA ancestry.com & Microfilm, PA State Library, Hbg, PA.

332 Angst household, 1810 United States Census, Berks Co, PA, ancestry.com & Microfilm, PA State Library, Hbg, PA.

333 Daniel Keefer.

334 Daniel Angst, Revolutionary War Military Abstract Card File, PA State Archives, www.digitalarchives.state.pu.us/archive.

335 Daniel Angst, Tax List: 1754-1785: Pine Grove Twp, Berks (now Schuylkill) Co, PA, Contributed for use in USGenWeb Archives by Richard Turnbach. Early [Colonial/Revolutionary] Tax and Census for Pine Grove Twp. Then Berks County, PA [now Schuylkill County], http://ftp.r.

Chapter Two

Our family's photos.

Some photographs of our family.
A picture is worth a thousand words.

Photos for Harper Thompson

Harper Bruce Thompson

Birth:	September 28, 1907	Father:	Abel Robert Thompson
Death:	July 23, 1981	Mother:	Augusta "Gussie" Mae Hensel
Marriage:	June 15, 1935	Spouse:	Myrtle Adeline Batdorf

8 Harper Thompson

8 Harper Thompson & Myrtle A Batdorf

8 Harper Thompson (2)

8 Harper Thompson (3)

8 Harper Thompson (4)

8 Harper Thompson (5)

8 Harper Thompson, with arrow

Photos for Abel Thompson

Abel Robert Thompson

Birth:	November 28, 1880	Father:	Robert Bruce Thompson
Death:	October 15, 1918	Mother:	Lydia Ann Goodman
Marriage:	June 15, 1904	Spouse:	Augusta "Gussie" Mae Hensel

16 Abel Thompson

16 Abel Thompson (2)

Abel & Gussie Thompson.

Augusta "Gussie" Mae Hensel

Birth:	February 16, 1885	
Death:	March 27, 1973	
Marriage:	June 15, 1904	

Father:	Howard Andrew Carson Hensel
Mother:	Clara Matilda Updegrove
Spouse:	Abel Robert Thompson

17 Augusta Hensel &
Lydia M Thompson

17 Augusta Hensel (2)

17 Augusta Hensel (3)

17 Augusta Hensel (4)

Photos for Robert Thompson

Robert Bruce Thompson

Birth:	September 24, 1847	Father:	Alexander Thompson
Death:	October 10, 1907	Mother:	Isabelle Stoddart Penman
Marriage:	Abt. 1873	Spouse:	Lydia Ann Goodman

32 Robert B Thompson &
33 Lydia A Goodman &
couple

32 Robert Thompson

Photos for Lydia Goodman

Lydia Ann Goodman

Birth:	February 20, 1856	Father:	Michael Goodman
Death:	October 09, 1883	Mother:	Mary Magdalena Brown
Marriage:	Abt. 1873	Spouse:	Robert Bruce Thompson

33 Lydia Goodman

Photos for Howard Hensel

Howard Andrew Carson Hensel

Birth:	September 02, 1858	Father:	Andrew Guise Hensel
Death:	June 06, 1927	Mother:	Catherine Workman
Marriage:	September 02, 1884	Spouse:	Clara Matilda Updegrove

34 Howard Hensel

34 Howard Hensel & Clara Updegrove

34 Howard Hensel & sibling

34 Howard Hensel, Clara Updegrove & children

Photos for Clara Updegrove

Clara Matilda Updegrove

Birth:	November 30, 1866	Father:	Daniel Updegrove
Death:	March 28, 1926	Mother:	Sarah "Salome" A Culp
Marriage:	September 02, 1884	Spouse:	Howard Andrew Carson Hensel

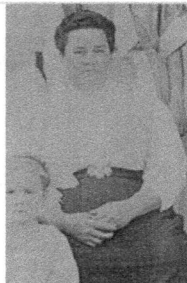

35 Clara Updegrove

35 Clara Updegrove & Lydia

35 Clara Updegrove & Lydia (2)

35 Clara Updegrove (2)

Photos for Alexander Thompson

Alexander Thompson

Birth:	October 22, 1805	Father:	Robert Thompson
Death:	December 04, 1873	Mother:	Janet Russell
Marriage:	January 01, 1835	Spouse:	Isabelle Stoddart Penman

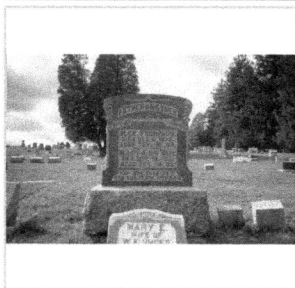

64 Alex Thompson

Photos for Michael Goodman

Michael Goodman

Birth:	June 10, 1806	Father:	Jacob Guteman
Death:	December 27, 1900	Mother:	Catherine Voller
Marriage:	Abt. 1832	Spouse:	Mary Magdalena Brown

66 Michael Goodman

Photos for Magdalena Brown

Mary Magdalena Brown

Birth:	1816	Father:	Peter Brown
Death:	December 17, 1884	Mother:	Anna Maria Schreckengast?
Marriage:	Abt. 1832	Spouse:	Michael Goodman

67 Mary Magd Goodman

Photos for Andrew G Hensel

Andrew Guise Hensel

Birth:	February 18, 1831	Father:	Andrew W Hensel
Death:	December 14, 1908	Mother:	Mary A Guise
Marriage:	May 17, 1853	Spouse:	Catherine Workman

68 Andrew Hensel

68 Andrew Hensel &
Catherine Workman

Photos for Catherine Workman

Catherine Workman

Birth:	May 17, 1838	Father:	Joseph Workman
Death:	February 10, 1877	Mother:	Susan Romberger
Marriage:	May 17, 1853	Spouse:	Andrew Guise Hensel

69 Catherine Workman

Photos for Daniel Updegrove

Daniel Updegrove

Birth:	June 28, 1839	Father:	John M Updegrove
Death:	March 25, 1899	Mother:	Elizabeth Trovinger
Marriage:	October 09, 1862	Spouse:	Sarah "Salome" A Culp

70 Daniel Updegrove

Photos for Sarah Culp

Sarah "Salome" A Culp

Birth:	June 30, 1844	Father:	Jacob Kulp
Death:	July 03, 1923	Mother:	Elizabeth Schneck
Marriage:	October 09, 1862	Spouse:	Daniel Updegrove

71 Augusta Hensel, Clara Updegrove, Sarah Culp & child

71 Sarah Culp

Photos for Andrew W Hensel

Andrew W Hensel

Birth:	June 28, 1793	Father:	John Casper Hensel
Death:	July 07, 1875	Mother:	Maria Eva
Marriage:	Abt. 1814	Spouse:	Mary A Guise

136 Andrew Hensel

136 Hensel memorial

Photos for Joseph Workman

Joseph Workman

Birth:	December 03, 1795	Father:	<No name>
Death:	May 23, 1857	Mother:	
Marriage:	Abt. 1818	Spouse:	Susan Romberger

138 Joseph & Susan
Workman

Chapter Three

Our family's places.

Where we're from, born, raised, lived and roamed through and what property value our ancestors had.

Place Report

$100

    Brown, Peter
                Propty: 1850
    Kulp, Jacob
                Propty: 1860
    Updegrove, Daniel
                Propty: 1870

$1000

    Goodman, Michael
                Propty: 1850

$1000 + $600

    Goodman, Michael
                Propty: 1860

$120

    Kulp, Jacob
                Propty: 1850

$1500

    Updegrove, Conrad
                Propty: 1850

$2000

    Thompson, Alexander
                Propty: 1850

$2000 + $200

    Goodman, Michael
                Propty: 1870

$250 + $123

    Hensel, Andrew Guise
                Propty: 1860

$294

    Workman, Joseph
                Propty: 1850

$340

    Hensel, Andrew Guise
                Propty: 1870

$3500

    Hensel, Augusta "Gussie" Mae
                Propty: 1930

$450

    Hensel, Andrew W
                Propty: 1850

$500

    Updegrove, John M
                Propty: 1850

$500 + $120
Hensel, Andrew W
          Propty: 1870

$5000 + $230
Thompson, Alexander
          Propty: 1860

$800 + $300
Hensel, Andrew W
          Propty: 1860

? St., Rush, Dauphin Co, PA
Thompson, Robert Bruce
          Res: 1880

25 West Grand Ave., Tower City, Schuylkill Co, PA
Culp, Sarah "Salome" A
          Res: 1920

2600 Green St., Harrisburg, Dauphin Co, PA
Thompson, Harper Bruce
          Res: 1981

2660A Green St., Harrisburg, Dauphin Co, PA
Batdorf, Myrtle Adeline
          Res: 1983

329 Main St., Highway Route 199, Sheridan, Schuylkill Co, PA
Hensel, Augusta "Gussie" Mae
          Res: 1930

329 Main St., Sheridan, Schuylkill Co, PA
Hensel, Augusta "Gussie" Mae
          Res: 1920

329 West Grand Ave., Tower City, Schuylkill Co, PA 17980
Hensel, Augusta "Gussie" Mae
          Res: 1973

914 ? St., Emmaus, Lehigh Co, PA
Thompson, Harper Bruce
          Res: 1930

Aaron Ralphsson, Williamstown, Dauphin Co, PA
Culp, Sarah "Salome" A
          Funrl: 1923

Adams Co, PA
Eva, Maria
          Death: Bet. 1800–1802
Guise, John Adam
          Will: 1834
          Death: Aft. 1800
Hensel, Casper
          Death: Abt. 1831
Maria?
          Death: Aft. 1801

Adams, PA

Guise, Mary A
>Marr: Abt. 1814

Hensel, Andrew W
>Marr: Abt. 1814

Allentown, Lehigh Co, PA
Hensel, Edna Boyer
>Death: October 14, 2001

Alsace, France
Braun, Peter
>Res: 1765

Annville, Dauphin (Lebanon) Co, PA
Romberger, John Balthaser
>Res: Bet. 1790–1800

Annville, Lebanon Co., PA
Romberger, John Balthaser
>Death: September 25, 1800

Beaufort Farms, Camp Curtain, Estherton, Fort Hunter, Harrisburg, Hecktown, Lucknow, Rockville, Uptown, Windsor farms, all Dauphin Co, PA
Batdorf, Myrtle Adeline
>Res: 1983

Thompson, Harper Bruce
>Res: 1981

Berks (Schuylkill) Co, PA
Brown, Peter
>Birth: 1775

Harman, Maria Elizabeth
>Death: Abt. 1810

Berks (Schuylkill), PA
Goodman, Michael
>Birth: June 10, 1806

Berks Co, PA
Benfield, Anna Maria Elizabeth
>Marr: Abt. 1755

Trovinger, Elizabeth
>Death: Bet. 1860–1870; Apoplexy (ie, Paralysis due to stroke)

Updegroff, John William
>Death: Bet. 1800–1804
>Marr: Abt. 1755

Updegrove, Edward Isaac
>Birth: November 27, 1771

Berks?, PA
Angst, John Daniel
>Marr: 1774

Harman, Maria Elizabeth
>Marr: 1774

Bethel, Dauphin Co, PA (Lehmey)
Lehman, Jacob
>Census: 1800

Bethel, Dauphin Co, PA (Lehmey) (con't)

Big Run, Dauphin Co, PA
Batdorf, Myrtle Adeline
> Birth: January 05, 1918

Bindagles Lutheran, Palmyra, Dauphin (Lebanon) Co, PA
Lehman, Jacob
> Burial: 1805

Borthwick, Newbattle, Midlothian, Scotland
Russell, Janet
> Marr: April 22, 1791
Thompson, Robert
> Marr: April 22, 1791

Brady, Lycoming Co, PA (Hullsizer)
Updegrove, Daniel
> Census: 1860

Buffalo, Union Co, PA
Culp, Sarah "Salome" A
> Census: 1860
Kulp, Jacob
> Census: 1860
Schneck, Elizabeth
> Census: 1860

Buffalo, Union Co, PA (Snook)
Schneck, Peter
> Census: 1820

Butler (Menallen), Adams Co, PA
Guise, John Adam
> Res: 1799

Calvary United Methodist, Wiconisco, Dauphin Co, PA
Hensel, Andrew Guise
> Burial: December 16, 1908
Romberger, Susan
> Burial: 1857
Workman, Catherine
> Burial: 1877
Workman, Joseph
> Burial: 1857

Centre, Northumberland (Centre) Co, PA
Schneck, Peter
> Census: 1830

Centre, Northumberland (Union) Co, PA
Schneck, Peter
> Census: 1810

Centre, Perry Co, PA
Guise, Mary A
> Census: 1850
> Census: 1860

Centre, Perry Co, PA (con't)
        Census: 1870
    Hensel, Andrew Guise
        Census: 1850
    Hensel, Andrew W
           Will: Bet. March–December 1864
        Census: 1850

Centre, Perry Co, PA (Hensley)
    Hensel, Andrew W
        Census: 1840

Centre, Perry Co, PA (Hentzelle)
    Hensel, Andrew W
        Census: 1870

Centre, Perry Co, PA (Miller)
    Hensel, Andrew W
        Census: 1860

Christ Church, Littlestown, York (Adams) Co, PA
    Hensel, John Casper
           Confir: April 21, 1776

Christ Reformed, Littlestown, York (Adams) Co, PA
    Hensel, Andrew W
           Baptism: August 11, 1793

Clarks Valley, Dauphin Co, PA
    Brown, Anna Maria
           Birth: February 17, 1815
    Goodman, Lydia Ann
           Birth: February 20, 1856

Clarks Valley, PA, now Charles Kessler farm
    Brown, Peter
           Res: 1916

Clinton, Lycoming Co, PA
    Trovinger, Elizabeth
        Census: 1860
    Updegrove, John M
        Census: 1860

Cochran, Scotland
    Thomson, Robert
           Birth: October 25, 1695

Cockpen, Midlothian, Scotland
    Muckle, Margaret
           Birth: November 05, 1756
           Marr: February 16, 1778
    Stoddart, David
           Marr: February 16, 1778

Collier
    Thomson, Robert
           Occu: Abt. 1760; Coal miner

Cranston, Midlothian, Scotland
    Thomson, Robert
               Birth: September 13, 1734

Cranston, Midlothian, Scotland
    Thompson, Alexander
               Baptism: November 03, 1805
    Thomson, Robert
               Baptism: September 15, 1734

Dalkeith Parish, Midlothian Scotland
    Keitchen, Agnes
               Marr: October 06, 1727
    Moffatt, David
               Marr: October 06, 1727

Dalkeith, Midlothian, Scotland
    Mason, Elizabeth
               Birth: May 15, 1709
    Moffatt, Christina
               Birth: December 11, 1731
               Baptism: December 19, 1731

Dauphin Co, PA
    Brown, Mary Magdalena
               Death: December 17, 1884
    Catherine
               Death: Bet. 1820–1830
    Culp, Sarah "Salome" A
               Marr: October 09, 1862
    Hensel, Andrew W
               Prob: May 24, 1878
    Hensel, Augusta "Gussie" Mae
               Baptism: April 05, 1885
    Lehman, Jacob
               Census: 1790
    Lehman, Susan
               Death: Aft. 1821
    Pennypacker, Martha
               Death: Aft. 1805
    Romberger, Balthasar
               Res: Bet. 1798–1811
    Romberger, Jacob
               Birth: 1806
    Romberger, Salome
               Birth: 1808
    Romberger, Samuel
               Birth: 1803
    Romberger, Susan
               Death: February 23, 1857
               Marr: Abt. 1818
    Schreckengast?, Anna Maria
               Birth: June 15, 1795
    Swab, Catherine "Kate"

Dauphin Co, PA (con't)

Death:

Trovinger, Elizabeth
    Marr: 1823

Updegrove, Daniel
    Res: Bet. 1864–1865
    Marr: October 09, 1862

Updegrove, John M
    Marr: 1823

Updegrove, Solomon
    Birth: 1809

Workman, Elizabeth
    Birth: 1829

Workman, Jacob
    Birth: 1819

Workman, Joseph
    Death: May 23, 1857
    Marr: Abt. 1818

Workman, Susan
    Birth: 1821

Dauphin Co, PA (listed in index only)

Romberger, Balthasar
    Prob: September 02, 1839

Workman, Joseph
    Prob: June 18, 1857

Dauphin Co?, PA

Brown, Mary Magdalena
    Birth: 1816

Brown, Peter
    Marr: Abt. 1812

Schreckengast?, Anna Maria
    Marr: Abt. 1812

Dauphin, PA

Brown, Anna Maria
    Death: September 07, 1891

Dayton, Dauphin Co, PA

Hensel, Arthur Preston
    Birth: 1886

Dean O Snyder, 304 E Grand Ave., Tower City, Schuylkill Co, PA

Hensel, Augusta "Gussie" Mae
    Funrl: 1973

Democrat

Batdorf, Myrtle Adeline
    PoliticalParty:

Dressler Cemetery, Susquehanna, Juniata, PA

Updegrove, Conrad
    Burial: 1865

Duane Snyder, 304 E Grand Ave., Tower City, Schuylkill Co, PA

Hensel, Howard Andrew Carson

Duane Snyder, 304 E Grand Ave., Tower City, Schuylkill Co, PA (con't)
> Funrl: 1927
> Updegrove, Clara Matilda
>> Funrl: 1926

East Hanover, Lancaster (Lebanon) Co, PA
> Angst, John Daniel
>> Birth: December 14, 1749

East Petersburg, Lancaster Co, PA
> Thompson, Abel Franklin
>> Death: June 1985

Edgehead, Cranston, Midlothian, Scotland
> Thompson, Robert
>> Birth: June 27, 1771

Edinburgh, Midlothian, Scotland
> Moffatt, Christina
>> Marr: January 13, 1750
> Russell, William
>> Marr: January 13, 1750

Emmaus, Lehigh Co, PA (Uncle James Knittle)
> Thompson, Harper Bruce
>> Census: 1930

Evangelical Lutheran Circuit, Lykens, Dauphin Co, PA
> Batdorf, Myrtle Adeline
>> Baptism: October 11, 1918

Exerter, Berks Co, PA
> Guteman, Jacob
>> Marr: April 26, 1801
> Voller, Catherine
>> Marr: April 26, 1801

Exeter, Berks Co, PA
> Benfield, Anna Maria Elizabeth
>> Prob: March 21, 1804
>> Death: February 23, 1804

family
> Workman, Catherine
>> Census: 1840; Not listed w

father
> Angst, Maria Elizabeth
>> Census: 1790; Pine Grove, Berks (Schuylkill) Co, PA w
> Brown, Mary Magdalena
>> Census: 1830; Rush, Dauphin Co, PA w
> Brown, Peter
>> Census: 1810; Lower Mahantango, Berks Co, PA w
> Hensel, Andrew W
>> Census: 1800; Maheim, York Co, PA w
> Lehman, Susan
>> Census: 1790; Dauphin Co, PA w
> Romberger, Susan

father (con't)
        Census: 1800; Upper Paxton, Dauphin Co, PA w
        Census: 1810; Upper Paxton, Dauphin Co, PA w
    Schneck, Elizabeth
        Census: 1810; Centre, Northumberland (Union) Co, PA w
    Thompson, Robert Bruce
        Census: 1870; Norwegian, Schuylkill Co, PA w
    Updegrove, Daniel
        Census: 1840; Wiconisco, Dauphin Co, PA w
    Updegrove, John M
        Census: 1810; Jonestown, Dauphin (Lebanon) Co, PA w
        Census: 1820; Lykens, Dauphin Co, PA w

father)
    Hensel, Casper
        Immigr: 1739; Germany to VA (w

Germantown, Philadelphia, PA
    Updegroff, John William
        Res: 1753

Germany
    Guise, John Adam
        Birth: Bet. 1756–1766
    Losch, Elisabeth Magdalena
        Birth: 1699

Germany to USA (ship Neptune)
    Romberger, John Balthaser
        Immigr: September 24, 1753

Germany, York Co, PA
    Hensel, Casper
        Res: 1779

Gladsmuir, East Lothian or, Newbattle, Midlothian, Scotland
    Penman, David
        Birth: December 31, 1775

Gladsmuir, East Lothian, Scotland
    Bowman, Margaret
        Birth: August 20, 1732

Greenwood Cemetery, Tower City, Schuylkill Co, PA
    Goodman, Lydia Ann
        Burial: October 14, 1883
    Hensel, Augusta "Gussie" Mae
        Burial: March 30, 1973
    Hensel, Howard Andrew Carson
        Burial: June 09, 1927
    Thompson, Abel Robert
        Burial: October 19, 1918
    Thompson, Alexander
        Burial: December 1873
    Thompson, Robert Bruce
        Burial: October 13, 1907
    Updegrove, Clara Matilda

Greenwood Cemetery, Tower City, Schuylkill Co, PA (con't)
    Burial: March 31, 1926

Haddington, East Lothian, Scotland
Cochran, Isabelle
    Res: Abt. 1720

Haddington, Scotland
Cochran, Isabelle
    Baptism: February 19, 1699
Thomson, Robert
    Baptism: November 19, 1695

Halifax, Dauphin Co, PA
Hensel, Andrew Guise
    Marr: May 17, 1853
Workman, Catherine
    Marr: May 17, 1853

Hand & Wiconisco Aves., Tower City, Schuylkill Co, PA
Hensel, Howard Andrew Carson
    Res: 1927

Hanover, Dauphin (Lebanon) Co, PA
Lehman, Jacob
    Death: October 20, 1805

Hanover, Dauphin Co, PA
Lehman, Jacob
    Will: December 13, 1800
    Prob: Bet. October 30–November 02, 1805

Harrisburg, Dauphin Co, PA
Batdorf, Myrtle Adeline
    Will: March 30, 1979
    Prob: Bet. May 10–19 1983
Culp, Sarah "Salome" A
    Prob: Bet. April 02–08 1927
Lehman, Susan
    Res: Abt. 1800
Thompson, Eugene Robert
    Death: March 21, 2007
Thompson, Harper Bruce
    Res: 1972

his 2 brothers)
Braun, Peter
    Immigr: 1770; Germany to VA (w

Home, New Bloomfield, Perry Co, PA
Hensel, Andrew Guise
    Birth: February 18, 1831
Hensel, Andrew W
    Death: July 07, 1875

Home, Tower City, Schuylkill Co, PA
Hensel, Augusta "Gussie" Mae

Home, Tower City, Schuylkill Co, PA (con't)

Death: March 27, 1973; Medullary paralysis w/thrombosis w/cerebral hemorrhage & arteriosclerosis

husband

Angst, Maria Elizabeth
Census: 1800; w
Census: 1810; Jonestown, Dauphin (Lebanon) Co, PA w
Census: 1820; Lykens, Dauphin Co, PA w
Census: 1830; Lykens, Dauphin Co, PA w
Census: 1840; Wiconisco, Dauphin Co, PA w

Benfield, Anna Maria Elizabeth
Census: 1790; w
Census: 1800; w

Brown, Mary Magdalena
Census: 1840; Lower Mahantango, Schuylkill Co, PA w

Catherine
Census: 1810; Lower Mahantango, Berks Co, PA w
Census: 1820; Rush, Dauphin Co, PA w

Eva, Maria
Census: 1790; w
Census: 1800; Manheim, York Co, PA w

Guise, Mary A
Census: 1820; Mount Joy, Adams Co, PA w
Census: 1830; Juniata, Perry Co, PA w
Census: 1840; Centre, Perry Co, PA w

Harman, Maria Elizabeth
Census: 1790; Pine Grove, Berks (Schuylkill) Co, PA w
Census: 1800; Pine Grove, Berks (Schuylkill) Co, PA w
Census: 1810; Pine Grove, Berks (Schuylkill) Co, PA w

Lehman, Susan
Census: 1800; Upper Paxton, Dauphin Co, PA w
Census: 1820; Lykens, Dauphin Co, PA w

Mary
Census: 1800; w
Census: 1810; Centre, Northumberland (Union) Co, PA w
Census: 1820; Centre, Union Co, PA w

Penman, Isabelle Stoddart
Census: 1840; Norwegian, Schuylkill Co, PA w

Pennypacker, Martha
Census: 1790; Dauphin Co, PA w
Census: 1800; w

Romberger, Susan
Census: 1820; Lykens, Dauphin Co, PA w
Census: 1840; Wiconisco, Dauphin Co, PA w

Schreckengast?, Anna Maria
Census: 1820; Rush, Dauphin Co, PA w
Census: 1830; Rush, Dauphin Co, PA w
Census: 1840; Rush, Dauphin Co, PA w

Trovinger, Elizabeth
Census: 1830; w
Census: 1840; Wiconisco, Dauphin Co, PA w

husband age 25
    Lehman, Susan
        Census: 1810; Upper Paxton, Dauphin Co, PA w

IL
    Hensel, George
        Death:

Ingolstadt, Bavaria, Germany
    Romberger, Balthasar
        Birth: July 05, 1747

Inveresk, Midlothian, Scotland
    Penman, Anne
        Birth: June 13, 1809

Inveresk, Scotland
    Moffatt, David
        Birth: September 14, 1700

Inversek, Scotland
    Black, George
        Marr: August 04, 1732
    Smith, Mary Helen
        Marr: August 04, 1732

Ireland
    Juliana
        Birth: 1841; PA

Jesse H Geigle, 2100 Linglestown Rd.,Harrisburg, Dauphin Co, PA
    Batdorf, Myrtle Adeline
        Funrl: 1983
    Thompson, Harper Bruce
        Funrl: 1981

John [F] Dreisingacer, Tower City, Schuylkill Co, PA
    Thompson, Robert Bruce
        Funrl: 1907

John F Dreisingacer, Tower City, Schuylkill Co, PA
    Thompson, Abel Robert
        Funrl: 1918

John Reiff, Lykens, Dauphin Co, PA
    Hensel, Andrew Guise
        Funrl: 1908

Joliett, Schuylkill Co, PA
    Workman, Catherine
        Death: February 10, 1877

Juniata, Perry Co, PA
    Hensel, Andrew W
        Census: 1830

Kirchberg Hunsruck, Rhineland-Palatinate, Germany
    Updegroff, John William
        Birth: February 24, 1732

Kirchberg Hunsruck, Rhineland-Palatinate, Germany (con't)
        Birth: April 24, 1732

Lancaster Co, PA
    Brucker, Anna Maria
        Marr: 1765
    Romberger, Adam
        Birth: 1775
    Romberger, Anna Catherine
        Birth: 1777
    Romberger, Balthasar
        Res: Bet. 1764–1783
    Romberger, Henry
        Birth: 1773
    Romberger, John Balthaser
        Res: Bet. 1780–1790
        Marr: 1765

Lasswade, Duddingston, Borthwick, Midlothian, Scotland
    Thomson, Robert
        Res: Abt. 1750

Lasswade, Midlothian, Scotland
    Muckle, Thomas
        Birth: February 15, 1718/19

Lassware, Midlothian, Scotland
    Brown, Catherine
        Marr: October 28, 1763
    Penman, John
        Birth: April 08, 1747
        Marr: October 28, 1763

Leacock, Lancaster Co, PA
    Romberger, John Balthaser
        Res: 1758

Libertan, Midloathian, Scotland
    Wilson, Isabelle
        Birth: Abt. 1720

Liberton, Midlothian, Scotland
    Brown, Catherine
        Birth: Abt. 1747
    Stoddart, Elizabeth
        Census: 1841

Littlestown, York (Adams) Co, PA
    Hensel, Andrew W
        Birth: June 28, 1793
    Hensel, Casper
        Res: 1776

Lower Mahantango, Berks Co, PA
    Braun, Peter
        Census: 1810

Lower Mahantango, Schuylkill Co, PA

Lower Mahantango, Schuylkill Co, PA (con't)
Goodman, Michael
Census: 1840

Lower Mahantango, Schuylkill Co, PA (son Philip Brown)
Braun, Peter
Census: 1830

Lower Ranch Creek, Tremont, Schuylkill Co, PA
Updegrove, Clara Matilda
Birth: November 30, 1866

Lykens, Dauphin Co, PA
Batdorf, Myrtle Adeline
Census: 1930
Hensel, John
Death:
Romberger, Susan
Birth: April 16, 1799
Updegrove, Conrad
Census: 1820
Census: 1830
Workman, Joseph
Birth: December 03, 1795
Census: 1820

Lykens, Dauphin Co, PA (James)
Workman, Joseph
Census: 1830

Lykens, Dauphin Co, PA (Rimberger)
Romberger, Balthasar
Census: 1820

Manallen, Adams Co, PA
Maria?
Census: 1800

Manheim Tp, Adams Co, PA
Hensel, John Casper
Death: January 1804

Manheim, York Co, PA
Hensel, John Casper
Prob: January 03, 1805
Will: April 28, 1800
Census: 1800

McCallister's Methodist Cemetery, Rush, Dauphin Co, PA
Schreckengast?, Anna Maria
Burial: April 1879

Menallan, Adams Co, PA
Guise, John Adam
Census: 1800

Middleport, Schuylkill Co, PA
Thompson, Alexander

Middleport, Schuylkill Co, PA (con't)
    Res: Abt. 1827

Midlothian, Scotland
    Keitchen, Agnes
            Birth: August 1701
    Russell, William
            Birth: September 28, 1725

Mifflin, Dauphin Co, PA
    Romberger, Balthasar
            Death: Abt. 1825
            Res: Abt. 1800

Mifflin, Dauphin Co, PA (Blthase)
    Romberger, Balthasar
            Census: 1830

Mifflin, Lancaster (Dauphin) Co, PA
    Brucker, Anna Maria
            Death: Bet. 1778–1798

Mount Joy, Adams Co, PA (Hensle)
    Hensel, Andrew W
            Census: 1820

Mt. Pleasant, York Co, PA
    Hensel, John Casper
            Res: Bet. 1798–1799

near Gettysburg, Adams Co, PA
    Guise, John Adam
            Res: 1813
            Res: 1824
    Hensel, Andrew W
            Res: 1823

New Holland, Lancaster Co, PA
    Haas, Anna Sabina
            Marr: 1761
    Romberger, John Balthaser
            Marr: 1761

Newbattle, Midlothian, Scotland
    Bowman, Margaret
            Marr: June 08, 1754
    Penman, Alexander
            Birth: October 24, 1820
    Penman, Catherine
            Birth: July 12, 1802
    Penman, Elizabeth
            Birth: February 22, 1807
    Penman, Isabelle Stoddart
            Birth: May 09, 1816
    Penman, James
            Birth: October 12, 1811
    Penman, John

Newbattle, Midlothian, Scotland (con't)
>> Birth: April 18, 1798
> Penman, Margaret
>> Birth: July 20, 1800
> Penman, Robert
>> Birth: December 11, 1824
> Russell, Janet
>> Birth: December 21, 1766
> Stoddart, David
>> Birth: May 19, 1754
>> Baptism: May 25, 1755
> Stoddart, John
>> Birth: December 25, 1728
>> Baptism: January 05, 1729
>> Marr: June 08, 1754

Newbattle, Scotland
> Russell, William
>> Death: 1792

Northampton Co, PA
> Guise, John Adam
>> Marr: Abt. 1784
> Guise, Mary A
>> Birth: December 16, 1791
> Maria?
>> Marr: Abt. 1784

Northumberland (Union) Co, PA
> Schneck, Elizabeth
>> Birth: August 13, 1805

Northumberland Co, PA
> Schneck, Peter
>> Death: Bet. 1830–1840

Norwegian, Schuylkill Co, PA
> Penman, Isabelle Stoddart
>> Census: 1850
> Stoddart, Elizabeth
>> Census: 1840
> Thompson, Alexander
>> Census: 1840
>> Census: 1850
>> Census: 1870
> Thompson, Robert Bruce
>> Census: 1850

NY
> Harman, Maria Elizabeth
>> Birth: Abt. 1749

OH
> Elizabeth
>> Birth: 1839

Old Lincoln, Dauphin Co, PA

Old Lincoln, Dauphin Co, PA (con't)
Workman, Catherine
> Birth: May 17, 1838

Oley, Berks Co, PA
Angst, Maria Elizabeth
> Marr: 1803

Updegrove, Conrad
> Birth: November 27, 1771
> Marr: 1803

Oley, Philadelphia (Berks) Co, PA
Benfield, Anna Maria Elizabeth
> Birth: April 01, 1729

Ormiston, East Lothian, Scotland
Cochran, Isabelle
> Marr: November 21, 1718

Thomson, Robert
> Marr: November 21, 1718

Orwin, Porter, Reinerton, Rush, Sheridan, Tower City, all Schuylkill Co, PA
Hensel, Augusta "Gussie" Mae
> Res: 1973

Orwin, Schuylkill Co, PA
Goodman, Michael
> Burial: 1900

PA
\<No name\>
> Birth: 1786

A, Mary
> Birth: 1836

A, Mary
> Birth: 1867

Angst, Jacob
> Birth: Abt. 1790

Angst, Juliana
> Birth: 1775

Angst, William
> Birth: 1794

Anna
> Birth: 1793

Bast, Mary A
> Birth: 1833

Beedle, Edward
> Birth: 1863

Brown
> Birth:

Brown
> Birth:

Brown, Elizabeth
> Birth: 1830

Brown, John
> Birth: 1812

Brown, Jonas
> Birth: Abt. 1790

Brown, Peter
> Birth: 1814

Brown, Philip
> Birth: 1821

Brown, Philip
> Birth: Abt. 1788

Brown, William
> Birth: 1818

Catherine
> Birth: 1820

Charlesworth, Blanche
> Birth: 1883

Coleman, Rosanna
> Birth: 1814

Culp, Elizabeth
> Birth: 1842

Culp, Fielta
> Birth: 1848

Culp, Jonas
> Birth: 1839

Culp, Sarah "Salome" A
> Pension: May 1899

Day, Sarah Elizabeth
> Birth: 1859

Elizabeth
> Birth: 1837

Esther
> Birth: 1814

Eva, Maria
> Birth: Abt. 1765

Faust, Agnes A
> Birth: 1855

Ferree, Margaret Rebecca
> Birth: 1810

Goodman, Anna Maria
> Birth: 1848

Goodman, Catherine
> Birth: 1846

Goodman, George H
> Birth: 1853

Goodman, George?
> Birth: Abt. 1800

Goodman, Jacob
> Birth: 1849

Goodman, Jane
> Birth: 1845

Goodman, John
> Birth: 1841

Goodman, Lydia Ann

Baptism: February 20, 1856
Goodman, Magdalena
Birth: 1839
Goodman, Mary
Birth: 1843
Goodman, Sarah "Sallie"
Birth: 1844
Goodman, Susan
Birth: 1837
Goodman, William
Birth: 1835
Guise, Peter?
Birth: 1795
Guteman, Jacob
Birth: 1780
Death: November 21, 1844
Hand, Christina "Dinah"
Birth: 1835
Hensel, Andrew Guise
Birth: February 20, 1832
Hensel, Anna Catherine
Birth: Abt. 1862
Hensel, Anna Maria Barbara
Birth: 1820
Hensel, Anne "Annie" Clarissa Workman
Birth: 1866
Hensel, Casper
Res: 1764
Hensel, Casper
Birth: Abt. 1790
Hensel, Edna Boyer
Birth: March 30, 1905
Hensel, Elmer Elsworth
Birth: 1891
Hensel, Emma
Birth: 1866
Hensel, George
Birth: 1796
Hensel, Helen Irene
Birth: 1888
Hensel, Ira Sylvester
Birth: 1856
Hensel, Jacob
Birth: 1795
Hensel, John Adam
Birth: 1814
Hensel, John Henry William
Birth: 1853
Hensel, Joseph Franklin
Birth: 1854
Hensel, Lawrence

Birth: Abt. 1791

Hensel, Lillian "Lillie" Emma Susan

Birth: 1864

Hensel, Lillian "Lillie" Verna

Birth: 1889

Hensel, Philip

Birth: Abt. 1800

Houtz, "Cassie"

Birth: 1841

Kulp, Jacob

Birth: Abt. 1802

Layman, Henry

Birth:

Layman, Jacob

Birth:

Layman, John

Birth:

Layman, Joseph

Birth:

Layman, Martha

Birth:

Layman, Mary

Birth:

Layman, Rebecca

Birth:

Lehman, Jacob

Marr: Abt. 1763

Losch, Elisabeth Magdalena

Death: 1763

Maria, Anna

Birth: 1810

Mary

Birth: 1826

McGough, Charles John

Birth: 1881

Miller, William

Birth: 1813

Moyer, Susan

Birth: 1833

Pennypacker, Martha

Marr: Abt. 1763

Rickert, Barbara Ellen

Birth: 1807

Romberger, Anna Maria

Birth: 1771

Romberger, Joseph

Birth: 1811

Sassaman, Emmanuel

Birth: 1827

Shadel, Henry L

Birth: 1865

PA (con't)

Sidnam
> Birth: 1824

Smink, Isaac
> Birth: 1828

Sophia
> Birth: 1835

Susan
> Birth: 1838

Susan
> Birth: 1790

Susan
> Birth: 1882

Swab, Catherine "Kate"
> Birth: 1788

Swartz, David
> Birth: 1816

Thompson, Abel Franklin
> Birth: October 19, 1910

Thompson, Alexander F
> Birth: 1845

Thompson, Benjamin
> Birth: 1874

Thompson, Blanche
> Birth: 1883

Thompson, David Penman
> Birth: 1837

Thompson, Elizabeth
> Birth: 1841

Thompson, Eugene Robert
> Birth: August 07, 1937

Thompson, George
> Birth: 1835

Thompson, Isabelle
> Birth: 1849

Thompson, James C
> Birth: 1851

Thompson, Janet "Jennie"
> Birth: 1844

Thompson, Oliver Charles
> Birth: 1875

Thompson, Robert
> Birth: 1836

Thompson, Virginia D
> Birth: 1905

Thompson, Wilbur Clark
> Birth: 1906

Thompson, William W
> Birth: 1839

Updegrove
> Birth: Abt. 1802

Updegrove, Anna

Birth: 1807

Updegrove, Anna M

Birth: 1864

Updegrove, Anna Magdalena

Birth: March 09, 1759

Updegrove, Catherine

Birth: 1833

Updegrove, Elizabeth

Birth: 1803

Updegrove, Ellen

Birth: Abt. 1812

Updegrove, Frances

Birth: September 10, 1756

Updegrove, Jacob

Birth: 1827

Updegrove, John Adam

Birth: 1761

Updegrove, John J

Birth: 1835

Updegrove, Nancy

Birth: 1838

Updegrove, Nellie

Birth: 1811

Updegrove, Nora Jane

Birth: 1874

Updegrove, Peter

Birth: May 01, 1766

Updegrove, Rebecca

Birth: 1847

Updegrove, Sarah

Birth: 1809

Updegrove, Solomon

Birth: 1845

Updegrove, William Henry

Birth: 1870

Voller, Catherine

Birth: 1780

Death: 1806

Birth: Abt. 1775

White, Lavinia Eva

Birth: 1890

Workman, Benjamin

Birth: 1787

Workman, Carolina

Birth: 1831

Workman, John

Birth: 1823

Workman, Joseph R

Birth: 1836

Workman, Nancy

Birth: 1826

PA (con't)
Zimmerman, Peter
> Birth: 1808

Palatinate, Germany
Hensel, Casper
> Birth: Abt. 1735

parents
Guise, Mary A
> Census: 1800; w
> Census: 1810; w

Hensel, Andrew W
> Census: 1810; w

Kulp, Jacob
> Census: 1830; w

Romberger, Balthasar
> Census: 1790; w
> Census: 1800; Upper Paxton, Dauphin Co, PA w

Schneck, Elizabeth
> Census: 1820; w
> Census: 1830; w

Schneck, Peter
> Census: 1790; w
> Census: 1800; w

Updegrove, Conrad
> Census: 1790; w

Perry Co, PA
Guise, Mary A
> Death: January 16, 1877

Hensel, Andrew Guise
> Census: 1840; Centre, Perry Co, PA w/father

Hensel, Andrew W
> Prob: August 13, 1875

Hensel, George
> Birth: 1825

Hensel, John
> Birth: 1824

Hensel, Michael
> Birth: 1834

Philadelphia (Montgomery) Co, PA
Pennypacker, Martha
> Birth: 1746

Philadelphia, PA
Romberger, John Balthaser
> Res: 1754

Pine Grove, Berks (Schuylkill) Co PA
Angst, John Daniel
> Res: Bet. 1773–1777
> Res: Bet. 1779–1786

Pine Grove, Berks (Schuylkill) Co, PA

Pine Grove, Berks (Schuylkill) Co, PA (con't)
Angst, Daniel
>> Birth: 1786

Angst, John
>> Birth: 1792

Angst, John Daniel
>> Census: 1790
>> Census: 1800
>> Census: 1810

Pine Grove, Berks (Schylkill) Co, PA
Updegrove, John M
>> Birth: March 23, 1805

Pine Grove, Schuylkill Co, PA
Angst, John Daniel
>> Death: June 11, 1815

Pittsburgh)
Hensel, Andrew Guise
>> Miltry: August 28, 1864; Civil War, Private, 155th Reg PA Inf, Co F (Harrisburg

Polyclinic Hospital, Harrisburg, Dauphin Co, PA
Batdorf, Myrtle Adeline
>> Death: May 08, 1983; Cardiorespiratory arrest w/ASHD w/pacemaker

Thompson, Harper Bruce
>> Death: July 23, 1981; Cardiorespiratory arrest w/subdural hematoma

Porter Tp, Schuylkill Co, PA
Thompson, Abel Robert
>> Prob: Bet. February–November 1919
>> Res: 1904

Thompson, Alexander
>> Will: December 03, 1873
>> Prob: December 17, 1873

Porter Tp, Schuylkill Co, PA (after Mary Thompson's death)
Thompson, Alexander
>> Prob: January 25, 1912

Porter Tp., Schuylkill Co, PA
Thompson, Abel Robert
>> Will: July 02, 1914

Porter, Schuylkill Co, PA
Hensel, Augusta "Gussie" Mae
>> Census: 1910
>> Census: 1920
>> Census: 1930
>> Census: 1940

Hensel, Howard Andrew Carson
>> Census: 1860

Thompson, Abel Robert
>> Census: 1910

Thompson, Alexander
>> Census: 1860
>> Res: 1854

Porter, Schuylkill Co, PA (con't)
Thompson, Harper Bruce
        Census: 1910
        Census: 1920
Thompson, Robert Bruce
        Census: 1860
Workman, Catherine
        Census: 1860

Porter, Schuylkill Co, PA (brother Oliver Thompson)
Thompson, Abel Robert
        Census: 1900

Porter, Schuylkill Co, PA (Hentzel)
Hensel, Andrew Guise
        Census: 1860

Pottsville Hospital, 500 Washington St, Pottsville, Schuylkill Co, PA
Thompson, Robert Bruce
        Res: 1900

Pottsville St., Williams, Dauphin Co, PA
Culp, Sarah "Salome" A
        Res: 1910

Pottsville, Schuylkill Co, PA
Penman, Isabelle Stoddart
        Death: April 18, 1851
        Marr: January 01, 1835
Stoddart, Elizabeth
        Death: December 25, 1849
Thompson, Alexander
        Marr: January 01, 1835
Thompson, Robert Bruce
        Census: 1900

Presbyterian Burial Grounds, Pottsville, Schuylkill Co, PA
Stoddart, Elizabeth
        Burial: 1849

Prestonpans, East Lothian, Scotland
Black, Mary
        Birth: 1737

Reading, Berks Co, PA
Updegroff, John William
        Res: Abt. 1770

Republican
Thompson, Alexander
        PoliticalParty:
Thompson, Harper Bruce
        PoliticalParty:

Rev. Brady, Schuylkill Co, PA
Updegrove, Clara Matilda
        Baptism: December 1866

Rev. Wm Yose, Dauphin Co, PA
Hensel, Howard Andrew Carson
Baptism: Abt. 1858

Rhineland-Palatinate, Germany
Braun, Peter
Birth: Abt. 1745

Richmond, York Co, PA
Hensel, John Casper
Birth: September 30, 1764

Rockland, Berks Co, PA
Angst, Maria Elizabeth
Birth: November 11, 1776

Rush Tp, Dauphin Co, PA (listed in index only)
Goodman, Michael
Prob: January 11, 1901

Rush, Dauphin Co, PA
Braun, Peter
Census: 1820
Brown, Mary Magdalena
Census: 1850
Census: 1870
Census: 1880
Brown, Peter
Death: 1861
Census: 1820
Census: 1830
Census: 1840
Census: 1850
Goodman, Lydia Ann
Census: 1870
Census: 1880
Goodman, Michael
Death: December 27, 1900; Old age
Census: 1850
Census: 1860
Census: 1870
Census: 1880
Schreckengast?, Anna Maria
Death: April 10, 1879
Census: 1850
Thompson, Robert Bruce
Census: 1880

Rush, Dauphin Co, PA (Margaret)
Brown, Mary Magdalena
Census: 1860

Rush, Dauphin Co, PA (son John Brown)
Schreckengast?, Anna Maria
Census: 1860

Rush, Dauphin Co, PA (son William Goodman)

Rush, Dauphin Co, PA (son William Goodman) (con't)

Goodman, Michael
> Census: 1900

Rush, Dauphin Co, PA (unlisted)

Brown, Mary Magdalena
> Census: 1820

Sauchenside Farm, Cranston, Midlothian, Scotland

Thompson, Alexander
> Birth: October 22, 1805

Schuylkill Co, PA

Goodman, Lydia Ann
> Marr: Abt. 1873

Goodman, Michael
> Confir: July 1825

Hensel, Augusta "Gussie" Mae
> Res: 1973
> Marr: June 15, 1904

Thompson, Abel Robert
> Marr: June 15, 1904

Thompson, Alexander
> Naturl: July 31, 1834

Thompson, Robert Bruce
> Marr: Abt. 1873

Schuylkill?, PA

Brown, Mary Magdalena
> Marr: Abt. 1832

Goodman, Michael
> Marr: Abt. 1832

Scotland

Black, George
> Birth: Abt. 1697
> Death: Aft. 1739

Black, John
> Birth: 1735

Black, Mary
> Death: Aft. 1779
> Marr: Abt. 1760

Black, Mary
> Birth: 1733

Black, William
> Birth: 1739

Bowman, Margaret
> Death: Aft. 1767

Brown, Catherine
> Death: Aft. 1775

Brown, Robert
> Birth: Abt. 1720
> Death: Aft. 1748
> Marr: July 12, 1747

Cochran, Isabelle

Birth: February 07, 1699
Death: Aft. 1744
Keitchen, Agnes
Death: Aft. 1745
Malcolm, Janet
Death: February 25, 1760
Marr: May 10, 1712
Moffatt, Agnes
Birth: 1740
Moffatt, Agnes
Birth: 1745
Moffatt, Allison
Birth: 1738
Moffatt, Andrew
Birth: 1728
Moffatt, Christina
Death: Aft. 1766
Moffatt, David
Death: Aft. 1745
Moffatt, Helen
Birth: 1729
Moffatt, Henry
Birth: 1734
Moffatt, John
Birth: 1736
Muckle, Margaret
Death: Aft. 1779
Penman, David
Death: Abt. 1826
Marr: Abt. 1800
Penman, John
Death: Aft. 1775
Penman, Miriam
Birth:
Russell, Janet
Death: Aft. 1811
Russell, John
Death: April 16, 1750
Marr: May 10, 1712
Russell, Mary
Birth: Abt. 1755
Russell, William
Birth: Abt. 1755
Smith, Mary Helen
Birth: Abt. 1707
Death: Aft. 1739
Stoddart, David
Death: Aft. 1779
Stoddart, Elizabeth
Marr: Abt. 1800
Stoddart, James

Scotland (con't)

Birth: 1767

Stoddart, John
 Death: Aft. 1767

Thompson, Anna
 Birth: 1779

Thompson, Christina
 Birth: 1792

Thompson, Elizabeth
 Birth: 1763

Thompson, George
 Birth: 1773

Thompson, George W
 Birth: 1802

Thompson, Grissel
 Birth: 1737

Thompson, Helen
 Birth: 1761

Thompson, Helen
 Birth: 1767

Thompson, Isabelle
 Birth: 1761

Thompson, Isabelle
 Birth: 1719

Thompson, Jacobina
 Birth: 1744

Thompson, James
 Birth: 1725

Thompson, James Smith
 Birth: 1811

Thompson, John
 Birth: 1804

Thompson, John
 Birth: 1808

Thompson, John
 Birth: 1728

Thompson, Margaret
 Birth: 1721

Thompson, Mary
 Birth: 1800

Thompson, Mary
 Birth: 1764

Thompson, Mary
 Birth: 1775

Thompson, Mary
 Birth: 1741

Thompson, Nicole
 Birth: 1777

Thompson, Robert
 Birth: 1795

Thompson, Robert
 Death: Aft. 1811

Scotland (con't)

Thompson, William
> Birth: 1797

Thomson, Robert
> Death: Aft. 1779
> Marr: Abt. 1760

Thomson, Robert
> Death: Abt. 1744

Wilson, Isabelle
> Death: Aft. 1748
> Marr: July 12, 1747

Scotland to New York, NY (ship Nimrod)

Thompson, Alexander
> Immigr: July 09, 1827

Seyberts (Old) Lutheran, Williamstown, Dauphin Co, PA

Angst, Maria Elizabeth
> Burial: Abt. 1850

Culp, Sarah "Salome" A
> Burial: July 06, 1923

Updegrove, Daniel
> Burial: March 28, 1899

Sheridan, Schuylkill Co, PA

Hensel, Augusta "Gussie" Mae
> Will: May 27, 1950

Thompson, Abel Robert
> Birth: November 28, 1880

Thompson, Harper Bruce
> Birth: September 28, 1907

Thompson, Lydia Mae
> Birth: February 07, 1914

Somerset Co, PA

Angst, Maria Elizabeth
> Death: Abt. 1850

Somerset County, PA

Trovinger, Elizabeth
> Birth: Abt. 1798

Updegrove, John M
> Death: 1864

Son Philip's home, Tower City, Schuylkill Co, PA

Braun, Peter
> Death: 1835

St Jacobs Lutheran, Pine Grove, Berks (Schuylkill) Co, PA

Updegrove, Conrad
> Confir: October 09, 1803

St John Hill (Quittaphilla) Lutheran, Cleona, Lancaster (Lebanon) Co, PA

Angst, John Daniel
> Baptism: January 02, 1751

St. Jacobs Lutheran, Pine Grove, Berks (Schuylkill) Co, PA

St. Jacobs Lutheran, Pine Grove, Berks (Schuylkill) Co, PA (con't)
Angst, Maria Elizabeth
>> Confir: October 09, 1803

Updegrove, John M
>> Baptism: April 14, 1805

St. Jacobs Lutheran, Pine Grove, Schuylkill Co, PA
Angst, John Daniel
>> Burial: 1815

St. Johns (Hill) Lutheran, Berrysburg, Dauphin Co, PA
Romberger, Balthasar
>> Burial: Abt. 1839

Romberger, Susan
>> Baptism: July 07, 1799

St. Johns (Hill) Lutheran, Lykens, Dauphin Co, PA
Batdorf, Myrtle Adeline
>> Marr: June 15, 1935

Thompson, Harper Bruce
>> Marr: June 15, 1935

St. Josephs Union (Oley Hill), Church, Berks Co, PA
Updegrove, Conrad
>> Baptism: December 29, 1771
>> Baptism: 1778

St. Lukes Reformed, Trappe, Philadelphia (Montgomery) Co, PA
Lehman, Susan
>> Baptism: Abt. 1771

St. Peters (Christ, Old Union) Cemetery, New Bloomfield, Perry Co, PA
Guise, Mary A
>> Burial: January 1877

Hensel, Andrew W
>> Burial: July 1875

St. Peters Reformed, Richmond, York Co, PA
Hensel, John Casper
>> Baptism: September 30, 1764

Stobgreen Temple, Edinburgh, Midlothian, Scotland
Stoddart, Elizabeth
>> Birth: January 05, 1779

Susquehanna, Juniata, PA (son Solomon Updegrove)
Updegrove, Conrad
>> Census: 1860

Theilheim, Bavaria, Germany
Brucker, Anna Maria
>> Birth: Abt. 1723

Theilheim, Schweinfurt, Bavaria, Germany
Romberger, John Balthaser
>> Birth: May 04, 1716

Thuringa, Germany
Braun, John Philip

Thuringa, Germany (con't)
          Birth: August 17, 1697

Tower City, Schuylkill Co, PA
  Batdorf, Myrtle Adeline
          Census: 1940
  Goodman, Lydia Ann
          Death: October 09, 1883; Complications of pregnancy
  Hensel, Augusta "Gussie" Mae
          Census: 1900
          Res: 1904
  Hensel, Howard Andrew Carson
          Will: January 17, 1918
          Death: June 06, 1927; Arteriosclerosis
          Census: 1900
          Census: 1910
          Census: 1920
  Thompson, Abel Robert
          Death: October 15, 1918; Pneumonia w/influenza
          Death: October 17, 1918
          Res: 1918
  Thompson, Alexander
          Death: December 04, 1873
  Thompson, Harper Bruce
          Census: 1940
  Thompson, Lydia Mae
          Death: January 1983
  Thompson, Robert Bruce
          Death: October 10, 1907; Typhoid fever w/contaminated water
  Updegrove, Clara Matilda
          Death: March 28, 1926; Metastatic carcinoma of medial atrium & left chest
                      w/carcinoma breast
          Census: 1900
          Census: 1910
          Census: 1920
  Updegrove, Daniel
          Res: 1890

Tower City, Schuylkill Co, PA (Weist)
  Culp, Sarah "Salome" A
          Census: 1920

Trappe, Philadelphia (Montgomery) Co, PA
  Lehman, Susan
          Birth: February 19, 1771

Tulpehocken, Berks, Pennsylvania, United States
  Braun, John Philip
          Death: August 16, 1767

Union Co, PA
  Culp, Sarah "Salome" A
          Birth: June 30, 1844
  Kulp, Jacob
          Death: Abt. 1865

Union Co, PA (con't)
>>> Marr: Abt. 1835
>> Mary
>>> Death: Aft. 1820
>> Schneck, Elizabeth
>>> Death: June 02, 1861
>>> Marr: Abt. 1835

Upper Paxton, Dauphin Co, PA
> Romberger, John Balthaser
>>> Census: 1800
>>> Census: 1810
> Updegrove, Conrad
>>> Census: 1810

Upper Paxton, Dauphin Co, PA age 44
> Romberger, Balthasar
>>> Census: 1810

VA
> Braun, Peter
>>> Res: Bet. 1775–1800
> Hensel, Casper
>>> Res: Abt. 1750
>>> Marr: Abt. 1755; PA
> Hensel, George
>>> Death: OH
> Walter, Maria Salome
>>> Birth: Abt. 1730
>>> Marr: Abt. 1755; PA

Washington, Dauphin Co, PA
> Batdorf, Myrtle Adeline
>>> Census: 1920

West Buffalo, Union Co, PA
> Culp, Sarah "Salome" A
>>> Census: 1850
> Kulp, Jacob
>>> Census: 1850
> Schneck, Elizabeth
>>> Census: 1850

Western Dt, Berks Co, PA
> Updegroff, John William
>>> Res: Bet. 1772–1775

Wiconisco Ave., Tower City, Schuylkill Co, PA
> Hensel, Howard Andrew Carson
>>> Res: Bet. 1910–1920

Wiconisco St., Sheridan, Schuylkill Co, PA
> Thompson, Abel Robert
>>> Res: 1900

Wiconisco, Dauphin Co, PA
> Angst, Maria Elizabeth

Wiconisco, Dauphin Co, PA (con't)

Census: 1850

Hensel, Andrew Guise
> Death: December 14, 1908; Bright's disease (ie, Chronic inflammation of kidneys) w/old age
> Census: 1870
> Census: 1880

Hensel, Augusta "Gussie" Mae
> Birth: February 16, 1885

Hensel, Howard Andrew Carson
> Birth: September 02, 1858
> Census: 1870
> Census: 1880
> Marr: September 02, 1884

Romberger, Susan
> Census: 1850

Trovinger, Elizabeth
> Census: 1850

Updegrove, Clara Matilda
> Marr: September 02, 1884

Updegrove, Conrad
> Census: 1840
> Census: 1850

Updegrove, Daniel
> Birth: June 28, 1839
> Census: 1850

Updegrove, John M
> Census: 1840
> Census: 1850

Workman, Catherine
> Census: 1850
> Census: 1870

Workman, Joseph
> Census: 1840
> Census: 1850

Wiconisco, Dauphin Co, PA (Weist-Heheel)

Hensel, Andrew Guise
> Census: 1900

Williams Valley, Dauphin Co, PA

Updegrove, Conrad
> Res: 1817

Williamstown, Dauphin Co, PA

Culp, Sarah "Salome" A
> Death: July 03, 1923; ? due to carcinoma of shoulder (recurrent) w/secondary ?
> Census: 1870
> Census: 1880

Updegrove, Clara Matilda
> Census: 1870
> Census: 1880

Updegrove, Conrad
> Death: April 1865

Williamstown, Dauphin Co, PA (con't)

Updegrove, Daniel
>> Death: 1899; Suffocated by mine gas
>> Death: March 25, 1899
>> Census: 1870
>> Census: 1880

Williamstown, Dauphin Co, PA (Shadel)

Culp, Sarah "Salome" A
>> Census: 1910

Windsor Tp, PA

Hensel, Casper
>> Res: 1767

Windsor, Berks Co, PA

Hensel, Casper
>> Naturl: September 15, 1765

Wisconsin, USA

Semrow, Loretta
>> Birth: 1900

Woodlawn Memorial Gardens, Harrisburg, Dauphin Co, PA

Batdorf, Myrtle Adeline
>> Burial: May 11, 1983
Thompson, Harper Bruce
>> Burial: 1981

York (Adams) Co, PA

Hensel, Catherine
>> Birth: 1792
Hensel, Maria Eva
>> Birth: 1792

York Co, PA

Eva, Maria
>> Marr: Abt. 1789
Hensel, Casper
>> Death: Abt. 1789
Hensel, John Casper
>> Res: Bet. 1778–1795
>> Marr: Abt. 1789
Walter, Maria Salome
>> Death: Aft. 1777

York Farm Burial Grounds, Pottsville, Schuylkill Co, PA

Penman, Isabelle Stoddart
>> Burial: April 19, 1851
Thompson, Alexander
>> Res: Aft. 1828
Thompson, Robert Bruce
>> Birth: September 24, 1847

Zion (Public Square) Lutheran Cemetery, Tower City, Schuylkill Co, PA

Brown, Mary Magdalena
>> Burial: 1884

Zion (Public Square) Lutheran Cemetery, Tower City, Schuylkill Co, PA (con't)
Goodman, Michael
Burial: 1900

Zion Lutheran, Harrisburg, Dauphin Co, PA
Lehman, Susan
Marr: June 15, 1798
Romberger, Balthasar
Marr: June 15, 1798

Zion Union, Tower City, Schuylkill Co, PA
Romberger, Susan
Confir: 1827
Workman, Joseph
Confir: 1827

Chapter Four

Our family's kinship.

How we are all related to one another from present to distant past and the outline descendants of Robert Thomson, our distant Scottish ancestor.

Kinship Report

Name:	Birth Date:	Relationship:
<No name>	1786	Wife of 2nd great grand uncle
<No name>		Wife of grand uncle
<No name>		3rd great grandmother
<No name>		3rd great grandfather
<No name>		3rd great grandfather
<No name>		4th great grandfather
<No name>		Wife of uncle
A, Mary	1836	Wife of grand uncle
A, Mary	1867	Wife of grand uncle
Albert, Jacob	Abt. 1770	Husband of 3rd great grandmother
Angst, Daniel	1786	3rd great grand uncle
Angst, Jacob	Abt. 1790	3rd great grand uncle
Angst, John	1792	3rd great grand uncle
Angst, John Daniel	December 14, 1749	4th great grandfather
Angst, Juliana	1775	3rd great grand aunt
Angst, Maria Elizabeth	November 11, 1776	3rd great grandmother
Angst, William	1794	3rd great grand uncle
Anna	1793	Wife of 2nd great grand uncle
Arrison, Grace	1823	Wife of great grandfather
Artz, Edgar Isaiah	1878	Husband of aunt
Bast, Mary A	1833	Wife of great grandfather
Batdorf, Myrtle Adeline	January 05, 1918	Wife
Beedle, Edward	1863	Husband of grand aunt
Bellis, Peter	1800	Husband of 2nd great grand aunt
Benfield, Anna Maria Elizabeth	April 01, 1729	4th great grandmother
Black, George	Abt. 1697	4th great grandfather
Black, John	1735	3rd great grand uncle
Black, Mary	1733	3rd great grand aunt
Black, Mary	1737	3rd great grandmother
Black, William	1739	3rd great grand uncle
Bowman, Margaret	August 20, 1732	4th great grandmother
Boyer, David Alfred	1860	Husband of grand aunt
Braun, John Philip	August 17, 1697	4th great grandfather
Braun, Peter	Abt. 1745	3rd great grandfather
Brown		2nd great grand aunt
Brown		2nd great grand aunt

Name:	Birth Date:	Relationship:
Brown, Anna Maria	February 17, 1815	Great grand aunt
Brown, Catherine	Abt. 1747	3rd great grandmother
Brown, Elizabeth	1830	Great grand aunt
Brown, John	1812	Great grand uncle
Brown, Jonas	Abt. 1790	2nd great grand uncle
Brown, Mary Elizabeth		1st cousin 3x removed
Brown, Mary Magdalena	1816	Great grandmother
Brown, Peter	1775	2nd great grandfather
Brown, Peter	1814	Great grand uncle
Brown, Philip	Abt. 1788	2nd great grand uncle
Brown, Philip	1821	Great grand uncle
Brown, Robert	Abt. 1720	4th great grandfather
Brown, William	1815	Husband of 2nd great grand aunt
Brown, William	1818	Great grand uncle
Brucker, Anna Maria	Abt. 1723	4th great grandmother
Catherine	Abt. 1760	Wife of 3rd great grand uncle
Catherine	Abt. 1760	3rd great grandmother
Catherine	1820	Wife of 1st great grand uncle
Charlesworth, Blanche	1883	Wife of uncle
Cleary, Living		Daughter-in-law
Cochran, Isabelle	February 07, 1699	4th great grandmother
Coleman, Rosanna	1814	Wife of 2nd great grand uncle
Cox, Almeda Ellen	1911	Sister-in-law
Craig, Living		Wife of uncle
Culp, Elizabeth	1842	Great grand aunt
Culp, Fielta	1848	Great grand aunt
Culp, Jonas	1839	Great grand uncle
Culp, Living		Great grand aunt
Culp, Living		Great grand aunt
Culp, Living		2nd great grand uncle
Culp, Sarah "Salome" A	June 30, 1844	Great grandmother
Curry, Living		Wife of grandson
Day, Sarah Elizabeth	1859	Wife of grand uncle
Doebler, David S	1816	Husband of 1st great grand aunt
Duncan, Living		Daughter-in-law
Elizabeth	1837	Wife of 1st great grand uncle
Elizabeth	1839	Wife of 1st great grand uncle
Esther	1814	Wife of 2nd great grand uncle
Eva, Maria	Abt. 1765	3rd great grandmother
Evans, Margaret "Peggy"	1935	Daughter-in-law

Name:	Birth Date:	Relationship:
Faust, Agnes A	1855	Wife of grand uncle
Ferree, Margaret Rebecca	1810	Wife of 2nd great grand uncle
Gabriell, Catherine		Wife of 4th great grandfather
Goodman, Anna Maria	1848	Grand aunt
Goodman, Catherine	1846	Grand aunt
Goodman, George H	1853	Grand uncle
Goodman, George?	Abt. 1800	Great grand uncle
Goodman, Jacob	1849	Grand uncle
Goodman, Jane	1845	Grand aunt
Goodman, John	1841	Grand uncle
Goodman, John?	Abt. 1805	Great grand uncle
Goodman, Lydia Ann	February 20, 1856	Paternal grandmother
Goodman, Magdalena	1839	Grand aunt
Goodman, Mary	1843	Grand aunt
Goodman, Michael	June 10, 1806	Great grandfather
Goodman, Sarah "Sallie"	1844	Grand aunt
Goodman, Susan	1837	Grand aunt
Goodman, William	1835	Grand uncle
Greene, Living		Husband of granddaughter
Greshammer, Louis A	1835	Husband of 1st great grand aunt
Guise, Abraham?	Abt. 1740	3rd great grand uncle
Guise, John Adam	Bet. 1756–1766	3rd great grandfather
Guise, John?		3rd great grand uncle
Guise, Living		2nd great grand uncle
Guise, Mary A	December 16, 1791	2nd great grandmother
Guise, Peter?		3rd great grand uncle
Guise, Peter?	1795	2nd great grand uncle
Guteman, Jacob	1780	2nd great grandfather
Haas, Anna Sabina		Wife of 4th great grandfather
Hamilton, Jean		4th great grandmother
Hand, Christina "Dinah"	1835	Wife of grand uncle
Harman, Maria Elizabeth	Abt. 1749	4th great grandmother
Hautz?, Catherine		Wife of 1st great grand uncle
Haverstick, Anna Maria		Wife of 1st great grand uncle
Hawk, Elizabeth		Wife of grand uncle
Helen		Wife of grand uncle
Hensel, Andrew Guise	February 18, 1831	Great grandfather
Hensel, Andrew W	June 28, 1793	2nd great grandfather
Hensel, Anna Catherine	Abt. 1862	Grand aunt

Name:	Birth Date:	Relationship:
Hensel, Anna Maria Barbara	1820	Great grand aunt
Hensel, Anne "Annie" Clarissa Workman	1866	Grand aunt
Hensel, Arthur Preston	1886	Uncle
Hensel, Augusta "Gussie" Mae	February 16, 1885	Mother
Hensel, Casper	Abt. 1735	4th great grandfather
Hensel, Casper	Abt. 1790	2nd great grand uncle
Hensel, Catherine	1768	3rd great grand aunt
Hensel, Catherine	1792	2nd great grand aunt
Hensel, Edna Boyer	March 30, 1905	Aunt
Hensel, Elmer Elsworth	1891	Uncle
Hensel, Emma	1866	Grand aunt
Hensel, George	1777	3rd great grand uncle
Hensel, George	1796	2nd great grand uncle
Hensel, George	1825	Great grand uncle
Hensel, Helen Irene	1888	Aunt
Hensel, Howard Andrew Carson	September 02, 1858	Maternal grandfather
Hensel, Ira Sylvester	1856	Grand uncle
Hensel, Jacob	Abt. 1773	3rd great grand uncle
Hensel, Jacob	1795	2nd great grand uncle
Hensel, John	1762	3rd great grand uncle
Hensel, John	1824	Great grand uncle
Hensel, John Adam	1814	Great grand uncle
Hensel, John Casper	September 30, 1764	3rd great grandfather
Hensel, John Henry William	1853	Grand uncle
Hensel, Joseph Franklin	1854	Grand uncle
Hensel, Lawrence	1766	3rd great grand uncle
Hensel, Lawrence	Abt. 1791	2nd great grand uncle
Hensel, Lillian "Lillie" Emma Susan	1864	Grand aunt
Hensel, Lillian "Lillie" Verna	1889	Aunt
Hensel, Living		Uncle
Hensel, Living		Aunt
Hensel, Living		Uncle
Hensel, Living		Aunt
Hensel, Living		Aunt
Hensel, Maria Eva	1792	2nd great grand aunt
Hensel, Michael	Abt. 1770	3rd great grand uncle
Hensel, Michael	1834	Great grand uncle
Hensel, Peter	Abt. 1770	3rd great grand uncle
Hensel, Philip	Abt. 1770	3rd great grand uncle

Name:	Birth Date:	Relationship:
Hensel, Philip	Abt. 1800	2nd great grand uncle
Hockley, Stephanie		Wife of grandson
Hoffman, Elizabeth		Wife of 3rd great grand uncle
Houtz, "Cassie"	1841	Wife of grand uncle
Houtz, Benjamin		Husband of grand aunt
Houtz, Living		Husband of aunt
Juliana	1841	Wife of 1st great grand uncle
Keitchen, Agnes	August 1701	4th great grandmother
Kimmel, Hiram		Husband of grand aunt
King, John		Husband of 1st great grand aunt
Knittle, Living		Husband of aunt
Kulp, Jacob	Abt. 1802	2nd great grandfather
Landis, Living		Wife of grandson
Layman, Elizabeth		3rd great grand aunt
Layman, Henry		3rd great grand uncle
Layman, Jacob		3rd great grand uncle
Layman, John		3rd great grand uncle
Layman, Joseph		3rd great grand uncle
Layman, Martha		3rd great grand aunt
Layman, Mary		3rd great grand aunt
Layman, Rebecca		3rd great grand aunt
Layman, Samuel		3rd great grand uncle
Lehman, Jacob	1744	4th great grandfather
Lehman, Susan	February 19, 1771	3rd great grandmother
Living		Husband of granddaughter
Living		Daughter-in-law
Losch, Elisabeth Magdalena	1699	4th great grandmother
M, Sarah	1810	Wife of 2nd great grandfather
Magdelena, Anna	Abt. 1760	Wife of 3rd great grandfather
Malcolm, Janet	Abt. 1690	4th great grandmother
Maria, Anna	1810	Wife of 1st great grand uncle
Maria?	Abt. 1765	3rd great grandmother
Mary	Abt. 1765	3rd great grandmother
Mary	1826	Wife of 1st great grand uncle
Mason, Elizabeth	May 15, 1709	4th great grandmother
Matter, Elva May	1911	Sister-in-law
Matter, John Michael		Husband of 3rd great grand aunt
McCracken, Jordan		Great grandson
McCracken, Kacie Jo		Great granddaughter
McCracken, Kristina		Great granddaughter

Name:	Birth Date:	Relationship:
McCracken, Mark		Husband of granddaughter
McCracken, Noah James		Great grandson
McCracken, Trista		Great granddaughter
McGough, Charles John	1881	Husband of aunt
McLeran, Margaret	1816	Wife of 1st great grand uncle
Miller, Elizabeth	Abt. 1775	Wife of 3rd great grand uncle
Miller, Martha		Wife of 3rd great grand uncle
Miller, William	1813	Husband of 1st great grand aunt
Moffatt, Agnes	1740	3rd great grand aunt
Moffatt, Agnes	1745	3rd great grand aunt
Moffatt, Allison	1738	3rd great grand aunt
Moffatt, Andrew	1728	3rd great grand uncle
Moffatt, Christina	December 11, 1731	3rd great grandmother
Moffatt, David	September 14, 1700	4th great grandfather
Moffatt, Helen	1729	3rd great grand aunt
Moffatt, Henry	1734	3rd great grand uncle
Moffatt, John	1736	3rd great grand uncle
Moses, Mary Margaret	1850	Step grandmother
Moyer, Susan	1833	Wife of 1st great grand uncle
Muckle, Margaret	November 05, 1756	3rd great grandmother
Muckle, Thomas	February 15, 1718/19	4th great grandfather
Penman, Alexander	October 24, 1820	Great grand uncle
Penman, Anna		Wife of 1st great grand uncle
Penman, Anne	June 13, 1809	Great grand aunt
Penman, Catherine	July 12, 1802	Great grand aunt
Penman, David	December 31, 1775	2nd great grandfather
Penman, Elizabeth	February 22, 1807	Great grand aunt
Penman, Isabelle Stoddart	May 09, 1816	Great grandmother
Penman, James	Abt. 1719	4th great grandfather
Penman, James	October 12, 1811	Great grand uncle
Penman, John	April 08, 1747	3rd great grandfather
Penman, John	April 18, 1798	Great grand uncle
Penman, Margaret	July 20, 1800	Great grand aunt
Penman, Miriam		Great grand aunt
Penman, Robert	December 11, 1824	Great grand uncle
Pennypacker, Martha	1746	4th great grandmother

Name:	Birth Date:	Relationship:
Potteiger, Living		Wife of grandson
Powell, George		Husband of grand aunt
Reedy, U	Abt. 1780	Husband of 2nd great grand aunt
Remp, Barbara		Wife of great grandfather
Rendall, Living		2nd great granddaughter
Rendall, Living		Husband of great granddaughter
Rickert, Barbara Ellen	1807	Wife of 2nd great grand uncle
Romano, Living		Wife of grandson
Romberger, Adam	1775	3rd great grand uncle
Romberger, Anna Catherine	1777	3rd great grand aunt
Romberger, Anna Maria	1771	3rd great grand aunt
Romberger, Balthasar	July 05, 1747	3rd great grandfather
Romberger, Henry	1773	3rd great grand uncle
Romberger, Jacob	1806	2nd great grand uncle
Romberger, John Balthaser	May 04, 1716	4th great grandfather
Romberger, Joseph	1811	2nd great grand uncle
Romberger, Salome	1808	2nd great grand aunt
Romberger, Samuel	1803	2nd great grand uncle
Romberger, Susan	April 16, 1799	2nd great grandmother
Russell, James	Abt. 1730	3rd great grand uncle
Russell, Janet	December 21, 1766	2nd great grandmother
Russell, John	Abt. 1690	4th great grandfather
Russell, Living		2nd great grand aunt
Russell, Mary		Wife of 2nd great grand uncle
Russell, Mary	Abt. 1755	2nd great grand aunt
Russell, William		Husband of 2nd great grand aunt
Russell, William	September 28, 1725	3rd great grandfather
Russell, William	Abt. 1755	2nd great grand uncle
Sassaman, Emmanuel	1827	Husband of 1st great grand aunt
Schneck		2nd great grand uncle
Schneck		2nd great grand uncle
Schneck, Elizabeth	August 13, 1805	2nd great grandmother
Schneck, Living		2nd great grand uncle
Schneck, Peter	Abt. 1765	3rd great grandfather
Schreckengast?, Anna Maria	June 15, 1795	2nd great grandmother
Semrow, Loretta	1900	Wife of uncle
Shadel, Henry L	1865	Husband of grand aunt
Shannon, Living		Husband of granddaughter
Sidnam	1824	Wife of 1st great grand uncle
Sikora, Living U		Husband of granddaughter

Name:	Birth Date:	Relationship:
Sikora, Living		Great granddaughter
Sikora, Living		Great granddaughter
Singer, Henry	1825	Husband of 1st great grand aunt
Smink, Isaac	1828	Husband of 1st great grand aunt
Smith, Mary Helen	Abt. 1707	4th great grandmother
Snoke	Abt. 1780	Husband of 2nd great grand aunt
Sophia	1835	Wife of 1st great grand uncle
St. Thompson, Living		Granddaughter
Sterner, Catherine	1890	Wife of uncle
Sterner, Living		Husband of aunt
Stoddart, David	May 19, 1754	3rd great grandfather
Stoddart, Elizabeth	January 05, 1779	2nd great grandmother
Stoddart, James	1767	3rd great grand uncle
Stoddart, John	December 25, 1728	4th great grandfather
Susan	1790	Wife of 2nd great grand uncle
Susan	1838	Wife of 1st great grand uncle
Susan	1882	Wife of uncle
Swab, Catherine "Kate"	1788	Wife of 2nd great grand uncle
Swartz, David	1816	Husband of 1st great grand aunt
Thompson, Abel Franklin	October 19, 1910	Brother
Thompson, Abel Robert	November 28, 1880	Father
Thompson, Alexander	October 22, 1805	Great grandfather
Thompson, Alexander F	1845	Grand uncle
Thompson, Anna	1779	2nd great grand aunt
Thompson, Benjamin	1874	Uncle
Thompson, Blanche	1883	Aunt
Thompson, Christina	1792	Great grand aunt
Thompson, David Penman	1837	Grand uncle
Thompson, Elizabeth	1763	2nd great grand aunt
Thompson, Elizabeth	1841	Grand aunt
Thompson, Eugene Robert	August 07, 1937	Son
Thompson, George	1773	2nd great grand uncle
Thompson, George	1835	Grand uncle
Thompson, George W	1802	Great grand uncle
Thompson, Grissel	1737	3rd great grand aunt
Thompson, Harper Bruce	September 28, 1907	Self
Thompson, Helen	1761	2nd great grand aunt
Thompson, Helen	1767	2nd great grand aunt
Thompson, Isabelle	1719	3rd great grand aunt

Name:	Birth Date:	Relationship:
Thompson, Isabelle	1761	2nd great grand aunt
Thompson, Isabelle	1849	Grand aunt
Thompson, Jacobina	1744	3rd great grand aunt
Thompson, James	1725	3rd great grand uncle
Thompson, James C	1851	Grand uncle
Thompson, James Smith	1811	Great grand uncle
Thompson, Janet "Jennie"	1844	Grand aunt
Thompson, John	1728	3rd great grand uncle
Thompson, John	1804	Great grand uncle
Thompson, John	1808	Great grand uncle
Thompson, Living		Granddaughter
Thompson, Living		Uncle
Thompson, Living		Great granddaughter
Thompson, Living		Granddaughter
Thompson, Living		Great granddaughter
Thompson, Living		Grandson
Thompson, Living		Aunt
Thompson, Living		Great granddaughter
Thompson, Living		Great grandson
Thompson, Living		Great granddaughter
Thompson, Living		Granddaughter
Thompson, Living		Son
Thompson, Living		Great grandson
Thompson, Living		Grandson
Thompson, Living		Son
Thompson, Living		Great grandson
Thompson, Living		Great grandson
Thompson, Living		Granddaughter
Thompson, Living		Great grandson
Thompson, Lydia Mae	February 07, 1914	Sister
Thompson, M		Grandson
Thompson, Margaret	1721	3rd great grand aunt
Thompson, Mary	1741	3rd great grand aunt
Thompson, Mary	1764	2nd great grand aunt
Thompson, Mary	1775	2nd great grand aunt
Thompson, Mary	1800	Great grand aunt
Thompson, Nicole	1777	2nd great grand aunt
Thompson, Oliver Charles	1875	Uncle
Thompson, Robert	June 27, 1771	2nd great grandfather
Thompson, Robert	1795	Great grand uncle

Name:	Birth Date:	Relationship:
Thompson, Robert	1836	Grand uncle
Thompson, Robert Bruce	September 24, 1847	Paternal grandfather
Thompson, Virginia D	1905	Sister
Thompson, Wilbur Clark	1906	Brother
Thompson, William	1797	Great grand uncle
Thompson, William W	1839	Grand uncle
Thomson, Robert	October 25, 1695	4th great grandfather
Thomson, Robert	September 13, 1734	3rd great grandfather
Trovinger, Elizabeth	Abt. 1798	2nd great grandmother
Tutto, Nancy	1938	Daughter-in-law
Underkoffler, Living		Husband of aunt
Updegroff, John William	February 24, 1732	4th great grandfather
Updegrove	Abt. 1802	2nd great grand uncle
Updegrove, Anna	1807	2nd great grand aunt
Updegrove, Anna M	1864	Grand aunt
Updegrove, Anna Magdalena	March 09, 1759	3rd great grand aunt
Updegrove, Catherine	1833	Great grand aunt
Updegrove, Clara Matilda	November 30, 1866	Maternal grandmother
Updegrove, Conrad	November 27, 1771	3rd great grandfather
Updegrove, Daniel	June 28, 1839	Great grandfather
Updegrove, Edward Isaac	November 27, 1771	3rd great grand uncle
Updegrove, Elizabeth	1803	2nd great grand aunt
Updegrove, Ellen	Abt. 1812	Wife of 1st great grand uncle
Updegrove, Frances	September 10, 1756	3rd great grand aunt
Updegrove, Jacob	1827	Great grand uncle
Updegrove, John Adam	1761	3rd great grand uncle
Updegrove, John J	1835	Great grand uncle
Updegrove, John M	March 23, 1805	2nd great grandfather
Updegrove, Nancy	1838	Great grand aunt
Updegrove, Nellie	1811	2nd great grand aunt
Updegrove, Nora Jane	1874	Grand aunt
Updegrove, Peter	May 01, 1766	3rd great grand uncle
Updegrove, Rebecca	1847	Great grand aunt
Updegrove, Sarah	1809	2nd great grand aunt
Updegrove, Solomon	1809	2nd great grand uncle
Updegrove, Solomon	1845	Great grand uncle

Name:	Birth Date:	Relationship:
Updegrove, William Henry	1870	Grand uncle
Voller, Catherine	1780	2nd great grandmother
Walter, Maria Salome	Abt. 1730	4th great grandmother
White, Lavinia Eva	1890	Wife of uncle
Wilson, Elizabeth		Wife of 1st great grand uncle
Wilson, Isabelle	Abt. 1720	4th great grandmother
Wilson, James		Husband of 1st great grand aunt
Wittle, Living		Wife of grandson
Workman, ?		Great grand uncle
Workman, Benjamin	1787	2nd great grand uncle
Workman, Carolina	1831	Great grand aunt
Workman, Catherine	May 17, 1838	Great grandmother
Workman, Elizabeth	1829	Great grand aunt
Workman, Jacob		2nd great grand uncle
Workman, Jacob	1819	Great grand uncle
Workman, James		2nd great grand uncle
Workman, John		2nd great grand uncle
Workman, John	1823	Great grand uncle
Workman, Joseph	December 03, 1795	2nd great grandfather
Workman, Joseph R	1836	Great grand uncle
Workman, Nancy	1826	Great grand aunt
Workman, Susan	1821	Great grand aunt
Yohe, John F	1887	Husband of aunt
Zimmerman, Peter	1808	Husband of 2nd great grand aunt

Outline Descendant Report for Robert Thomson

1 Robert Thomson b: October 25, 1695 in Cochran, Scotland, d: Abt. 1744 in Scotland
... + Isabelle Cochran b: February 07, 1699 in Scotland, m: November 21, 1718 in Ormiston, East Lothian, Scotland, d: Aft. 1744 in Scotland
......2 Isabelle Thompson b: 1719 in Scotland
......2 Margaret Thompson b: 1721 in Scotland
......2 James Thompson b: 1725 in Scotland
......2 John Thompson b: 1728 in Scotland
......2 Robert Thomson b: September 13, 1734 in Cranston, Midlothian, Scotland, d: Aft. 1779 in Scotland
...... + Mary Black b: 1737 in Prestonpans, East Lothian, Scotland, m: Abt. 1760 in Scotland, d: Aft. 1779 in Scotland
.........3 Helen Thompson b: 1761 in Scotland
.........3 Isabelle Thompson b: 1761 in Scotland
.........3 Elizabeth Thompson b: 1763 in Scotland
.........3 Mary Thompson b: 1764 in Scotland
.........3 Helen Thompson b: 1767 in Scotland
.........3 Robert Thompson b: June 27, 1771 in Edgehead, Cranston, Midlothian, Scotland, d: Aft. 1811 in Scotland
.... + Janet Russell b: December 21, 1766 in Newbattle, Midlothian, Scotland, m: April 22, 1791 in Borthwick, Newbattle, Midlothian, Scotland, d: Aft. 1811 in Scotland
............4 Christina Thompson b: 1792 in Scotland
.... + John King
...............5 Robert King b: 1810
...............5 William King b: 1812
...............5 John King b: 1814
...............5 Janet King b: 1817
...............5 Beatrice King b: 1822
............4 Robert Thompson b: 1795 in Scotland
.... + Elizabeth Wilson
...............5 James Thompson b: 1814
...............5 Robert Thompson b: 1816
...............5 William Thompson b: 1819
...............5 John King Thompson b: 1822
...............5 Living Thompson
...............5 Living Thompson
...............5 Living Thompson
...............5 Mary Thompson b: 1830
...............5 Elizabeth Thompson b: 1833
............4 William Thompson b: 1797 in Scotland
.... + Anna Penman
...............5 Living Thompson
...............5 Living Thompson
.... + Helen Patterson
...............5 Living Thompson
.... + Robert Wilson
..................6 Living Wilson

..................6 Living Wilson
...............5 Living Thompson
...............5 Living Thompson
...............5 William D Thompson b: 1831
...............5 Robert Thompson
....   + Helen Lawson
..................6 Margaret Blythe Thompson
....   + Martin Tait
.....................7 Joseph Tait
....   + Elsie Weir
........................8 Margaret Tait
........................8 Living Tait
...............5 Anna Thompson b: 1835
...............5 Mary Thompson b: 1837
...............5 Isabelle Thompson b: 1839
...............5 Elizabeth Thompson b: 1842
...........4 Mary Thompson b: 1800 in Scotland
....   + James Wilson
...............5 Robert Wilson b: 1822
...............5 Living Wilson
...............5 Alexander Wilson b: 1829
...............5 Charles Wilson b: 1832
...............5 William Wilson b: 1834
...............5 George Wilson b: 1837
...............5 Living Wilson
...........4 George W Thompson b: 1802 in Scotland
....   + Catherine Penman b: July 12, 1802 in Newbattle, Midlothian, Scotland
...............5 Elizabeth Thompson b: 1826
....   + Margaret McLeran b: 1816
...........4 John Thompson b: 1804 in Scotland
...........4 Alexander Thompson b: October 22, 1805 in Sauchenside Farm, Cranston, Midlothian,
        Scotland, d: December 04, 1873 in Tower City, Schuylkill Co, PA
....   + Isabelle Stoddart Penman b: May 09, 1816 in Newbattle, Midlothian, Scotland, m: January
        01, 1835 in Pottsville, Schuylkill Co, PA, d: April 18, 1851 in Pottsville, Schuylkill Co, PA
...............5 George Thompson b: 1835 in PA
...............5 Robert Thompson b: 1836 in PA
....   + Helen
..................6 William Thompson b: 1859
..................6 Anna Thompson b: 1864
..................6 John Thompson b: 1866
..................6 David Lawson Thompson b: 1869, d: 1935
..................6 Christina Thompson b: 1871
..................6 Helen Thompson b: 1874
..................6 Robert Thompson b: 1876
..................6 Richard Thompson b: 1878
..................6 Mary F Thompson b: 1879
...............5 David Penman Thompson b: 1837 in PA, d: 1912
....   + "Cassie" Houtz b: 1841 in PA, d: 1883
..................6 Walter S Thompson b: 1862 in PA
....   + Cordelia Henry b: 1867 in PA
.....................7 Living Thompson
....   + Living Milk

......................7 Living Thompson
....   + Living DeWitt
......................7 Living Thompson
....   + Living Conrad
.......................8 Living Conrad
.......................8 Living Conrad
....   + Dorothy "Dot" Winefred Jay
......................7 Living Thompson
......................7 Lucilla Thompson
......................7 Maria Thompson
......................7 Ruth Thompson
......................7 Donald Thompson
...................6 William A Thompson b: 1864
...................6 David P Thompson b: 1866 in PA
....   + Ida Strohecker b: 1866 in PA
......................7 Grant R Thompson b: 1889
....   + Ethel
......................7 Martha Myrtle Thompson b: 1890
....   + Harvey Reisch
.......................8 Eldon Reisch
.......................8 Roy Reisch
......................7 Living Thompson
....   + Living
.......................8 Living Thompson
.......................8 Living Thompson
.......................8 Living Thompson
.......................8 Living Thompson
.......................8 Living Thompson
...................6 Grant C Thompson b: 1869 in PA, d: 1880
...................6 Ulysses Schuyler Thompson b: 1871
....   + Edith
......................7 Ruth Thompson
......................7 Catherine Thompson
...................6 Harry Snyder Thompson b: 1872
....   + Alice Barker
......................7 Ruth Jane Thompson
......................7 Harry Thompson
......................7 Erma May Thompson
...................6 Milton S Thompson b: 1874
...................6 "Carrie" Isabella Thompson b: 1876, d: 1877
...................6 Nettie M Thompson b: 1878
....   + Walter Shackley
......................7 Living Shackley
...................6 Jane "Jennie" B Thompson b: 1879, d: 1882
...................6 Erma Agnes Thompson b: 1880
....   + Edgar Chapman b: 1875
......................7 Living Chapman
......................7 Living Chapman
......................7 Living Chapman
......................7 Living Chapman
......................7 Living Chapman
......................7 Mildred Agnes Chapman

....................7 Arvilla Betty Chapman
...............5 William W Thompson b: 1839 in PA
....   + Mary A b: 1836 in PA
..................6 David A Thompson b: 1859 in PA
..................6 Mary Agnes Thompson b: 1861 in PA
..................6 George E Thompson b: 1864 in PA
....   + Mary A Shumber b: 1871 in PA
....................7 Mary A Thompson b: 1892
....................7 Living Thompson
....................7 Living Thompson
....................7 Living Thompson
..................6 Abraham L Thompson b: 1866 in PA
..................6 Albert Thompson b: 1867 in PA
....   + Sarah Beene b: 1867 in PA
..................6 Harry Thompson b: 1869 in PA
....   + Barbara b: 1878 in PA
..................6 Edwin Thompson b: 1872 in PA
....   + Catherine b: 1876 in PA
....................7 Living Thompson
....   + Living
....................7 Living Thompson
....................7 Living Thompson
..................6 Helen Thompson b: 1875 in PA
..................6 Joseph W Thompson b: 1876 in PA, d: 1982
....   + Lucy E Gamber b: 1882 in PA, d: 1982
....................7 Living Thompson
....................7 Harold L Thompson b: 1921, d: 1941
...............5 Elizabeth Thompson b: 1841 in PA
....   + Hiram Kimmel
...............5 Janet "Jennie" Thompson b: 1844 in PA
....   + Benjamin Houtz
..................6 Clara Houtz
..................6 Reno Houtz
..................6 Harry Houtz U
....   + Annie Martz
....................7 William Houtz
....................7 Mark Houtz
..................6 Emma Houtz
....   + Edwin Kantner
....................7 Lola Kantner
....................7 Thelma Kantner
..................6 Elizabeth Houtz
....   + Percy Fornwalt
....................7 Maude Fornwalt
....................7 Margaret Fornwalt
....................7 Ethel Fornwalt
....................7 Helen Fornwalt
....................7 Edwin Fornwalt
..................6 Edwin Houtz
...............5 Alexander F Thompson b: 1845 in PA
....   + Elizabeth Hawk
..................6 William Calude Thompson b: 1873

..................6 Warren Ray Thompson b: 1877
.... + Margaret Gum
.... + Mary A b: 1867 in PA
..................6 May Buckenbill b: 1891 in PA (Adopted)
...............5 Robert Bruce Thompson b: September 24, 1847 in York Farm Burial Grounds, Pottsville, Schuylkill Co, PA, d: October 10, 1907 in Tower City, Schuylkill Co, PA; Typhoid fever w/contaminated water
.... + Lydia Ann Goodman b: February 20, 1856 in Clarks Valley, Dauphin Co, PA, m: Abt. 1873 in Schuylkill Co, PA, d: October 09, 1883 in Tower City, Schuylkill Co, PA; Complications of pregnancy
..................6 Benjamin Thompson b: 1874 in PA, d: 1875
..................6 Oliver Charles Thompson b: 1875 in PA, d: 1918
.... + Blanche Charlesworth b: 1883 in PA
.....................7 Living Thompson
.... + Living Harvey
.....................8 Living Harvey
.....................8 Living Harvey
.....................8 Living Harvey
.....................7 Living Thompson
.... + Living Heiss
.....................8 Living Heiss
.....................8 Living Heiss
.....................7 Living Thompson
.....................7 Living Thompson
.... + Living Cleaver
.....................8 Living Cleaver
.....................8 Living Cleaver
.....................7 Living Thompson
.... + Living Slear
.....................8 Living Slear
.... + <No name>
.....................7 Allen Thompson b: 1891 in PA
..................6 Abel Robert Thompson b: November 28, 1880 in Sheridan, Schuylkill Co, PA, d: October 15, 1918 in Tower City, Schuylkill Co, PA; Pneumonia w/influenza
.... + Augusta "Gussie" Mae Hensel b: February 16, 1885 in Wiconisco, Dauphin Co, PA, m: June 15, 1904 in Schuylkill Co, PA, d: March 27, 1973 in Home, Tower City, Schuylkill Co, PA; Medullary paralysis w/thrombosis w/cerebral hemorrhage & arteriosclerosis
.....................7 Virginia D Thompson b: 1905 in PA, d: 1905
.....................7 Wilbur Clark Thompson b: 1906 in PA, d: 1963
.... + Elva May Matter b: 1911, d: 1999
.....................8 no issue
.....................7 Harper Bruce Thompson b: September 28, 1907 in Sheridan, Schuylkill Co, PA, d: July 23, 1981 in Polyclinic Hospital, Harrisburg, Dauphin Co, PA; Cardiorespiratory arrest w/subdural hematoma
.... + Myrtle Adeline Batdorf b: January 05, 1918 in Big Run, Dauphin Co, PA, m: June 15, 1935 in St. Johns (Hill) Lutheran, Lykens, Dauphin Co, PA, d: May 08, 1983 in Polyclinic Hospital, Harrisburg, Dauphin Co, PA; Cardiorespiratory arrest w/ASHD w/pacemaker
.....................8 Living Thompson
.... + Living Duncan
.....................9 M Thompson
.... + Living Curry
.... + Living Romano
.... + Living Wittle
.....................9 Living St. Thompson

.... + Living Shannon
.........................9 Living Thompson
.... + Living
........................8 Eugene Robert Thompson b: August 07, 1937 in PA, d: March 21, 2007 in Harrisburg, Dauphin Co, PA
.... + Margaret "Peggy" Evans b: 1935, d: July 31, 2005
.........................9 Living Thompson
.... + Living Potteiger
.... + Stephanie Hockley
........................8 Living Thompson
.... + Nancy Tutto b: 1938, d: 1988
.........................9 Living Thompson
.... + Living Sikora U
.... + Living Cleary
.........................9 Living Thompson
.... + Mark McCracken
.........................9 Living Thompson
.... + Living Greene
.........................9 Living Thompson
.... + Living Landis
.... + Living
.....................7 Abel Franklin Thompson b: October 19, 1910 in PA, d: June 1985 in East Petersburg, Lancaster Co, PA
.... + Almeda Ellen Cox b: 1911, m: 1931, d: 1991
........................8 Living Thompson
.... + Living Paris
.........................9 Living Thompson
.... + Living Rudisill
.........................9 Living Thompson
.... + Living Potter
.... + Living Hauck
........................8 Darryl E Thompson b: 1939, d: 2009
.... + Mary Ann Hoover
.........................9 Living Thompson
.... + Living Kulp
.........................9 Living Thompson
.... + Stanley L Shive d: Abt. 2005
.....................7 Lydia Mae Thompson b: February 07, 1914 in Sheridan, Schuylkill Co, PA, d: January 1983 in Tower City, Schuylkill Co, PA
..................6 Blanche Thompson b: 1883 in PA, d: 1915
..................6 Living Thompson
.... + Susan b: 1882 in PA
.....................7 Living Thompson
.... + Living
.....................7 Living Thompson
.....................7 Living Thompson
.....................7 Living Thompson
.....................7 Living Thompson
.....................7 Living Thompson
.....................7 Living Thompson
..................6 Living Thompson
.... + Charles John McGough b: 1881 in PA
.... + Mary Margaret Moses b: 1850

..................6 Living Thompson
..................6 Lillian "Lillie" R Thompson b: 1889 in PA
....   + Charles I Haubenstein b: 1878 in PA
..................7 Living Haubenstein
..................7 Elizabeth Haubenstein
..................7 Living Haubenstein
..................7 James Haubenstein
..................6 Allen Herbert Thompson b: 1891 in PA, d: 1962
...............5 Isabelle Thompson b: 1849 in PA
....   + George Powell
..................6 Sarah Powell
..................6 Elizabeth Powell
..................6 Richard Powell
..................6 John Powell
..................6 "Carrie" Powell b: 1872
..................6 Walter Alfred Powell b: 1879
....   + Kathryn Blanche Antes
..................7 Margaret Powell
..................7 Elva Mae Powell
..................7 Martha Isabel Powell
..................7 Walter Alfred Powell
..................7 Thomas Robert Powell
..................7 Richard W Powell
..................7 John Charles Powell
..................7 Corine Isabel Powell
..................6 George Powell b: 1881
....   + Sara
..................6 Thomas J Powell b: 1884
....   + Edith
..................6 Mary A Powell b: 1888
....   + Gilbert Knecht
...............5 James C Thompson b: 1851 in PA
....   + Mary A Bast b: 1833 in PA, m: 1853, d: 1910
...............5 Isaac B Thompson b: 1853 in PA
....   + Mary Goodman b: 1857 in PA
..................6 Cora Thompson b: 1876 in PA
....   + Francis W Shomber
....   + Lester Beningo
..................6 Arthur W Thompson b: 1878 in PA, d: 1937
....   + Caroline Shomper b: 1881 in PA, d: 1967
..................7 Living Thompson
....   + Living Shreffler
..................7 Martha Thompson b: 1900 in PA, d: 1901
..................7 Living Thompson
....   + Living Machamer
..................8 Living Machamer
..................8 Living Machamer
..................8 Living Machamer
..................7 Clyde Thompson b: 1904, d: 1910
..................7 Isaac Thompson b: 1909, d: 1910
..................7 Living Thompson
....   + Living Meyers

.....................7 Living Thompson
.... + Living Bailey
.................6 Charles Thompson b: 1879 in PA
.................6 Mary Thompson b: 1889 in PA
.... + Wilbur Kaufman b: 1888 in PA
.....................7 Living Kaufman
.....................7 Living Kaufman
.....................7 Living Kaufman
.....................7 Living Kaufman
.....................7 Living Kaufman
.....................7 Living Kaufman
.................6 "Lillie" Thompson
.................6 "Carrie" A Thompson b: 1891 in PA
.... + Harry L Shomber b: 1892 in PA
.....................7 Living Shomber
.... + Richard Daughtery
.................6 Living Thompson
.................6 Lester Thompson
.................6 Living Thompson
.... + Living Lenkert
.....................7 Living Lenkert
.....................7 Living Lenkert
.....................7 Living Lenkert
.....................7 Living Lenkert
.....................7 Living Lenkert
.....................7 Living Lenkert
.....................7 Living Lenkert
.....................7 Living Lenkert
.................6 Ralph I Thompson b: 1882
.... + Cora Peters b: 1886
.....................7 Hazel Thompson
.....................7 Russell Thompson
.................6 Living Thompson
.... + Living Slingwine
.....................7 Living Thompson
.....................7 Living Thompson
.....................7 Living Thompson
.....................7 Living Thompson
.....................7 Living Thompson
.....................7 Living Thompson
.................6 Living Thompson
.............5 George Thompson b: 1854 in PA
.............5 Mary Isabelle Thompson b: 1856 in PA
.... + Harry Daniel Stout
.............5 Mary A Thompson b: 1857 in PA
.............5 John K Thompson b: 1858 in PA
.... + Elizabeth "Lizzie" Ann Kimmel b: 1860 in PA
.................6 Elizabeth "Bessie" M Thompson b: 1892 in PA
.... + Harvey Fetterhoff
.............5 Andrew R Thompson b: 1862 in PA
.... + Bertha
.................6 Jesse Thompson

.... + Elizabeth Kinsey
....................7 Virginia "Virgie" Thompson
....................7 Betty Thompson
....................7 Ione Thompson
.................6 Blanche Thompson
.................6 Earl Thompson
.................6 Ruth Thompson
..............5 Charles W Thompson b: 1864 in PA, d: 1879
..............5 Abraham L Thompson b: 1865 in PA, d: 1912
.... + Maclada Strohecker b: 1864, d: 1954
..............5 Winfield S Thompson b: 1868 in PA
.... + Ella M O'Brien b: 1874 in PA
..............5 William USG Thompson b: 1869 in PA
.... + Sarah "Sadie" J Miller b: 1879 in PA
.................6 Living Thompson
.................6 Living Thompson
.................6 Thelma E Thompson b: 1904, d: 1910
..............5 Elmer Edwin Thompson b: 1871 in PA
.... + Fielta Daniels b: 1863 in PA
.................6 Living Thompson
.... + Living
....................7 Living Thompson
....................7 Living Thompson
.................6 Dora D Thompson b: 1895 in PA, d: 1946
.................6 Living Thompson
..............5 Rebecca M Thompson b: 1873
.... + Hopkins Evans
.................6 Living Evans
.................6 Charles Evans
............4 John Thompson b: 1808 in Scotland
............4 James Smith Thompson b: 1811 in Scotland
.........3 George Thompson b: 1773 in Scotland
.... + Mary Russell
.........3 Mary Thompson b: 1775 in Scotland
.........3 Nicole Thompson b: 1777 in Scotland
.........3 Anna Thompson b: 1779 in Scotland
.... + William Russell
......2 Grissel Thompson b: 1737 in Scotland
......2 Mary Thompson b: 1741 in Scotland
......2 Jacobina Thompson b: 1744 in Scotland

Chapter Five

Our family's calendar.

Important annual dates of birth, marriage and death.

January 2014

	January 2014							February 2014					
S	M	T	W	T	F	S	S	M	T	W	T	F	S
			1	2	3	4							1
5	6	7	8	9	10	11	2	3	4	5	6	7	8
12	13	14	15	16	17	18	9	10	11	12	13	14	15
19	20	21	22	23	24	25	16	17	18	19	20	21	22
26	27	28	29	30	31		23	24	25	26	27	28	

Sunday	Monday	Tuesday	Wednesday	Thursday	Friday	Saturday
			1 Isabelle S. and Alexander Thompson	2	3	4
5 Myrtle A. Batdorf Thompson Elizabeth Stoddart Penman	6	7	8	9	10	11
12	13 Christina and William Russell	14	15	16 Mary A. Guise Hensel	17	18
19	20	21	22	23	24	25
26	27	28	29	30	31	

February 2014

February 2014							March 2014						
S	M	T	W	T	F	S	S	M	T	W	T	F	S
						1							1
2	3	4	5	6	7	8	2	3	4	5	6	7	8
9	10	11	12	13	14	15	9	10	11	12	13	14	15
16	17	18	19	20	21	22	16	17	18	19	20	21	22
23	24	25	26	27	28		23	24	25	26	27	28	29
							30	31					

Sunday	Monday	Tuesday	Wednesday	Thursday	Friday	Saturday
						1
2	3	4	5	6	7 Isabelle Cochran Thomson	8
9	10 Catherine Workman Hensel	11	12	13	14	15 Thomas Muckle
16 Augusta ".M. Hensel Thompson Margaret and David Stoddart	17	18 Andrew G. Hensel	19 Susan Lehman Romberger	20 Lydia A. Goodman Thompson	21	22
23 Anna M.E. Benfield Updegroff Susan Romberger Workman	24 John W. Updegroff	25 Janet Malcolm Russell	26	27	28	

March 2014

March 2014

S	M	T	W	T	F	S
						1
2	3	4	5	6	7	8
9	10	11	12	13	14	15
16	17	18	19	20	21	22
23	24	25	26	27	28	29
30	31					

April 2014

S	M	T	W	T	F	S
		1	2	3	4	5
6	7	8	9	10	11	12
13	14	15	16	17	18	19
20	21	22	23	24	25	26
27	28	29	30			

Sunday	Monday	Tuesday	Wednesday	Thursday	Friday	Saturday
						1
2	3	4	5	6	7	8
9	10	11	12	13	14	15
16	17	18	19	20	21 Eugene R. Thompson	22
23 John M. Updegrove	24	25 Daniel Updegrove	26	27 Augusta ".M. Hensel Thompson	28 Clara M. Updegrove Hensel	29
30	31					

April 2014

April 2014								May 2014						
S	M	T	W	T	F	S		S	M	T	W	T	F	S
		1	2	3	4	5						1	2	3
6	7	8	9	10	11	12		4	5	6	7	8	9	10
13	14	15	16	17	18	19		11	12	13	14	15	16	17
20	21	22	23	24	25	26		18	19	20	21	22	23	24
27	28	29	30					25	26	27	28	29	30	31

Sunday	Monday	Tuesday	Wednesday	Thursday	Friday	Saturday
		1 Anna M.E. Benfield Updegroff	**2**	**3**	**4**	**5**
6	**7**	**8** John Penman	**9**	**10** Anna M. Schreckengast? Brown	**11**	**12**
13	**14**	**15**	**16** Susan Romberger Workman John Russell	**17**	**18** Isabelle S. Penman Thompson	**19**
20	**21**	**22** Janet and Robert Thompson	**23**	**24**	**25**	**26** Catherine and Jacob Guteman
27	**28**	**29**	**30**			

May 2014

May 2014
S M T W T F S
1 2 3
4 5 6 7 8 9 10
11 12 13 14 15 16 17
18 19 20 21 22 23 24
25 26 27 28 29 30 31

June 2014
S M T W T F S
1 2 3 4 5 6 7
8 9 10 11 12 13 14
15 16 17 18 19 20 21
22 23 24 25 26 27 28
29 30

Sunday	Monday	Tuesday	Wednesday	Thursday	Friday	Saturday
				1	2	3
4 John B. Romberger	5	6	7	8 Myrtle A. Batdorf Thompson	9 Isabelle S. Penman Thompson	10 Janet and John Russell
11	12	13	14	15 Elizabeth Mason Muckle	16	17 Catherine and Andrew G. Hensel Catherine Workman Hensel
18	19 David Stoddart	20	21	22	23 Joseph Workman	24
25	26	27	28	29	30	31

June 2014

June 2014

S	M	T	W	T	F	S
1	2	3	4	5	6	7
8	9	10	11	12	13	14
15	16	17	18	19	20	21
22	23	24	25	26	27	28
29	30					

July 2014

S	M	T	W	T	F	S
		1	2	3	4	5
6	7	8	9	10	11	12
13	14	15	16	17	18	19
20	21	22	23	24	25	26
27	28	29	30	31		

Sunday	Monday	Tuesday	Wednesday	Thursday	Friday	Saturday
1	2 Elizabeth Schneck Kulp	3	4	5	6 Howard A.C. Hensel	7
8 Margaret and John Stoddart	9	10 Michael Goodman	11 John D. Angst	12	13	14
15 Myrtle A. and Harper B. Thompson / Augusta ".M. and Abel R. Thompson / Susan and Balthasar Romberger	16	17	18	19	20	21
22	23	24	25	26	27 Robert Thompson	28 Andrew W. Hensel / Daniel Updegrove
29	30 Sarah ".A. Culp Updegrove					

July 2014

July 2014						
S	M	T	W	T	F	S
		1	2	3	4	5
6	7	8	9	10	11	12
13	14	15	16	17	18	19
20	21	22	23	24	25	26
27	28	29	30	31		

August 2014						
S	M	T	W	T	F	S
					1	2
3	4	5	6	7	8	9
10	11	12	13	14	15	16
17	18	19	20	21	22	23
24	25	26	27	28	29	30
31						

Sunday	Monday	Tuesday	Wednesday	Thursday	Friday	Saturday
		1	2	3 Sarah ".A. Culp Updegrove	4	5 Balthasar Romberge
6	7 Andrew W. Hensel	8	9	10	11	12 Isabelle and Robert Brown
13	14	15	16	17	18	19
20	21	22	23 Harper B. Thompson	24	25	26
27	28	29	30	31 Margaret ". Evans Thompson		

August 2014

August 2014

S	M	T	W	T	F	S
					1	2
3	4	5	6	7	8	9
10	11	12	13	14	15	16
17	18	19	20	21	22	23
24	25	26	27	28	29	30
31						

September 2014

S	M	T	W	T	F	S
	1	2	3	4	5	6
7	8	9	10	11	12	13
14	15	16	17	18	19	20
21	22	23	24	25	26	27
28	29	30				

Sunday	Monday	Tuesday	Wednesday	Thursday	Friday	Saturday
					1	2
3	4 Mary H. and George Black	5	6	7 Eugene R. Thompson	8	9
10	11	12	13 Elizabeth Schneck Kulp	14	15	16 John P. Braun
17 John P. Braun	18	19	20 Margaret Bowman Stoddart	21	22	23
24	25	26	27	28	29	30
31						

September 2014

September 2014

S	M	T	W	T	F	S
	1	2	3	4	5	6
7	8	9	10	11	12	13
14	15	16	17	18	19	20
21	22	23	24	25	26	27
28	29	30				

October 2014

S	M	T	W	T	F	S
			1	2	3	4
5	6	7	8	9	10	11
12	13	14	15	16	17	18
19	20	21	22	23	24	25
26	27	28	29	30	31	

Sunday	Monday	Tuesday	Wednesday	Thursday	Friday	Saturday
	1	2 Howard A.C. Hensel Clara M. and Howard A.C. Hensel	3	4	5	6
7	8	9	10	11	12	13 Robert Thomson
14 David Moffatt	15	16	17	18	19	20
21	22	23	24 Robert B. Thompson	25 John B. Romberger	26	27
28 William Russell Harper B. Thompson	29	30 John C. Hensel				

October 2014

October 2014

S	M	T	W	T	F	S
			1	2	3	4
5	6	7	8	9	10	11
12	13	14	15	16	17	18
19	20	21	22	23	24	25
26	27	28	29	30	31	

November 2014

S	M	T	W	T	F	S
						1
2	3	4	5	6	7	8
9	10	11	12	13	14	15
16	17	18	19	20	21	22
23	24	25	26	27	28	29
30						

Sunday	Monday	Tuesday	Wednesday	Thursday	Friday	Saturday
			1	2	3	4
5	6 Agnes and David Moffatt	7	8	9 Sarah ".A. and Daniel Updegrove Lydia A. Goodman Thompson	10 Robert B. Thompson	11
12	13	14	15 Abel R. Thompson	16	17	18
19	20 Jacob Lehman	21	22 Alexander Thompson	23	24	25 Robert Thomson
26	27	28 Catherine and John Penman	29	30	31	

November 2014

November 2014

S	M	T	W	T	F	S
						1
2	3	4	5	6	7	8
9	10	11	12	13	14	15
16	17	18	19	20	21	22
23	24	25	26	27	28	29
30						

December 2014

S	M	T	W	T	F	S
	1	2	3	4	5	6
7	8	9	10	11	12	13
14	15	16	17	18	19	20
21	22	23	24	25	26	27
28	29	30	31			

Sunday	Monday	Tuesday	Wednesday	Thursday	Friday	Saturday
						1
2	3	4	5 Margaret Muckle Stoddart	6	7	8
9	10	11 Maria E. Angst Updegrove	12	13	14	15
16	17	18	19	20	21 Isabelle and Robert Thomson Jacob Guteman	22
23	24	25	26	27 Conrad Updegrove	28 Abel R. Thompson	29
30 Clara M. Updegrove Hensel						

December 2014

December 2014

S	M	T	W	T	F	S
	1	2	3	4	5	6
7	8	9	10	11	12	13
14	15	16	17	18	19	20
21	22	23	24	25	26	27
28	29	30	31			

January 2015

S	M	T	W	T	F	S
				1	2	3
4	5	6	7	8	9	10
11	12	13	14	15	16	17
18	19	20	21	22	23	24
25	26	27	28	29	30	31

Sunday	Monday	Tuesday	Wednesday	Thursday	Friday	Saturday
	1	2	3 Joseph Workman	4 Alexander Thompson	5	6
7	8	9	10	11 Christina Moffatt Russell	12	13
14 John D. Angst Andrew G. Hensel	15	16 Mary A. Guise Hensel	17 Mary M. Brown Goodman	18	19	20
21 Janet Russell Thompson	22	23	24	25 Elizabeth Stoddart Penman John Stoddart	26	27 Michael Goodman
28	29	30	31 David Penman			

Chapter Six

The Afterword, Sources Report, and the Author's Bio.

Afterword

Without my ancestors, I would have been had the chance to experience the wonders of life. Thank you grandma and grandpa, you have allowed me to see beautiful places, do wonderful things and meet amazing people. This is my testament.

Source Title: **Abel F Thompson**

Citation: Abel F Thompson, Bob Averell Family Tree, Entries: 7956, Updated: 2004-08-01 00:29:03 UTC (Sun), Contact: Bob Averell.

Thompson, Abel Franklin
> Death: June 1985 in East Petersburg, Lancaster Co, PA

Source Title: **Abel R Thompson**

Citation: Abel R Thompson, 1918, Schuylkill County Register of Wills, Schuylkill Co, PA, #284.

Thompson, Abel Robert
> Will: July 02, 1914 in Porter Tp., Schuylkill Co, PA

Citation: Abel R Thompson, Probate file, 1918, unnumbered original papers, 34pp, Schuylkill Co Courthouse, Schuylkill, PA, Norman Nicol, Apr 2008.

Thompson, Abel Robert
> Death: October 15, 1918 in Tower City, Schuylkill Co, PA; Pneumonia w/influenza
> Prob: Bet. February–November 1919 in Porter Tp, Schuylkill Co, PA
> Will: July 02, 1914 in Porter Tp., Schuylkill Co, PA

Source Title: **Abel Robert Thompson**

Citation: Abel Robert Thompson, WW I Draft Reg Cards, 1917-1918 Record, www.ancestry.com.

Thompson, Abel Robert
> Occu: September 15, 1918; Miner (PR CSJ Co, West Brookside, Tower City, Schuylkill Co, PA)
> Res: 1918 in Tower City, Schuylkill Co, PA
> Birth: November 28, 1880 in Sheridan, Schuylkill Co, PA
> Medical: Height Tall, Build Medium, Eyes Gray, Hair Dark

Source Title: **Abel Thompson**

Citation: Abel Thompson, Greenwood Cemetery, Tower City, Schuylkill Co, PA, John Barket, Tower City, PA, B-3-1.

Thompson, Abel Robert
> Death: October 17, 1918 in Tower City, Schuylkill Co, PA
> Burial: October 19, 1918 in Greenwood Cemetery, Tower City, Schuylkill Co, PA

Source Title: **Abel Thompson death certificate**

Citation: Abel Thompson death certificate, #0506211, #133775-93, January 1918, Department of Vital Records, New castle, PC.

Thompson, Abel Robert
> Occu: 1918; Miner
> Birth: November 28, 1880 in Sheridan, Schuylkill Co, PA
> Death: October 15, 1918 in Tower City, Schuylkill Co, PA; Pneumonia w/influenza
> Burial: October 19, 1918 in Greenwood Cemetery, Tower City, Schuylkill Co, PA
> Funrl: 1918 in John F Dreisingacer, Tower City, Schuylkill Co, PA

Source Title: **Adam Gice**

Citation: Adam Gice, Adams Co Centinel, Gettysburg, PA, October 8, 1823.

Guise, John Adam

Source Title: **Adam Gice (con't)**

Citation: Adam Gice, Adams Co Centinel, Gettysburg, PA, October 8, 1823.

Guise, John Adam
  Res: 1813 in near Gettysburg, Adams Co, PA
  Res: 1824 in near Gettysburg, Adams Co, PA

Source Title: **Adam Gise**

Citation: Adam Gise, 1799 Menallan Twp. Tax List, Histopry of Adams Co County, Donna Zinn, djzinnn@@pa.net.

Guise, John Adam
  Occu: 1799; Weaver
  Res: 1799 in Butler (Menallen), Adams Co, PA

Citation: Adam Gise, 1834, A1784, Index to Wills and Administration Bonds of Adams Co, PA 1800-1864, SCPGS, York, PA 1997, c/o Gene Smith, GSmithsan@@aolom.

Guise, John Adam
  Will: 1834 in Adams Co, PA

Citation: Adam Gise, PA State Archives, Rev War Index, http://www.digitalarchives.state.pa.us/archive.asp?view=ArchiveItems&ArchiveID=13&FID=478075&LID=478174&FL=&p=4.

Guise, John Adam
  Miltry: 1780; American Revolution, Private 6th PA Reg, 4th Co, 6th class (Northampton, Capt. Andrew Dapper)

Citation: Adam Gise, Revolutionary War Military Abstract Card File, PA State Archives, www.digitalarchives.state.pu.us/archive.

Guise, John Adam
  Immigr: Bef. 1780

Source Title: **Alexander Thompson**

Citation: Alexander Thompson, Dauphin Co Biograhpical Encyclopedia.

Thompson, Alexander
  Occu: Abt. 1860; Superintendent (Potts & Co)
  Occu: Bet. 1865–1871; Contract work (Mines)

Citation: Alexander Thompson, Greenwood Cemetery, Tower City, Schuylkill Co, PA, John Barket, Tower City, PA, A-4-2.

Thompson, Alexander
  Burial: December 1873 in Greenwood Cemetery, Tower City, Schuylkill Co, P

Citation: Alexander Thompson, Miners Journal, December 5, 1873.

Thompson, Alexander
  Death: December 04, 1873 in Tower City, Schuylkill Co, PA

Citation: Alexander Thompson, November 1836, Court of Common Pleas, Schuylkill Co, PA.

Thompson, Alexander
  Naturl: July 31, 1834 in Schuylkill Co, PA

Citation: Alexander Thompson, Reg of Wills, Bk 4, pp 142-3; probate file, 1873, unnumbered original papers, 10pp, Schuylkill Co Courthouse, Schuylkill, PA, Norman Nicol, Apr 2008.

Thompson, Alexander
  Prob: December 17, 1873 in Porter Tp, Schuylkill Co, PA
  Prob: January 25, 1912 in Porter Tp, Schuylkill Co, PA (after Mary Thompson's death)
  Will: December 03, 1873 in Porter Tp, Schuylkill Co, PA

Citation: Alexander Thompson, Schuylkill County, PA, p 1054.

Goodman, Lydia Ann

Source Title: **Alexander Thompson (con't)**

Citation: Alexander Thompson, Schuylkill County, PA, p 1054.

Goodman, Lydia Ann
    Death: October 09, 1883 in Tower City, Schuylkill Co, PA; Complications of pregnancy
    Burial: October 14, 1883 in Greenwood Cemetery, Tower City, Schuylkill Co, PA

Thompson, Robert Bruce
    Occu: Bet. 1899–1901; Supervisor (Porter Tp)
    Occu: Abt. 1900; Tax collector
    Burial: October 13, 1907 in Greenwood Cemetery, Tower City, Schuylkill Co, PA

Citation: Alexander Thompson, Schuylkill County, PA, p 668-669.

Thompson, Alexander
    Occu: 1854; Laid out town of Sheridan, PA
    Res: Aft. 1828 in York Farm Burial Grounds, Pottsville, Schuylkill Co, PA
    Res: 1854 in Porter, Schuylkill Co, PA
    Death: December 04, 1873 in Tower City, Schuylkill Co, PA
    Burial: December 1873 in Greenwood Cemetery, Tower City, Schuylkill Co, P
    Res: Abt. 1827 in Middleport, Schuylkill Co, PA

Citation: Alexander Thompson, Sheridan, Pottsville & Schuylkill Co, PA, J.H. Zerbey, pp 1131-1132.

Thompson, Alexander
    PoliticalParty: Republican

Source Title: **Ancestors of John Wedgewood White**

Citation: Ancestors of John Wedgewood White, Ancestors of John Wedgewood White, jwcotton, Russellville, Arkansas ancestry Tree, ancestry.com.

Keitchen, Agnes
    Birth: August 1701 in Midlothian, Scotland

Malcolm, Janet
    Marr: May 10, 1712 in Scotland
    Death: February 25, 1760 in Scotland

Moffatt, Christina
    Birth: December 11, 1731 in Dalkeith, Midlothian, Scotland

Russell, John
    Marr: May 10, 1712 in Scotland
    Death: April 16, 1750 in Scotland

Russell, William
    Birth: September 28, 1725 in Midlothian, Scotland
    Death: 1792 in Newbattle, Scotland

Source Title: **Ancestry Public Tree**

Citation: Ancestry Public Tree, Goodman Family Tree, Robert Goodman, Phila, PA, ancestry,com.

Guteman, Jacob
    Birth: 1780 in PA
    Death: November 21, 1844 in PA

Source Title: **Andreas Hansel**

Citation: Andreas Hansel, Baptism, York Co, PA library, cards on file.

Hensel, Andrew W
    Birth: June 28, 1793 in Littlestown, York (Adams) Co, PA

Source Title: **Andreas Hansel (con't)**

Citation: Andreas Hansel, Baptism, York Co, PA library, cards on file.

Hensel, Andrew W
> Baptism: August 11, 1793 in Christ Reformed, Littlestown, York (Adams) Co, PA

Source Title: **Andrew Gise Hensel**

Citation: Andrew Gise Hensel, #0036891, #115081, Reg # 84, December 1908, Department of Vital records, New Castle, PA.

Hensel, Andrew Guise
> Birth: February 20, 1832 in PA

Source Title: **Andrew Gise Hensel death certificate**

Citation: Andrew Gise Hensel death certificate, #0036891, #115081, Reg # 84, December 1908, Department of Vital records, New Castle, PA.

Hensel, Andrew Guise
> Occu: 1908; Mason & School teacher
> Death: December 14, 1908 in Wiconisco, Dauphin Co, PA; Bright's disease (ie, Chronic inflammation of kidneys) w/old age
> Funrl: 1908 in John Reiff, Lykens, Dauphin Co, PA

Source Title: **Andrew Hensel**

Citation: Andrew Hensel, 1878, August 02, 1875, Dauphin County Register of Wills, Harrisburg, PA.

Hensel, Andrew W
> Prob: May 24, 1878 in Dauphin Co, PA

Citation: Andrew Hensel, Christ Church, Littlestown, PA, Adams Co County 18th records lookup, Virginia, vperry1@@shawneelink.net.

Hensel, Andrew W
> Birth: June 28, 1793 in Littlestown, York (Adams) Co, PA
> Baptism: August 11, 1793 in Christ Reformed, Littlestown, York (Adams) Co, PA

Citation: Andrew Hensel, Death of an Old Soldier, Obituary, New Bloomfield newspaper, July 1875.

Hensel, Andrew W
> Death: July 07, 1875 in Home, New Bloomfield, Perry Co, PA
> Miltry: February 1814; War of 1812, Private, 5th Reg PA Militia (Fentons), detachment (Adams, Capt. John McMillan)
> Relgn: 1875; Lutheran & German Reformed Church

Citation: Andrew Hensel, Probate files, 1875, rep 49, Perry County Historicans, Newport, PA, Deborah Hershey, Elizabethtown, PA, Jan 2009.

Hensel, Andrew W
> Prob: August 13, 1875 in Perry Co, PA
> Will: Bet. March–December 1864 in Centre, Perry Co, PA

Citation: Andrew Hensel, Source 146, index card, Perry County Historians.

Hensel, Andrew W
> Death: July 07, 1875 in Home, New Bloomfield, Perry Co, PA

Citation: Andrew Hensel, Union Lutheran Cemetery, New Bloomfield, Perry Co, PA, 30 Perry Co PA Cemetery Records, Closson Press, Apollo, PA, 1992.

Hensel, Andrew W
> Burial: July 1875 in St. Peters (Christ, Old Union) Cemetery, New Bloomfield, Perry Co, PA

Citation: Andrew Hensel, War of 1812 Records, DDC, 1999-, www.ancestry.com.

Hensel, Andrew W

Source Title: **Andrew Hensel (con't)**

Citation: Andrew Hensel, War of 1812 Records, DDC, 1999-, www.ancestry.com.

Hensel, Andrew W
>> Miltry: February 1814; War of 1812, Private, 5th Reg PA Militia (Fentons), detachment (Adams, Capt. John McMillan)

Source Title: **Andrew Hentzell**

Citation: Andrew Hentzell, Adams Co Centinel, Gettysburg, PA, October 8, 1823.

Hensel, Andrew W
>> Res: 1823 in near Gettysburg, Adams Co, PA

Source Title: **Andrew Henzel**

Citation: Andrew Henzel, Anton Hentschel, Civil war Soldier & Sailor System, M554, Roll 53, http://www.itd.nps.gov/cwss/soldiers.cfm.

Hensel, Andrew Guise
>> Miltry: August 28, 1864 in Pittsburgh); Civil War, Private, 155th Reg PA Inf, Co F (Harrisburg

Citation: Andrew Henzel, US Civil War Soldiers, 1861-1865, M554 roll 53, www.ancestry.com.

Hensel, Andrew Guise
>> Miltry: August 28, 1864 in Pittsburgh); Civil War, Private, 155th Reg PA Inf, Co F (Harrisburg

Source Title: **Angst household**

Citation: Angst household, 1790 United States Census, Berks Co, PA, Roll M637 8, p 38, Image 0201, ancestry.com & Microfilm, PA State Library, Hbg, PA.

Angst, John Daniel
>> Census: 1790 in Pine Grove, Berks (Schuylkill) Co, PA

Citation: Angst household, 1800 United States Census, Berks Co, PA ancestry.com & Microfilm, PA State Library, Hbg, PA.

Angst, John Daniel
>> Census: 1800 in Pine Grove, Berks (Schuylkill) Co, PA

Citation: Angst household, 1810 United States Census, Berks Co, PA, ancestry.com & Microfilm, PA State Library, Hbg, PA.

Angst, John Daniel
>> Census: 1810 in Pine Grove, Berks (Schuylkill) Co, PA

Source Title: **Balser Ramberger**

Citation: Balser Ramberger, PA State Archives, Rev War Index, http://www.digitalarchives.state.pa.us/archive.asp?view=ArchiveItems&ArchiveID=13&FID=478075&LID=478174&FL=&p=4.

Romberger, John Balthaser
>> Miltry: Abt. 1775; American Revolution, Private 1st PA Reg, 5th Co, 3rd class (Lancaster)

Source Title: **Balthaser Romberger**

Citation: Balthaser Romberger, & Anna Marie Bricker, Bob Salzman, Beavertown, OR, www.e-familytree.net/f2850.htm.

Brucker, Anna Maria
>> Marr: 1765 in Lancaster Co, PA
Romberger, John Balthaser
>> Marr: 1765 in Lancaster Co, PA

Citation: Balthaser Romberger, Debbie Ferguson's Family Tree, 2006, debbief56@@myfamily.com, worldconnect.genealogy.rootsweb.com.

Source Title:	**Balthaser Romberger (con't)**
Citation:	Balthaser Romberger, Debbie Ferguson's Family Tree, 2006, debbief56@@myfamily.com, worldconnect.genealogy.rootsweb.com.
	Brucker, Anna Maria
	Death: Bet. 1778–1798 in Mifflin, Lancaster (Dauphin) Co, PA
Citation:	Balthaser Romberger, Probate files, 1839, Letter of Admin, Dauphin County Courthouse, Reg of Wills, Deborah Hershey, Elizabethtown, PA, Mar 2008.
	Romberger, Balthasar
	Prob: September 02, 1839 in Dauphin Co, PA (listed in index only)

Source Title:	**Baltzer Romberger**
Citation:	Baltzer Romberger, Tax list, 1798, Dauphin Co, PA, John Romberger.
	Lehman, Susan
	Marr: June 15, 1798 in Zion Lutheran, Harrisburg, Dauphin Co, PA
	Romberger, Balthasar
	Marr: June 15, 1798 in Zion Lutheran, Harrisburg, Dauphin Co, PA

Source Title:	**Bartel Raumberger**
Citation:	Bartel Raumberger, PA Census, 1772-1890, Philadelphia, PA, www.ancestry.com.
	Romberger, John Balthaser
	Res: 1754 in Philadelphia, PA
Citation:	Bartel Raumberger, Passenger and Immigration Lists Index, 1500-1900, myfamily.com, P. William Filby, ancestry.com.
	Romberger, John Balthaser
	Immigr: September 24, 1753 in Germany to USA (ship Neptune)

Source Title:	**Bastoe household**
Citation:	Bastoe household, 1850 United States Census, Dauphin Co, PA ancestry.com & Microfilm, PA State Library, Hbg, PA.
	Updegrove, Daniel
	Census: 1850 in Wiconisco, Dauphin Co, PA

Source Title:	**Batdorf household**
Citation:	Batdorf household, 1920 United States Census, Dauphin Co, PA, Roll T625 1559, p 3A, ED 148, Image 1081, ancestry.com & Microfilm, PA State Library, Hbg, PA.
	Batdorf, Myrtle Adeline
	Census: 1920 in Washington, Dauphin Co, PA
Citation:	Batdorf household, 1930 United States Census, Dauphin Co, PA, Roll T626 2027, p 19A, ED 76, Image 0959, ancestry.com & Microfilm, PA State Library, Hbg, PA.
	Batdorf, Myrtle Adeline
	Educ: 1930; School
Citation:	Batdorf household, 1930 United States Census, Dauphin Co, PA, Roll T626 2027, p 19A, ED 76, Image 0959, ancestry.com & Microfilm, PA State Library, Hbg, PA.
	Batdorf, Myrtle Adeline
	Census: 1930 in Lykens, Dauphin Co, PA

Source Title:	**Benfield Family information**
Citation:	Benfield Family information, MihnBu@@aol.com.
	Benfield, Anna Maria Elizabeth
	Death: February 23, 1804 in Exeter, Berks Co, PA
	Updegroff, John William
	Birth: February 24, 1732 in Kirchberg Hunsruck, Rhineland-Palatinate, Germany

| Source Title: | **Berks County Early Church Records** |

Citation: Berks County Early Church Records, Volume 2, Diana Quinones, audianaq@@msn.com.

Hensel, Casper
      Res: 1764 in PA
      Res: 1767 in Windsor Tp, PA
Hensel, John Casper
      Birth: September 30, 1764 in Richmond, York Co, PA
      Baptism: September 30, 1764 in St. Peters Reformed, Richmond, York Co, PA

| Source Title: | **Bob Averell Family Tree** |

Citation: Bob Averell Family Tree, Bob Averell, raverell@@carolina.rr.com, awt.ancestry.com.

Hensel, Andrew Guise
      Birth: February 18, 1831 in Home, New Bloomfield, Perry Co, PA
      Death: December 14, 1908 in Wiconisco, Dauphin Co, PA; Bright's disease
            (ie, Chronic inflammation of kidneys) w/old age
      Burial: December 16, 1908 in Calvary United Methodist, Wiconisco, Dauphin
            Co, PA
Hensel, Howard Andrew Carson
      Marr: September 02, 1884 in Wiconisco, Dauphin Co, PA
      Birth: September 02, 1858 in Wiconisco, Dauphin Co, PA
      Death: June 06, 1927 in Tower City, Schuylkill Co, PA; Arteriosclerosis
      Burial: June 09, 1927 in Greenwood Cemetery, Tower City, Schuylkill Co, PA
Lehman, Susan
      Birth: February 19, 1771 in Trappe, Philadelphia (Montgomery) Co, PA
Romberger, Balthasar
      Death: Abt. 1825 in Mifflin, Dauphin Co, PA
      Burial: Abt. 1839 in St. Johns (Hill) Lutheran, Berrysburg, Dauphin Co, PA
Romberger, Susan
      Birth: April 16, 1799 in Lykens, Dauphin Co, PA
      Death: February 23, 1857 in Dauphin Co, PA
      Burial: 1857 in Calvary United Methodist, Wiconisco, Dauphin Co, PA
Updegrove, Clara Matilda
      Marr: September 02, 1884 in Wiconisco, Dauphin Co, PA
      Birth: November 30, 1866 in Lower Ranch Creek, Tremont, Schuylkill Co, P
      Death: March 28, 1926 in Tower City, Schuylkill Co, PA; Metastatic carcinoma
            of medial atrium & left chest w/carcinoma breast
      Burial: March 31, 1926 in Greenwood Cemetery, Tower City, Schuylkill Co, P
Workman, Catherine
      Birth: May 17, 1838 in Old Lincoln, Dauphin Co, PA
      Death: February 10, 1877 in Joliett, Schuylkill Co, PA
      Burial: 1877 in Calvary United Methodist, Wiconisco, Dauphin Co, PA
Workman, Joseph
      Birth: December 03, 1795 in Lykens, Dauphin Co, PA
      Death: May 23, 1857 in Dauphin Co, PA
      Burial: 1857 in Calvary United Methodist, Wiconisco, Dauphin Co, PA

| Source Title: | **Brown family information** |

Citation: Brown family information, Peter Brown descedants, Deb Kandybowksi, debkandy@@epix.net.

Brown, Anna Maria
      Birth: February 17, 1815 in Clarks Valley, Dauphin Co, PA
      Death: September 07, 1891 in Dauphin, PA

Source Title: **Brown family information (con't)**

Citation: Brown family information, Peter Brown descedants, Deb Kandybowksi, debkandy@@@epix.net.

Schreckengast?, Anna Maria
      Birth: June 15, 1795 in Dauphin Co, PA
      Death: April 10, 1879 in Rush, Dauphin Co, PA

Citation: Brown family information, Schuylkill County, USgenweb.com, p 156.

Braun, Peter
      Res: 1765 in Alsace, France

Source Title: **Brown household**

Citation: Brown household, 1790 United States Census, Berks Co, PA, ancestry.com & Microfilm, PA State Library, Hbg, PA.

Brown, Peter
      Census: 1790

Citation: Brown household, 1810 United States Census, Berks Co, PA ancestry.com & Microfilm, PA State Library, Hbg, PA.

Braun, Peter
      Census: 1810 in Lower Mahantango, Berks Co, PA

Brown, Peter
      Census: 1810 in father; Lower Mahantango, Berks Co, PA w

Citation: Brown household, 1820 United States Census, Berks Co, PA, Roll, ancestry.com & Microfilm, PA State Library, Hbg, PA.

Braun, Peter
      Census: 1820 in Rush, Dauphin Co, PA

Citation: Brown household, 1820 United States Census, Dauphin Co, PA, ancestry.com & Microfilm, PA State Library, Hbg, PA.

Brown, Peter
      Census: 1820 in Rush, Dauphin Co, PA

Citation: Brown household, 1820 United States Census, Schuylkill Co, PA, ancestry.com & Microfilm, PA State Library, Hbg, PA.

Brown, Mary Magdalena
      Census: 1820 in Rush, Dauphin Co, PA (unlisted)

Citation: Brown household, 1820 United States Census, York Co, PA, ancestry.com.

Brown, Peter
      Census: 1800

Citation: Brown household, 1830 United States Census, Dauphin Co, PA ancestry.com & Microfilm, PA State Library, Hbg, PA.

Braun, Peter
      Census: 1830 in Lower Mahantango, Schuylkill Co, PA (son Philip Brown)

Brown, Peter
      Census: 1830 in Rush, Dauphin Co, PA

Citation: Brown household, 1830 United States Census, Dauphin Co, PA, ancestry.com & Microfilm, PA State Library, Hbg, PA.

Brown, Mary Magdalena
      Census: 1830 in father; Rush, Dauphin Co, PA w

Citation: Brown household, 1840 United States Census, Dauphin Co, PA ancestry.com & Microfilm, PA State Library, Hbg, PA.

Brown, Peter
      Census: 1840 in Rush, Dauphin Co, PA

Citation: Brown household, 1850 United States Census, Dauphin Co, PA, 338, ancestry.com & Microfilm, PA State Library, Hbg, PA.

Source Title: **Brown household (con't)**

Citation: Brown household, 1850 United States Census, Dauphin Co, PA, 338, ancestry.com & Microfilm, PA State Library, Hbg, PA.

Brown, Peter
      Propty: 1850 in $100

Citation: Brown household, 1850 United States Census, Dauphin Co, PA, 338, ancestry.com & Microfilm, PA State Library, Hbg, PA.

Brown, Peter
      Census: 1850 in Rush, Dauphin Co, PA

Citation: Brown household, 1850 United States Census, Dauphin Co, PA, p 336, Kathleen M Fagnani, katfagn@@erols.com.

Brown, Peter
      Census: 1850 in Rush, Dauphin Co, PA
       Occu: 1850; Weaver

Citation: Brown household, 1860 United States Census, Dauphin Co, PA, ancestry.com & Microfilm, PA State Library, Hbg, PA.

Schreckengast?, Anna Maria
      Census: 1860 in Rush, Dauphin Co, PA (son John Brown)

Source Title: **Burials 1782-1807**

Citation: Burials 1782-1807, Rev. John William Boos, Ind. reformed Minister, Central Berks Co, BCGS, Berks Co, PA.

Benfield, Anna Maria Elizabeth
      Birth: April 01, 1729 in Oley, Philadelphia (Berks) Co, PA
      Death: February 23, 1804 in Exeter, Berks Co, PA

Source Title: **Capser Hensel**

Citation: Capser Hensel, Adams Co Church Records, PA of the 18th Century, Family Line Prod., NY, c/o Gene Smith, GSmithsan@@aolom.

Hensel, John Casper
      Confir: April 21, 1776 in Christ Church, Littlestown, York (Adams) Co, PA

Citation: Capser Hensel, Descendants of Casper (LaHentzelle) Hensel, Evelyn S. Hartman.

Eva, Maria
      Death: Bet. 1800–1802 in Adams Co, PA

Source Title: **Caspar Haenssel**

Citation: Caspar Haenssel, FGS, York PA library.

Eva, Maria
      Birth: Abt. 1765 in PA
Hensel, John Casper
      Census: 1800 in Manheim, York Co, PA

Source Title: **Caspar Hentsell**

Citation: Caspar Hentsell, September 1765,. Naturalizations, PA, p 113.

Hensel, Casper
      Naturl: September 15, 1765 in Windsor, Berks Co, PA

Source Title: **Casper Hansel**

Citation: Casper Hansel, Descendants of Casper (LaHentzelle) Hensel, Evelyn S Hartman, deanh@@voicenet.com.

Arrison, Grace
      Death: 1893
Semrow, Loretta

Source Title: **Casper Hansel (con't)**

Citation: Casper Hansel, Descendants of Casper (LaHentzelle) Hensel, Evelyn S Hartman, deanh@@voicenet.com.

    Semrow, Loretta
        Death: 1933

Citation: Casper Hansel, Tax List of York County 1779, PA Archives 3rd Ed., Family Line Production, 1989, Gene Smith, GSmithan@@aol.com.

    Hensel, Casper
        Res: 1779 in Germany, York Co, PA

Source Title: **Casper Hensel**

Citation: Casper Hensel, 1767 Pennsylvania Tax Lists, http://freepages.genealogy.rootsweb.com/~genbel/sept/patowshp1767.htm.

    Hensel, Casper
        Res: 1767 in Windsor Tp, PA

Citation: Casper Hensel, Christ Church commnuicants, Littlestown, Adams Co, PA, 1776, p 86, Victoria Cawood Thompson, thompst7@@yahoo.com.

    Hensel, Casper
        Relgn: April 21, 1776; Christ Church (Conewago), Littlestown, York (Adams)
               Co, PA

Citation: Casper Hensel, Christ Church, Littlestown, PA, Adams Co County 18th records lookup, Virginia, vperry1@@shawneelink.net.

    Hensel, Casper
        Res: 1776 in Littlestown, York (Adams) Co, PA

Citation: Casper Hensel, Descendants of Casper (LaHentzelle) Hensel, Evelyn S. Hartman.

    Hensel, John Casper
        Death: January 1804 in Manheim Tp, Adams Co, PA

Citation: Casper Hensel, H.J. Young, Christ Reformed Church 1747-1871, Littlestown, Adams Co, PA.

    Hensel, John Casper
        Confir: April 21, 1776 in Christ Church, Littlestown, York (Adams) Co, PA

Citation: Casper Hensel, Hensels of Adams Co County, Adams Co County Historical Society.

    Walter, Maria Salome
        Death: Aft. 1777 in York Co, PA

Citation: Casper Hensel, Muster Roll of the 4th Company York County, 1785, Capt.M Will, Lt H Shilt, footnote.com.

    Hensel, John Casper
        Miltry: Abt. 1780; American Revolution, Private PA Reg, 4th Co, ? class
               (York, Capt. Martin Will)

Source Title: **Casper Hentzel**

Citation: Casper Hentzel, Abstract of York County, PA Wills, 1749-1819, F.E. Wright, Family lIne Productions, 1995, Gene Smith, GSmithan@@aol.com.

    Hensel, John Casper
        Death: January 1804 in Manheim Tp, Adams Co, PA

Citation: Casper Hentzel, April 28, 1800, 1805, OCI 257, L25, 7-5, York PA library.

    Hensel, John Casper
        Prob: January 03, 1805 in Manheim, York Co, PA

Citation: Casper Hentzel, April 28, 1800, January 3, 1805, York County Will Abstracts, York County, PA.

    Hensel, John Casper
        Prob: January 03, 1805 in Manheim, York Co, PA

Source Title: **Casper Hentzel (con't)**

Citation: Casper Hentzel, Probate files, 1800, Rep 37, York County Archives, York, PA, Deborah Hershey, Elizabethtown, PA, Dec 2008.

Hensel, John Casper

    Will: April 28, 1800 in Manheim, York Co, PA

    Occu: Bet. 1799–1800; Weaver

Citation: Casper Hentzel, Probate files, 1805, Rep 37, York County Archives, York, PA, Deborah Hershey, Elizabethtown, PA, Dec 2008.

Hensel, John Casper

    Prob: January 03, 1805 in Manheim, York Co, PA

Source Title: **Churches Between the Mountains**

Citation: Churches Between the Mountains, A History of the Lutheran Congregatioons in Perry County, PA,. D.H. Focht.

Hensel, Andrew W

    Occu: Bet. 1850–1855; Deacon (Christ's Church, Bloomfield, Perry Co, PA)

Source Title: **Clara Hensel**

Citation: Clara Hensel, Greenwood Cemetery, Tower City, Schuylkill Co, PA, John Barket, Tower City, PA, B-3-1.

Updegrove, Clara Matilda

    Death: March 30, 1926

    Burial: March 31, 1926 in Greenwood Cemetery, Tower City, Schuylkill Co, P

Source Title: **Clara M Hensel death certificate**

Citation: Clara M Hensel death certificate, #0042528, #37124, Reg # 29, March 1926, Department of Vital records, New Castle, PA.

Updegrove, Clara Matilda

    Death: March 28, 1926 in Tower City, Schuylkill Co, PA; Metastatic carcinoma of medial atrium & left chest w/carcinoma breast

    Burial: March 31, 1926 in Greenwood Cemetery, Tower City, Schuylkill Co, P

    Funrl: 1926 in Duane Snyder, 304 E Grand Ave., Tower City, Schuylkill Co, PA

    Occu: 1926; Housewife

Source Title: **Conrad Updegrove**

Citation: Conrad Updegrove, Church records, St. Pauls Church, Tower City, PA, Marie Rodichok, Church Secretary.

Updegrove, Conrad

    Birth: November 27, 1771 in Oley, Berks Co, PA

    Death: April 1865 in Williamstown, Dauphin Co, PA

Source Title: **Culp household**

Citation: Culp household, 1850 United States Census, Union Co, PA, ancestry.com & Microfilm, PA State Library, Hbg, PA.

Culp, Sarah "Salome" A

    Census: 1850 in West Buffalo, Union Co, PA

Kulp, Jacob

    Census: 1850 in West Buffalo, Union Co, PA

    Occu: 1850; Carpenter

Citation: Culp household, 1850 United States Census, Union Co, PA, ancestry.com & Microfilm, PA State Library, Hbg, PA.

Culp, Sarah "Salome" A

    Educ: 1850; School

Source Title: **Culp household (con't)**

Citation: Culp household, 1850 United States Census, Union Co, PA, ancestry.com & Microfilm, PA State Library, Hbg, PA.

Kulp, Jacob
      Propty: 1850 in $120

Citation: Culp household, 1850 United States Census, Union Co, PA, FTM CD 305, Disk 10, film 831.

Kulp, Jacob
      Census: 1850 in West Buffalo, Union Co, PA
      Occu: 1850; Carpenter

Citation: Culp household, 1860 United States Census, Union Co, PA, ancestry.com & Microfilm, PA State Library, Hbg, PA.

Kulp, Jacob
      Propty: 1860 in $100
      Occu: 1860; Laborer

Citation: Culp household, 1860 United States Census, Union Co, PA, ancestry.com & Microfilm, PA State Library, Hbg, PA.

Culp, Sarah "Salome" A
      Census: 1860 in Buffalo, Union Co, PA

Kulp, Jacob
      Census: 1860 in Buffalo, Union Co, PA

Source Title: **Daniel Angst**

Citation: Daniel Angst, Revolutionary War Military Abstract Card File, PA State Archives, www.digitalarchives.state.pu.us/archive.

Angst, John Daniel
      Miltry: Bet. 1777–1779; American Revolution, Private 6th PA Reg, 5th Co, ? class (Berks, Capt. Michael Bretz)

Citation: Daniel Angst, Tax List: 1754-1785: Pine Grove Twp, Berks (now Schuylkill) Co, PA, Contributed for use in USGenWeb Archives by Richard Turnbach. Early [Colonial/Revolutionary] Tax and Census for Pine Grove Twp. Then Berks County, PA [now Schuylkill County], http://ftp.r.

Angst, John Daniel
      Res: Bet. 1779–1786 in Pine Grove, Berks (Schuylkill) Co PA
      Res: Bet. 1773–1777 in Pine Grove, Berks (Schuylkill) Co PA

Source Title: **Daniel Keefer**

Citation: Daniel Keefer.

Angst, John Daniel
      Miltry: Bet. 1777–1779; American Revolution, Private 6th PA Reg, 5th Co, ? class (Berks, Capt. Michael Bretz)

Source Title: **Daniel Updegrave**

Citation: Daniel Updegrave, 1864-5 service, 1890 Veterans Schedule, private, Tower City, Schuylkill Co, PA, Roll 83, p 3, ED 215, www.ancestry.com.

Updegrove, Daniel
      Miltry: August 16, 1864; Civil War, Private, 9th Reg PA Cav, Co B, 92nd Volunteers (Harrisburg, Capt. Edward Savage)
      Res: 1890 in Tower City, Schuylkill Co, PA

Source Title: **Daniel Updegrove**

Citation: Daniel Updegrove, Civil War Pension Index, K 39 PA infantry, filed 1899, www.ancestry.com.

Updegrove, Daniel

Source Title: **Daniel Updegrove (con't)**

Citation: Daniel Updegrove, Civil War Pension Index, K 39 PA infantry, filed 1899, www.ancestry.com.

Updegrove, Daniel
> Miltry: August 16, 1864; Civil War, Private, 9th Reg PA Cav, Co B, 92nd Volunteers (Harrisburg, Capt. Edward Savage)

Citation: Daniel Updegrove, Civil War Pension Index, www.ancestry.com.

Updegrove, Daniel
> Miltry: August 16, 1864; Civil War, Private, 9th Reg PA Cav, Co B, 92nd Volunteers (Harrisburg, Capt. Edward Savage)

Citation: Daniel Updegrove, Civil War Pension Index: General Index to Pension Files, 1861-1934, www.ancestry.com.

Culp, Sarah "Salome" A
> Pension: May 1899 in PA

Citation: Daniel Updegrove, Civil War Veterans Card File, 1861-1866, PA State Archives, www.digitalarchives.state.pa.us.

Updegrove, Daniel
> Occu: Bet. 1864–1865; Miner
> Res: Bet. 1864–1865 in Dauphin Co, PA

Citation: Daniel Updegrove, Schuylkill Countians captured in the Civil War, rootsweb.com.

Updegrove, Daniel
> Miltry: August 16, 1864; Civil War, Private, 9th Reg PA Cav, Co B, 92nd Volunteers (Harrisburg, Capt. Edward Savage)

Citation: Daniel Updegrove, Vital records, Dauphin County, p 26.

Updegrove, Daniel
> Burial: March 28, 1899 in Seyberts (Old) Lutheran, Williamstown, Dauphin Co, PA
> Miltry: August 16, 1864; Civil War, Private, 9th Reg PA Cav, Co B, 92nd Volunteers (Harrisburg, Capt. Edward Savage)

Citation: Daniel Updegrove, Vital records, Dauphin County, p 26.

Updegrove, Daniel
> Death: 1899 in Williamstown, Dauphin Co, PA; Suffocated by mine gas

Source Title: **Daniel Updegrove death certificate**

Citation: Daniel Updegrove death certificate, #1071, March 1899, Dauphin County Register of Wills, Harrisburg, PA.

Updegrove, Daniel
> Occu: 1899; Miner (Brookside Colliery)
> Birth: June 28, 1839 in Wiconisco, Dauphin Co, PA
> Burial: March 28, 1899 in Seyberts (Old) Lutheran, Williamstown, Dauphin Co, PA

Source Title: **David Penman**

Citation: David Penman, FHL, Pedigree chart, www.ancestry.com.

Penman, David
> Birth: December 31, 1775 in Gladsmuir, East Lothian or, Newbattle, Midlothian, Scotland

Stoddart, Elizabeth
> Birth: January 05, 1779 in Stobgreen Temple, Edinburgh, Midlothian, Scotland
> Death: December 25, 1849 in Pottsville, Schuylkill Co, PA

Source Title: **David Stoddard**

Source Title: **David Stoddard (con't)**

Citation: David Stoddard, FHL, Individual record, AFN 148J-5NB, www.familysearch.com.

Muckle, Margaret
        Marr: February 16, 1778 in Cockpen, Midlothian, Scotland
Stoddart, David
        Marr: February 16, 1778 in Cockpen, Midlothian, Scotland

Source Title: **David Stoddart**

Citation: David Stoddart, FHL, IGI Individual record, www.familysearch.org.

Stoddart, David
        Birth: May 19, 1754 in Newbattle, Midlothian, Scotland

Source Title: **Descedants of Herman OpDenGraeff**

Citation: Descedants of Herman OpDenGraeff, Cathy Berger, Bedford, PA.

Updegroff, John William
        Res: Abt. 1770 in Reading, Berks Co, PA
        Res: Bet. 1772–1775 in Western Dt, Berks Co, PA
      Immigr: 1753
        Res: 1753 in Germantown, Philadelphia, PA

Source Title: **Descendants of Johann Pfannebecker**

Citation: Descendants of Johann Pfannebecker, Pfennebaker History & John A. Romberger manuscript, 1997.

Lehman, Jacob
        Birth: 1744
        Death: October 20, 1805 in Hanover, Dauphin (Lebanon) Co, PA
Lehman, Susan
        Marr: June 15, 1798 in Zion Lutheran, Harrisburg, Dauphin Co, PA
Romberger, Balthasar
        Marr: June 15, 1798 in Zion Lutheran, Harrisburg, Dauphin Co, PA
        Death: Abt. 1825 in Mifflin, Dauphin Co, PA

Source Title: **Direct Descendants of John Bartholomus Romberger**

Citation: Direct Descendants of John Bartholomus Romberger, Weiss, Shreffler & Romberg, Roger Cramer, members.aol.com/roghistory.

Lehman, Susan
        Marr: June 15, 1798 in Zion Lutheran, Harrisburg, Dauphin Co, PA
Romberger, Balthasar
        Marr: June 15, 1798 in Zion Lutheran, Harrisburg, Dauphin Co, PA
        Birth: July 05, 1747 in Ingolstadt, Bavaria, Germany
Romberger, John Balthaser
        Death: September 25, 1800 in Annville, Lebanon Co., PA
      Immigr: September 24, 1753 in Germany to USA (ship Neptune)

Source Title: **Direct Descendants of John Bartholomus Romberger to Roger Cramer**

Citation: Direct Descendants of John Bartholomus Romberger to Roger Cramer, Roger Cramer, October 10, 2004.

Romberger, John Balthaser
        Birth: May 04, 1716 in Theilheim, Schweinfurt, Bavaria, Germany

Source Title: **Elizabeth Penman**

Citation: Elizabeth Penman, 1841 Scotland Census Record, Midlothian, SCO, www.ancestry.com.

Stoddart, Elizabeth

Source Title: **Elizabeth Penman (con't)**

Citation: Elizabeth Penman, 1841 Scotland Census Record, Midlothian, SCO, www.ancestry.com.

Stoddart, Elizabeth
Census: 1841 in Liberton, Midlothian, Scotland
Occu: 1841; Pauper sup by children

Source Title: **Elizabeth Updegroff**

Citation: Elizabeth Updegroff, Probate file, 1804, unnumbered original papers, 4pp, Berks Co Courthouse, Berks, PA, Norman Nicol, Apr 2008.

Benfield, Anna Maria Elizabeth
Prob: March 21, 1804 in Exeter, Berks Co, PA

Source Title: **Gise household**

Citation: Gise household, 1790 United States Census, Northampton Co, PA, ancestry.com & Microfilm, PA State Library, Hbg, PA.

Guise, John Adam
Census: 1790

Citation: Gise household, 1800 United States Census, Adams Co, PA, ancestry.com & Microfilm, PA State Library, Hbg, PA.

Guise, John Adam
Census: 1800 in Menallan, Adams Co, PA
Maria?
Census: 1800 in Manallen, Adams Co, PA

Source Title: **Goodman household**

Citation: Goodman household, 1840 United States Census, Schuylkill Co, PA, Roll M704 492, p 79, Image 159, ancestry.com & Microfilm, PA State Library, Hbg, PA.

Goodman, Michael
Census: 1840 in Lower Mahantango, Schuylkill Co, PA

Citation: Goodman household, 1850 United States Census, Dauphin Co, PA, 338, ancestry.com & Microfilm, PA State Library, Hbg, PA.

Goodman, Michael
Propty: 1850 in $1000
Occu: 1850; Carpenter

Citation: Goodman household, 1850 United States Census, Dauphin Co, PA, 338, ancestry.com & Microfilm, PA State Library, Hbg, PA.

Goodman, Michael
Census: 1850 in Rush, Dauphin Co, PA

Citation: Goodman household, 1860 United States Census, Dauphin Co, PA, ancestry.com & Microfilm, PA State Library, Hbg, PA.

Goodman, Michael
Propty: 1860 in $1000 + $600
Occu: Bet. 1860–1880; Farmer

Citation: Goodman household, 1860 United States Census, Dauphin Co, PA, ancestry.com & Microfilm, PA State Library, Hbg, PA.

Goodman, Michael
Census: 1860 in Rush, Dauphin Co, PA

Citation: Goodman household, 1870 United States Census, Dauphin Co, PA, ancestry.com & Microfilm, PA State Library, Hbg, PA.

Goodman, Lydia Ann
Census: 1870 in Rush, Dauphin Co, PA
Goodman, Michael
Census: 1870 in Rush, Dauphin Co, PA

Source Title: **Goodman household (con't)**

Citation: Goodman household, 1870 United States Census, Dauphin Co, PA, ancestry.com & Microfilm, PA State Library, Hbg, PA.

Goodman, Michael
    Occu: Bet. 1860–1880; Farmer

Citation: Goodman household, 1870 United States Census, Dauphin Co, PA, ancestry.com & Microfilm, PA State Library, Hbg, PA.

Brown, Mary Magdalena
    Census: 1870 in Rush, Dauphin Co, PA
    Occu: 1870; Keeping house

Goodman, Michael
    Propty: 1870 in $2000 + $200

Citation: Goodman household, 1880 United States Census, Dauphin Co, PA, www.ancestry.com and 1880 United States Census, Dauphin Co, PA, FHL 1255124, Film T9-1124, p 432B, www.familysearch.org.

Goodman, Michael
    Occu: Bet. 1860–1880; Farmer

Citation: Goodman household, 1880 United States Census, Dauphin Co, PA, www.ancestry.com and 1880 United States Census, Dauphin Co, PA, FHL 1255124, Film T9-1124, p 432B, www.familysearch.org.

Brown, Mary Magdalena
    Occu: 1880; Keeping house

Goodman, Michael
    Census: 1880 in Rush, Dauphin Co, PA

Citation: Goodman household, 1900 United States Census, Dauphin Co, PA, www.ancestry.com and 1900 United States Census, Dauphin Co, PA, Pa State Library microfilm image.

Goodman, Michael
    Census: 1900 in Rush, Dauphin Co, PA (son William Goodman)
    Occu: 1900; Retired

Source Title: **Guise household**

Citation: Guise household, 1800 United States Census, Adams Co, PA, ancestry.com & Microfilm, PA State Library, Hbg, PA.

Guise, Mary A
    Census: 1800 in parents; w

Citation: Guise household, 1810 United States Census, Adams Co, PA, ancestry.com & Microfilm, PA State Library, Hbg, PA.

Guise, Mary A
    Census: 1810 in parents; w

Citation: Guise household, 1820 United States Census, Adams Co, PA, ancestry.com & Microfilm, PA State Library, Hbg, PA.

Guise, Mary A
    Census: 1820 in husband; Mount Joy, Adams Co, PA w

Source Title: **Gussie M. Thompson**

Citation: Gussie M. Thompson, Greenwood Cemetery, Tower City, Schuylkill Co, PA, John Barket, Tower City, PA, B-3-1.

Hensel, Augusta "Gussie" Mae
    Death: March 27, 1973 in Home, Tower City, Schuylkill Co, PA; Medullary paralysis w/thrombosis w/cerebral hemorrhage & arteriosclerosis
    Burial: March 30, 1973 in Greenwood Cemetery, Tower City, Schuylkill Co, P

Citation: Gussie M. Thompson, Reg of Will book, Book 145, pp578-82, May 27, 1950, probated Sept 11, 1973, Schuylkill Co Courthouse, Schuylkill, PA, Norman Nicol, Apr 2008.

Source Title: **Gussie M. Thompson (con't)**

Citation: Gussie M. Thompson, Reg of Will book, Book 145, pp578-82, May 27, 1950, probated Sept 11, 1973, Schuylkill Co Courthouse, Schuylkill, PA, Norman Nicol, Apr 2008.

Hensel, Augusta "Gussie" Mae
 Death: March 27, 1973 in Home, Tower City, Schuylkill Co, PA; Medullary paralysis w/thrombosis w/cerebral hemorrhage & arteriosclerosis
 Will: May 27, 1950 in Sheridan, Schuylkill Co, PA

Source Title: **Gussie Mae Thompson**

Citation: Gussie Mae Thompson, Obituary, Pottsville Repulbican, Pottsville, PA, March 28, 1973.

Hensel, Augusta "Gussie" Mae
 Relgn: 1973; Wesley United Methodist, Tower City, PA
 Res: 1973 in 329 West Grand Ave., Tower City, Schuylkill Co, PA 17980
 Birth: February 16, 1885 in Wiconisco, Dauphin Co, PA
 Funrl: 1973 in Dean O Snyder, 304 E Grand Ave., Tower City, Schuylkill Co, PA

Source Title: **Gussie May Hensel**

Citation: Gussie May Hensel, Funeral obituary, March 1973.

Hensel, Augusta "Gussie" Mae
 Birth: February 16, 1885 in Wiconisco, Dauphin Co, PA
 Death: March 27, 1973 in Home, Tower City, Schuylkill Co, PA; Medullary paralysis w/thrombosis w/cerebral hemorrhage & arteriosclerosis
 Burial: March 30, 1973 in Greenwood Cemetery, Tower City, Schuylkill Co, P

Source Title: **Gussie May Thompson**

Citation: Gussie May Thompson, #0506187, #31982, March 1973, Department of Vital Records, New Castle, PA.

Hensel, Augusta "Gussie" Mae
 Res: 1973 in 329 West Grand Ave., Tower City, Schuylkill Co, PA 17980

Citation: Gussie May Thompson, Funeral obituary, March 1973.

Hensel, Augusta "Gussie" Mae
 Funrl: 1973 in Dean O Snyder, 304 E Grand Ave., Tower City, Schuylkill Co, PA

Source Title: **Gussie May Thompson death certificate**

Citation: Gussie May Thompson death certificate, #0506187, #31982, March 1973, Department of Vital Records, New Castle, PA.

Hensel, Augusta "Gussie" Mae
 Occu: 1973; Housewife
 Birth: February 16, 1885 in Wiconisco, Dauphin Co, PA
 Death: March 27, 1973 in Home, Tower City, Schuylkill Co, PA; Medullary paralysis w/thrombosis w/cerebral hemorrhage & arteriosclerosis
 Burial: March 30, 1973 in Greenwood Cemetery, Tower City, Schuylkill Co, P
 Funrl: 1973 in Dean O Snyder, 304 E Grand Ave., Tower City, Schuylkill Co, PA
 SSN: 1973; 173-46-1535

Source Title: **Gussie Thompson**

Citation: Gussie Thompson, March 1973, PA, Social Security Death Index, www.familysearch.org.

Hensel, Augusta "Gussie" Mae
 Res: 1973 in Orwin, Porter, Reinerton, Rush, Sheridan, Tower City, all Schuylkill Co, PA

Source Title: **Gussie Thompson (con't)**

Citation: Gussie Thompson, March 1973, PA, Social Security Death Index, www.familysearch.org.

Hensel, Augusta "Gussie" Mae
    SSN: 1973; 173-46-1535

Source Title: **Harper B Thompson**

Citation: Harper B Thompson, Obituary, Harrisburg Patriot Newspaper, July 1981.

Thompson, Harper Bruce
    Occu: 1981; Retired mail handler (Harrisburg Post Office)
    Birth: September 28, 1907 in Sheridan, Schuylkill Co, PA
    Death: July 23, 1981 in Polyclinic Hospital, Harrisburg, Dauphin Co, PA; Cardiorespiratory arrest w/subdural hematoma
    Burial: 1981 in Woodlawn Memorial Gardens, Harrisburg, Dauphin Co, PA
    Funrl: 1981 in Jesse H Geigle, 2100 Linglestown Rd.,Harrisburg, Dauphin Co, PA
    Relgn: 1981; Lakeside Lutheran Church

Citation: Harper B Thompson, Social Seurity numident record, application for SS-5, SSA, Nov 2006, Baltimore, MD.

Thompson, Harper Bruce
    Res: 1972 in Harrisburg, Dauphin Co, PA

Source Title: **Harper B Thompson death certificate**

Citation: Harper B Thompson death certificate, #2501265, Department of Vital Records, New Castle, PA.

Thompson, Harper Bruce
    Res: 1981 in 2600 Green St., Harrisburg, Dauphin Co, PA
    Birth: September 28, 1907 in Sheridan, Schuylkill Co, PA
    Death: July 23, 1981 in Polyclinic Hospital, Harrisburg, Dauphin Co, PA; Cardiorespiratory arrest w/subdural hematoma

Source Title: **Harper Bruce Thompson birth record**

Citation: Harper Bruce Thompson birth record, #344701, #122649-07, September 1907, Schuylkill Co, PA, Department of Vital Records, New Castle, PA.

Thompson, Harper Bruce
    Birth: September 28, 1907 in Sheridan, Schuylkill Co, PA

Source Title: **Harper Thompson**

Citation: Harper Thompson, July 1981, PA, Social Security Death Index, www.familysearch,org.

Thompson, Harper Bruce
    Res: 1981 in Beaufort Farms, Camp Curtain, Estherton, Fort Hunter, Harrisburg, Hecktown, Lucknow, Rockville, Uptown, Windsor farms, all Dauphin Co, PA
    SSN: 1981; 205-05-3254

Source Title: **Heheel household**

Citation: Heheel household, 1900 United States Census, Dauphin Co, PA, Roll T623 1404, p 2A, ED 190, ancestry.com & Microfilm, PA State Library, Hbg, PA.

Hensel, Andrew Guise
    Occu: 1900; Boarder

Source Title: **Hensel family information**

Citation: Hensel family information, Dauphin Co Marriages, 1852-1855, CAGS.

Hensel, Andrew Guise
    Marr: May 17, 1853 in Halifax, Dauphin Co, PA

Source Title: **Hensel family information (con't)**

Citation: Hensel family information, Dauphin Co Marriages, 1852-1855, CAGS.

Hensel, Andrew Guise
       Occu: 1853; Plasterer
       Birth: February 18, 1831 in Home, New Bloomfield, Perry Co, PA
Workman, Catherine
       Marr: May 17, 1853 in Halifax, Dauphin Co, PA

Citation: Hensel family information, H Andrew Brown, habraun2@@netscape.net, Los Angeles, CA, 2007.

Hensel, John Casper
       Death: January 1804 in Manheim Tp, Adams Co, PA

Citation: Hensel family information, History of Michael Hensel (Hentzel) Sr. & His Related Families, R. Longtin-Thompson.

Guise, Mary A
       Marr: Abt. 1814 in Adams, PA
       Burial: January 1877 in St. Peters (Christ, Old Union) Cemetery, New Bloomfield, Perry Co, PA
Hensel, Andrew Guise
       Birth: February 18, 1831 in Home, New Bloomfield, Perry Co, PA
Hensel, Andrew W
       Marr: Abt. 1814 in Adams, PA
       Burial: July 1875 in St. Peters (Christ, Old Union) Cemetery, New Bloomfield, Perry Co, PA
       Miltry: February 1814; War of 1812, Private, 5th Reg PA Militia (Fentons), detachment (Adams, Capt. John McMillan)
       Relgn: 1875; Lutheran & German Reformed Church
Hensel, John Casper
       Death: January 1804 in Manheim Tp, Adams Co, PA

Citation: Hensel family information, Victor Hensel, NJ.

Hensel, Howard Andrew Carson
       Marr: September 02, 1884 in Wiconisco, Dauphin Co, PA
       Occu: Abt. 1915; Deacon (Methodist)
       Res: 1927 in Hand & Wiconisco Aves., Tower City, Schuylkill Co, PA
       Birth: September 02, 1858 in Wiconisco, Dauphin Co, PA
       Death: June 06, 1927 in Tower City, Schuylkill Co, PA; Arteriosclerosis
Updegrove, Clara Matilda
       Marr: September 02, 1884 in Wiconisco, Dauphin Co, PA
       Birth: November 30, 1866 in Lower Ranch Creek, Tremont, Schuylkill Co, P
       Death: March 28, 1926 in Tower City, Schuylkill Co, PA; Metastatic carcinoma of medial atrium & left chest w/carcinoma breast
       Baptism: December 1866 in Rev. Brady, Schuylkill Co, PA

Citation: Hensel family information, York Co, History of Michael Hensel (Hentzel) Sr. & His Related Families, R. Longtin-Thompson.

Hensel, John Casper
       Miltry: Abt. 1780; American Revolution, Private PA Reg, 4th Co, ? class (York, Capt. Martin Will)

Source Title: **Hensel household**

Citation: Hensel household, 1800 United States Census, York Co, PA, ancestry.com & Microfilm, PA State Library, Hbg, PA.

Hensel, Andrew W
       Census: 1800 in father; Maheim, York Co, PA w

Source Title: **Hensel household (con't)**

Citation: Hensel household, 1840 United States Census, Perry Co, PA, ancestry.com & Microfilm, PA State Library, Hbg, PA.

Hensel, Andrew Guise
Census: 1840 in Perry Co, PA; Centre, Perry Co, PA w/father

Citation: Hensel household, 1870 United States Census, Dauphin Co, PA, M593-1335, 997-566, ancestry.com & Microfilm, PA State Library, Hbg, PA.

Hensel, Andrew Guise
Census: 1870 in Wiconisco, Dauphin Co, PA

Citation: Hensel household, 1870 United States Census, Dauphin Co, PA, M593-1335, 997-566, ancestry.com & Microfilm, PA State Library, Hbg, PA.

Hensel, Andrew Guise
Propty: 1870 in $340

Citation: Hensel household, 1870 United States Census, Dauphin Co, PA, PA State library microfilm.

Hensel, Andrew Guise
Census: 1870 in Wiconisco, Dauphin Co, PA

Hensel, Howard Andrew Carson
Census: 1870 in Wiconisco, Dauphin Co, PA

Workman, Catherine
Occu: 1870; Keeping house

Citation: Hensel household, 1870 United States Census, Dauphin Co, PA, PA State library microfilm.

Hensel, Andrew Guise
Occu: Bet. 1850–1900; Plasterer

Citation: Hensel household, 1880 United States Census, Dauphin Co, PA, FHL 1255124, Film T9-1124, p 270D, 71-76, www.familysearch.org.

Hensel, Andrew Guise
Census: 1880 in Wiconisco, Dauphin Co, PA

Citation: Hensel household, 1880 United States Census, Dauphin Co, PA, FHL 1255124, Film T9-1124, p 270D, www.familysearch.org.

Hensel, Andrew Guise
Occu: Bet. 1850–1900; Plasterer

Hensel, Howard Andrew Carson
Occu: 1880; Laborer

Citation: Hensel household, 1880 United States Census, Dauphin Co, PA, FHL 1255124, Film T9-1124, p 270D, www.familysearch.org.

Hensel, Howard Andrew Carson
Census: 1880 in Wiconisco, Dauphin Co, PA

Citation: Hensel household, 1900 United States Census, Schuylkill Co, PA, ww.ancestry.com and 1900 United States Census, Schuylkill Co, PA, PA State library microfilm image.

Hensel, Augusta "Gussie" Mae
Census: 1900 in Tower City, Schuylkill Co, PA
Educ: 1900; School

Hensel, Howard Andrew Carson
Census: 1900 in Tower City, Schuylkill Co, PA
Occu: 1900; Coal miner

Citation: Hensel household, 1910 United States Census, Schuylkill Co, PA, www.ancestry.com and 1910 United States Census, Schuylkill Co, PA, ED 102, Sheet 4, PA State Library.

Hensel, Howard Andrew Carson
Census: 1910 in Tower City, Schuylkill Co, PA
Occu: 1910; Engineer (P? Mill)

Source Title: **Hensel household (con't)**

Citation: Hensel household, 1910 United States Census, Schuylkill Co, PA, www.ancestry.com and 1910 United States Census, Schuylkill Co, PA, ED 102, Sheet 4, PA State Library.

Hensel, Howard Andrew Carson
> Res: Bet. 1910–1920 in Wiconisco Ave., Tower City, Schuylkill Co, PA

Citation: Hensel household, 1920 United States Census, Schuylkill Co, PA, T625 1652, p 17A, ED 143, Image 0877, www.ancestry.com and 1920 United States Census, Schuylkill Co, PA, PA State Libraray, microfilm image.

Hensel, Howard Andrew Carson
> Res: Bet. 1910–1920 in Wiconisco Ave., Tower City, Schuylkill Co, PA

Citation: Hensel household, 1920 United States Census, Schuylkill Co, PA, T625 1652, p 17A, ED 143, Image 0877, www.ancestry.com and 1920 United States Census, Schuylkill Co, PA, PA State Libraray, microfilm image.

Hensel, Howard Andrew Carson
> Census: 1920 in Tower City, Schuylkill Co, PA
> Occu: 1920; Fireman (Coal mine)

Source Title: **Hensel-Workman marriage record**

Citation: Hensel-Workman marriage record, 1853, Register of Wills, Dauphin Co, PA.

Hensel, Andrew Guise
> Marr: May 17, 1853 in Halifax, Dauphin Co, PA
> Occu: 1853; Plasterer
> Birth: February 18, 1831 in Home, New Bloomfield, Perry Co, PA
> Relgn: 1853; Methodist Episcopal

Workman, Catherine
> Marr: May 17, 1853 in Halifax, Dauphin Co, PA

Source Title: **Hensil household**

Citation: Hensil household, 1850 United States Census, Perry Co, PA, Roll M432-805, p 433, Image 283, ancestry.com & Microfilm, PA State Library, Hbg, PA.

Hensel, Andrew W
> Propty: 1850 in $450

Citation: Hensil household, 1850 United States Census, Perry Co, PA, Roll M432-805, p 433, Image 283, ancestry.com & Microfilm, PA State Library, Hbg, PA.

Hensel, Andrew Guise
> Census: 1850 in Centre, Perry Co, PA
> Occu: Bet. 1850–1900; Plasterer

Hensel, Andrew W
> Census: 1850 in Centre, Perry Co, PA
> Occu: 1850; Laborer

Source Title: **Hensley household**

Citation: Hensley household, 1840 United States Census, Perry Co, PA, ancestry.com & Microfilm, PA State Library, Hbg, PA.

Hensel, Andrew W
> Census: 1840 in Centre, Perry Co, PA (Hensley)

Source Title: **Hentzel household**

Citation: Hentzel household, 1860 United States Census, Schuylkill Co, PA, ancestry.com & Microfilm, PA State Library, Hbg, PA.

Hensel, Howard Andrew Carson
> Census: 1860 in Porter, Schuylkill Co, PA

Citation: Hentzel household, 1860 United States Census, Schuylkill Co, PA, M653-1181, 628-9, ancestry.com & Microfilm, PA State Library, Hbg, PA.

Source Title:	**Hentzel household (con't)**
Citation:	Hentzel household, 1860 United States Census, Schuylkill Co, PA, M653-1181, 628-9, ancestry.com & Microfilm, PA State Library, Hbg, PA.
	Hensel, Andrew Guise
	Census: 1860 in Porter, Schuylkill Co, PA (Hentzel)
Citation:	Hentzel household, 1860 United States Census, Schuylkill Co, PA, PA State library microfilm.
	Hensel, Andrew Guise
	Census: 1860 in Porter, Schuylkill Co, PA (Hentzel)
	Hensel, Howard Andrew Carson
	Census: 1860 in Porter, Schuylkill Co, PA
Citation:	Hentzel household, 1860 United States Census, Schuylkill Co, PA, PA State library microfilm.
	Hensel, Andrew Guise
	Occu: Bet. 1850–1900; Plasterer
	Propty: 1860 in $250 + $123
Source Title:	**Hentzelle household**
Citation:	Hentzelle household, 1870 United States Census, Perry Co, PA, PA State library microfilm.
	Guise, Mary A
	Occu: 1870; Invalid
	Hensel, Andrew W
	Census: 1870 in Centre, Perry Co, PA (Hentzelle)
	Propty: 1870 in $500 + $120
	Occu: 1870; Laborer
Source Title:	**Henzell household**
Citation:	Henzell household, 1830 United States Census, Perry Co, PA, ancestry.com & Microfilm, PA State Library, Hbg, PA.
	Hensel, Andrew W
	Census: 1830 in Juniata, Perry Co, PA
Source Title:	**Hinsle household**
Citation:	Hinsle household, 1820 United States Census, Adams Co, PA, ancestry.com & Microfilm, PA State Library, Hbg, PA.
	Hensel, Andrew W
	Census: 1820 in Mount Joy, Adams Co, PA (Hensle)
Source Title:	**Howard A.C. Hensel**
Citation:	Howard A.C. Hensel, #0036895, #63360, Reg # 66, June 1927, Department of Vital records, New Castle, PA.
	Hensel, Howard Andrew Carson
	Occu: 1927; Fireman (Bestock Underwear Mills, Tower City, PA)
	Birth: September 02, 1858 in Wiconisco, Dauphin Co, PA
	Death: June 06, 1927 in Tower City, Schuylkill Co, PA; Arteriosclerosis
	Burial: June 09, 1927 in Greenwood Cemetery, Tower City, Schuylkill Co, PA
	Funrl: 1927 in Duane Snyder, 304 E Grand Ave., Tower City, Schuylkill Co, PA
Citation:	Howard A.C. Hensel, Greenwood Cemetery, Tower City, Schuylkill Co, PA, John Barket, Tower City, PA, B-3-1.
	Hensel, Howard Andrew Carson
	Burial: June 09, 1927 in Greenwood Cemetery, Tower City, Schuylkill Co, PA

Source Title: **Howard Andrew Carson Hensel**

Citation: Howard Andrew Carson Hensel, Howard Andrew Carson Hensel probate file, 1927, unnumbered orginal papers, 21pp, probated June 29, 1927, Schuylkill Co Courthouse, Schuylkill, PA, Norman Nicol, Apr 2008.

Hensel, Howard Andrew Carson
  Res: 1927 in Hand & Wiconisco Aves., Tower City, Schuylkill Co, PA
  Death: June 06, 1927 in Tower City, Schuylkill Co, PA; Arteriosclerosis
  Will: January 17, 1918 in Tower City, Schuylkill Co, PA

Source Title: **Hullsizer household**

Citation: Hullsizer household, 1860 United States Census, Lycoming Co, PA, ancestry.com & Microfilm, PA State Library, Hbg, PA.

Updegrove, Daniel
  Census: 1860 in Brady, Lycoming Co, PA (Hullsizer)
  Occu: 1860; Blksmith App.

Source Title: **Isabel Penman**

Citation: Isabel Penman, Vital records Index, British Isles, Intellectual Reserve Inc, 8/5/2010.

Thompson, Alexander
  Birth: October 22, 1805 in Sauchenside Farm, Cranston, Midlothian, Scotland

Source Title: **Jacob Leman**

Citation: Jacob Leman, December 13, 1800, November 2, 1805, Abstracts of Wills, PA, p 290.

Lehman, Jacob
  Will: December 13, 1800 in Hanover, Dauphin Co, PA

Citation: Jacob Leman, Probate files, 1805, Bk B, p291, File 1, Dauphin County Courthouse, Reg of Wills, Deborah Hershey, Elizabethtown, PA, Mar 2008.

Lehman, Jacob
  Prob: Bet. October 30–November 02, 1805 in Hanover, Dauphin Co, PA
  Will: December 13, 1800 in Hanover, Dauphin Co, PA

Source Title: **Jacob Leyman**

Citation: Jacob Leyman, Revolutonary War Soldiers buried at Bindnagles Cemetery, Vaughn Hostettler, Palmyra, PA.

Lehman, Jacob
  Birth: 1744
  Death: October 20, 1805 in Hanover, Dauphin (Lebanon) Co, PA
  Burial: 1805 in Bindagles Lutheran, Palmyra, Dauphin (Lebanon) Co, PA
  Miltry: Bet. 1775–1781; American Revolution, Ensign, 2nd PA Reg, 8th Co (Lancaster)

Source Title: **Johann Uptegrav**

Citation: Johann Uptegrav, 1805, Jacobs Church, Pine Grove, Swedberg, SCUR III, p 240.

Updegrove, John M
  Birth: March 23, 1805 in Pine Grove, Berks (Schylkill) Co, PA
  Baptism: April 14, 1805 in St. Jacobs Lutheran, Pine Grove, Berks (Schuylkill) Co, PA

Source Title: **John Penman**

Citation: John Penman, FHL, IGI Individual record, www.familysearch.com.

Brown, Catherine
  Marr: October 28, 1763 in Lassware, Midlothian, Scotland
Penman, John

Source Title: **John Penman (con't)**

Citation: John Penman, FHL, IGI Individual record, www.familysearch.com.

Penman, John
        Marr: October 28, 1763 in Lassware, Midlothian, Scotland

Citation: John Penman, FHL, IGI Individual record, www.familysearch.org.

Penman, John
        Birth: April 08, 1747 in Lassware, Midlothian, Scotland

Citation: John Penman, Vital records Index, British Isles, Intellectual Reserve Inc, 8/5/2010.

Penman, John
        Birth: April 18, 1798 in Newbattle, Midlothian, Scotland

Source Title: **John Romberger**

Citation: John Romberger, Romberger family, Onetree, ancestry.com.

Brucker, Anna Maria
        Death: Bet. 1778–1798 in Mifflin, Lancaster (Dauphin) Co, PA

Source Title: **John William Op Den Graeff**

Citation: John William Op Den Graeff, Descendants of Herman Op den Graef, www.kevin-sholder.net.

Benfield, Anna Maria Elizabeth
        Death: February 23, 1804 in Exeter, Berks Co, PA

Updegroff, John William
        Birth: February 24, 1732 in Kirchberg Hunsruck, Rhineland-Palatinate, Germany

Citation: John William Op Den Graeff, Descendants of Herman Op den Graef, www.kevin-sholder.net.

Benfield, Anna Maria Elizabeth
        Birth: April 01, 1729 in Oley, Philadelphia (Berks) Co, PA

Citation: John William Op Den Graeff, Updegrove History, Kevin L Sholder, Dayton, OH, www.scholderer.org, June 2010.

Updegroff, John William
        Birth: April 24, 1732 in Kirchberg Hunsruck, Rhineland-Palatinate, Germany

Source Title: **Joseph Workman**

Citation: Joseph Workman, Descendants of Joseph Workman, Evelyn S. Hartman.

Hensel, Howard Andrew Carson
        Baptism: Abt. 1858 in Rev. Wm Yose, Dauphin Co, PA

Romberger, Susan
        Baptism: July 07, 1799 in St. Johns (Hill) Lutheran, Berrysburg, Dauphin Co, PA

Updegrove, Clara Matilda
        Baptism: December 1866 in Rev. Brady, Schuylkill Co, PA

Citation: Joseph Workman, Wiconisco Calvary Cemetery, Rhonda, yeahbaby@@penn.com, Row 4.

Workman, Joseph
        Death: May 23, 1857 in Dauphin Co, PA
        Burial: 1857 in Calvary United Methodist, Wiconisco, Dauphin Co, PA

Source Title: **Joseph Workman Sr**

Citation: Joseph Workman Sr, Probate files, 1857, Letter of Admin, A-35, Dauphin County Courthouse, Reg of Wills, Deborah Hershey, Elizabethtown, PA, Mar 2008.

Workman, Joseph
        Prob: June 18, 1857 in Dauphin Co, PA (listed in index only)

Source Title:	**Katherine Brown**	

Citation: Katherine Brown, FHL, IGI Individual record, www.familysearch.com and FHL, IGi Individual record, CD 54, Pin 16549, www.ancestry.com.

Brown, Catherine
      Birth: Abt. 1747 in Liberton, Midlothian, Scotland

Source Title:	**Knittle household**	

Citation: Knittle household, 1930 United States Census, Lehigh Co, PA, ancestry.com & Microfilm, PA State Library, Hbg, PA.

Thompson, Harper Bruce
      Census: 1930 in Emmaus, Lehigh Co, PA (Uncle James Knittle)
      Occu: 1930; Lineman (Telephone Co)
      Res: 1930 in 914 ? St., Emmaus, Lehigh Co, PA

Source Title:	**Kulp family information**	

Citation: Kulp family information, J. Wagner, Union County.

Kulp, Jacob
      Census: 1850 in West Buffalo, Union Co, PA
Schneck, Elizabeth
      Birth: August 13, 1805 in Northumberland (Union) Co, PA
      Death: June 02, 1861 in Union Co, PA

Source Title:	**Lehman family information**	

Citation: Lehman family information, Sherry L Johnson, sherrjo@@tenet.edu.

Pennypacker, Martha
      Birth: 1746 in Philadelphia (Montgomery) Co, PA

Source Title:	**Lehmey household**	

Citation: Lehmey household, 1800 United States Census, Dauphin Co, PA, ancestry.com & Microfilm, PA State Library, Hbg, PA.

Lehman, Jacob
      Census: 1800 in Bethel, Dauphin Co, PA (Lehmey)

Source Title:	**Leman household**	

Citation: Leman household, 1790 United States Census, Dauphin Co, PA ancestry.com & Microfilm, PA State Library, Hbg, PA.

Lehman, Jacob
      Census: 1790 in Dauphin Co, PA

Source Title:	**Lydia B. Thompson**	

Citation: Lydia B. Thompson, Greenwood Cemetery, Tower City, Schuylkill Co, PA, John Barket, Tower City, PA, B-1-1.

Goodman, Lydia Ann
      Death: October 09, 1883 in Tower City, Schuylkill Co, PA; Complications of pregnancy

Citation: Lydia B. Thompson, Greenwood Cemetery, Tower City, Schuylkill Co, PA, John Barket, Tower City, PA, B-3-1.

Goodman, Lydia Ann
      Burial: October 14, 1883 in Greenwood Cemetery, Tower City, Schuylkill Co, PA

Source Title:	**Lydia Mae Thompson**	

Citation: Lydia Mae Thompson, Obituary, Pottsville Repulbican, Pottsville, PA, Jan 18, 1983.

Thompson, Lydia Mae

Source Title: **Lydia Mae Thompson (con't)**

     Citation: Lydia Mae Thompson, Obituary, Pottsville Repulbican, Pottsville, PA, Jan 18, 1983.

         Thompson, Lydia Mae
                Birth: February 07, 1914 in Sheridan, Schuylkill Co, PA

Source Title: **Margaret Bowman**

     Citation: Margaret Bowman, One tree, from WFT collection, trees.ancestry.com/owt, www.ancestry.com.

         Bowman, Margaret
                Marr: June 08, 1754 in Newbattle, Midlothian, Scotland
                Birth: August 20, 1732 in Gladsmuir, East Lothian, Scotland
         Stoddart, John
                Marr: June 08, 1754 in Newbattle, Midlothian, Scotland
                Birth: December 25, 1728 in Newbattle, Midlothian, Scotland

Source Title: **Maria Brown**

     Citation: Maria Brown, McCallister's Methodist Cemetery, Barbara, Homelybin@@aol.com.

         Schreckengast?, Anna Maria
                Burial: April 1879 in McCallister's Methodist Cemetery, Rush, Dauphin Co, PA

Source Title: **Mary A Guise**

     Citation: Mary A Guise, Family pedigree, www.rootsweb.com, tiana.geo@@yahoo.com.

         Guise, John Adam
                Birth: Bet. 1756–1766 in Germany

Source Title: **Mary Hensel**

     Citation: Mary Hensel, Union Lutheran Cemetery, New Bloomfield, Perry Co, PA, 30 Perry Co PA Cemetery Records, Closson Press, Apollo, PA, 1992.

         Guise, Mary A
                Burial: January 1877 in St. Peters (Christ, Old Union) Cemetery, New Bloomfield, Perry Co, PA

Source Title: **Michael Goodman**

     Citation: Michael Goodman, Descendants of Michael Goodman, Evelyn S Hartman, deanh@@voicenet.com.

         Matter, Elva May
                Death: 1999
         Thompson, Lydia Mae
                Death: January 1983 in Tower City, Schuylkill Co, PA
         Thompson, Wilbur Clark
                Death: 1963

     Citation: Michael Goodman, Probate files, 1901, Inventory, 3-173, Aff. of Death, Bk D, p434, Dauphin County Courthouse, Reg of Wills, Deborah Hershey, Elizabethtown, PA, Mar 2008.

         Goodman, Michael
                Prob: January 11, 1901 in Rush Tp, Dauphin Co, PA (listed in index only)

     Citation: Michael Goodman, Tower City, Porter Centennial, 1868-1968, p 188.

         Brown, Mary Magdalena
                Death: December 17, 1884 in Dauphin Co, PA
         Goodman, Michael
                Birth: June 10, 1806 in Berks (Schuylkill), PA
                Death: December 27, 1900 in Rush, Dauphin Co, PA; Old age
                Confir: July 1825 in Schuylkill Co, PA

Source Title: **Michael Goodman death certificate**

Citation: Michael Goodman death certificate, #1252, May 1901, Dauphin County Register of Wills, Harrisburg, PA.

Goodman, Michael
        Occu: 1901; Farmer
        Death: December 27, 1900 in Rush, Dauphin Co, PA; Old age
        Burial: 1900 in Zion (Public Square) Lutheran Cemetery, Tower City, Schuylkill Co, PA

Citation: Michael Goodman death certificate, #1252, May 1901, Dauphin County Register of Wills, Harrisburg, PA.

Goodman, Michael
        Burial: 1900 in Orwin, Schuylkill Co, PA

Source Title: **Michael Gutman**

Citation: Michael Gutman, St. Peter's Evangelical Lutheran Church, Reinertown, PA, Pastor Arthur Sonnenberg, July 6, 2005.

Goodman, Michael
        Confir: July 1825 in Schuylkill Co, PA

Source Title: **Miller household**

Citation: Miller household, 1860 United States Census, Perry Co, PA, PA State library microfilm.

Hensel, Andrew W
        Census: 1860 in Centre, Perry Co, PA (Miller)
        Occu: 1860; Farmer

Citation: Miller household, 1860 United States Census, Perry Co, PA, PA State library microfilm.

Hensel, Andrew W
        Propty: 1860 in $800 + $300

Source Title: **Mrs Hensel**

Citation: Mrs Hensel, Source 140 & 146, index cards, Perry County Historians.

Guise, Mary A
        Death: January 16, 1877 in Perry Co, PA

Source Title: **Mrs Mary Hensel**

Citation: Mrs Mary Hensel, New Bloomfield Times, January 20, 1877.

Guise, Mary A
        Death: January 16, 1877 in Perry Co, PA

Source Title: **Mrs Sarah Updegrove death certificate**

Citation: Mrs Sarah Updegrove death certificate, #0042525, #81494, File 42, Reg 2193, July 1923, Department of Vital Records, New Castle, PA.

Culp, Sarah "Salome" A
        Occu: 1923; Domestic
        Birth: June 30, 1844 in Union Co, PA
        Death: July 03, 1923 in Williamstown, Dauphin Co, PA; ? due to carcinoma of shoulder (recurrent) w/secondary ?
        Burial: July 06, 1923 in Seyberts (Old) Lutheran, Williamstown, Dauphin Co, PA
        Funrl: 1923 in Aaron Ralphsson, Williamstown, Dauphin Co, PA

Source Title: **Mrs. Thompson**

Citation: Mrs. Thompson, Burial record, Miners Journal deaths, 1851.

Penman, Isabelle Stoddart

Source Title: **Mrs. Thompson (con't)**

Citation: Mrs. Thompson, Burial record, Miners Journal deaths, 1851.

Penman, Isabelle Stoddart
> Death: April 18, 1851 in Pottsville, Schuylkill Co, PA

Citation: Mrs. Thompson, Burial record, Miners Journal deaths, April 1851.

Penman, Isabelle Stoddart
> Burial: April 19, 1851 in York Farm Burial Grounds, Pottsville, Schuylkill Co, PA

Source Title: **Myrtle A Thompson**

Citation: Myrtle A Thompson, Obituary, Harrisburg Patriot newspaper, 1983.

Batdorf, Myrtle Adeline
> Funrl: 1983 in Jesse H Geigle, 2100 Linglestown Rd.,Harrisburg, Dauphin Co, PA

Citation: Myrtle A Thompson, Probate files, 1983, File 424-1983, Dauphin County Courthouse, Reg of Wills, Deborah Hershey, Elizabethtown, PA, Mar 2008.

Batdorf, Myrtle Adeline
> Prob: Bet. May 10–19 1983 in Harrisburg, Dauphin Co, PA
> Will: March 30, 1979 in Harrisburg, Dauphin Co, PA

Source Title: **Myrtle A Thompson death certificate**

Citation: Myrtle A Thompson death certificate, #3455802, Department of Vital records, New Castle, PA.

Batdorf, Myrtle Adeline
> Res: 1983 in 2660A Green St., Harrisburg, Dauphin Co, PA
> Death: May 08, 1983 in Polyclinic Hospital, Harrisburg, Dauphin Co, PA; Cardiorespiratory arrest w/ASHD w/pacemaker
> Occu: 1983; Housewife
> SSN: 1983; 165-26-7303

Source Title: **Myrtle A. Batdorf birth certificate**

Citation: Myrtle A. Batdorf birth certificate, January 1918, Department of Vital records, New Castle, PA.

Batdorf, Myrtle Adeline
> Birth: January 05, 1918 in Big Run, Dauphin Co, PA

Source Title: **Myrtle Thompson**

Citation: Myrtle Thompson, Gerald G Thompson.

Batdorf, Myrtle Adeline
> Relgn: 1983; Lakeside Lutheran Church

Citation: Myrtle Thompson, May 1983, PA, Social Security Death Index, www.familysearch.org.

Batdorf, Myrtle Adeline
> Res: 1983 in Beaufort Farms, Camp Curtain, Estherton, Fort Hunter, Harrisburg, Hecktown, Lucknow, Rockville, Uptown, Windsor farms, all Dauphin Co, PA
> SSN: 1983; 165-26-7303

Citation: Myrtle Thompson, Obituary, Harrisburg Patriot newspaper, 1983.

Batdorf, Myrtle Adeline
> Res: 1983 in 2660A Green St., Harrisburg, Dauphin Co, PA
> Death: May 08, 1983 in Polyclinic Hospital, Harrisburg, Dauphin Co, PA; Cardiorespiratory arrest w/ASHD w/pacemaker
> Relgn: 1983; Lakeside Lutheran Church

Source Title: **Our Coal Mining Ancestors**

Citation: Our Coal Mining Ancestors, Lindsay Reeks, pp 161-172, c/o Tammy Tarbet, Bennington, ID.

Keitchen, Agnes
>Marr: October 06, 1727 in Dalkeith Parish, Midlothian Scotland

Moffatt, Christina
>Marr: January 13, 1750 in Edinburgh, Midlothian, Scotland
>Birth: December 11, 1731 in Dalkeith, Midlothian, Scotland
>Baptism: December 19, 1731 in Dalkeith, Midlothian, Scotland

Moffatt, David
>Marr: October 06, 1727 in Dalkeith Parish, Midlothian Scotland
>Birth: September 14, 1700 in Inveresk, Scotland
>Occu: 1734; Collier

Russell, William
>Marr: January 13, 1750 in Edinburgh, Midlothian, Scotland

Source Title: **Penman family information**

Citation: Penman family information, Jim Thompson, jbthompson@@compuserve.com.

Moffatt, Christina
>Marr: January 13, 1750 in Edinburgh, Midlothian, Scotland
>Birth: December 11, 1731 in Dalkeith, Midlothian, Scotland

Penman, David
>Birth: December 31, 1775 in Gladsmuir, East Lothian or, Newbattle, Midlothian, Scotland
>Death: Abt. 1826 in Scotland

Penman, Isabelle Stoddart
>Immigr: 1828

Russell, William
>Marr: January 13, 1750 in Edinburgh, Midlothian, Scotland

Stoddart, Elizabeth
>Birth: January 05, 1779 in Stobgreen Temple, Edinburgh, Midlothian, Scotland
>Death: December 25, 1849 in Pottsville, Schuylkill Co, PA

Citation: Penman family information, John Penman, JCPenman@@aol.com.

Stoddart, Elizabeth
>Burial: 1849 in Presbyterian Burial Grounds, Pottsville, Schuylkill Co, PA

Citation: Penman family information, John Penman, PenmanJC@@aol.com.

Stoddart, David
>Baptism: May 25, 1755 in Newbattle, Midlothian, Scotland

Stoddart, John
>Baptism: January 05, 1729 in Newbattle, Midlothian, Scotland

Citation: Penman family information, Penman family information, John Penman, PenmanJC@@aol.com.

Brown, Catherine
>Marr: October 28, 1763 in Lassware, Midlothian, Scotland

Penman, John
>Marr: October 28, 1763 in Lassware, Midlothian, Scotland

Source Title: **Pennman household**

Citation: Pennman household, 1840 United States Census, Schuylkill Co, PA, ancestry.com & Microfilm, PA State Library, Hbg, PA.

Stoddart, Elizabeth

Source Title: **Pennman household (con't)**

Citation: Pennman household, 1840 United States Census, Schuylkill Co, PA, ancestry.com & Microfilm, PA State Library, Hbg, PA.

Stoddart, Elizabeth
    Census: 1840 in Norwegian, Schuylkill Co, PA

Source Title: **Peter Braun**

Citation: Peter Braun, Brown/Braun Family Line, Gayle T. Clews, gclews@@aessuccess.org.

Braun, Peter
    Miltry: 1775 American Revolution, Private Co B (British Army)

Citation: Peter Braun, Schuylkill County, PA, Chicago, JH Beers & Co, 1916, vol II, p 1071, Historical Society of Schuykill County.

Braun, Peter
    Miltry: 1775 American Revolution, Private Co B (British Army)

Brown, Peter
    Res: 1916 in Clarks Valley, PA, now Charles Kessler farm

Source Title: **Pottsville Hospital**

Citation: Pottsville Hospital, 1900 United States Census, Schuylkill Co, PA, T623, Roll 1485, p 189, www.ancestry.com and 1900 United States Census, Schuylkill Co, PA, PA State library microfilm image.

Thompson, Robert Bruce
    Census: 1900 in Pottsville, Schuylkill Co, PA
    Occu: Bet. 1899–1901; Supervisor (Porter Tp)

Source Title: **Public Family Tree**

Citation: Public Family Tree, Ancestry Famnily Tree, carolcaroll115, Carol Weanfeb, CA, ancestry.com.

Brown, Peter
    Birth: 1775 in Berks (Schuylkill) Co, PA
    Death: 1861 in Rush, Dauphin Co, PA

Source Title: **Robert B Thompson**

Citation: Robert B Thompson, Greenwood Cemetery, Tower City, Schuylkill Co, PA, John Barket, Tower City, PA, B-1-1.

Thompson, Robert Bruce
    Death: October 10, 1907 in Tower City, Schuylkill Co, PA; Typhoid fever w/contaminated water

Source Title: **Robert B Thompson death certificate**

Citation: Robert B Thompson death certificate, #0042512, #102079, Reg # 102, October 1907, Department of Vital records, New Castle, PA.

Thompson, Robert Bruce
    Occu: 1907; Business
    Birth: September 24, 1847 in York Farm Burial Grounds, Pottsville, Schuylkill Co, PA
    Death: October 10, 1907 in Tower City, Schuylkill Co, PA; Typhoid fever w/contaminated water
    Funrl: 1907 in John [F] Dreisingacer, Tower City, Schuylkill Co, PA

Source Title: **Robert B. Thomspon**

Citation: Robert B. Thomspon, Greenwood Cemetery, Tower City, Schuylkill Co, PA, John Barket, Tower City, PA, B-3-1.

Thompson, Robert Bruce

Source Title: **Robert B. Thomspon (con't)**

Citation: Robert B. Thomspon, Greenwood Cemetery, Tower City, Schuylkill Co, PA, John Barket, Tower City, PA, B-3-1.

Thompson, Robert Bruce
       Burial: October 13, 1907 in Greenwood Cemetery, Tower City, Schuylkill Co, PA

Source Title: **Romberger All-Family History Site**

Citation: Romberger All-Family History Site, http://freepages.genealogy.rootsweb.ancestry.com/~rombergerfamily/, Dr John Romberger, Jan 2010.

Romberger, Balthasar
       Birth: July 05, 1747 in Ingolstadt, Bavaria, Germany
       Death: Abt. 1825 in Mifflin, Dauphin Co, PA

Romberger, John Balthaser
       Birth: May 04, 1716 in Theilheim, Schweinfurt, Bavaria, Germany
       Death: September 25, 1800 in Annville, Lebanon Co., PA

Source Title: **Romberger Family**

Citation: Romberger Family, Gratz History, p 207.

Romberger, Balthasar
       Death: Abt. 1825 in Mifflin, Dauphin Co, PA

Citation: Romberger Family, p 261.

Romberger, Balthasar
       Occu: Abt. 1785; Laborer

Citation: Romberger Family, St. John's Lutheran Church, p 10, John Romberger.

Romberger, Balthasar
       Occu: Bet. 1806–1809; Deacon
       Occu: Bet. 1813–1815; Elder

Romberger, Susan
       Birth: April 16, 1799 in Lykens, Dauphin Co, PA

Source Title: **Romberger Family information**

Citation: Romberger Family information, Carol Mallory, wamcam@@cjnetworks.com.

Romberger, John Balthaser
       Birth: May 04, 1716 in Theilheim, Schweinfurt, Bavaria, Germany

Citation: Romberger Family information, Family Group sheet, Corethel J. Vinup, Shaomkin, PA.

Romberger, Balthasar
       Birth: July 05, 1747 in Ingolstadt, Bavaria, Germany

Romberger, John Balthaser
       Birth: May 04, 1716 in Theilheim, Schweinfurt, Bavaria, Germany
       Death: September 25, 1800 in Annville, Lebanon Co., PA

Citation: Romberger Family information, John A Romberger, Elizabethville, PA.

Romberger, Balthasar
       Occu: Bet. 1806–1809; Deacon

Romberger, John Balthaser
       Res: 1758 in Leacock, Lancaster Co, PA
       Res: Bet. 1790–1800 in Annville, Dauphin (Lebanon) Co, PA
       Immigr: September 24, 1753 in Germany to USA (ship Neptune)

Citation: Romberger Family information, John Romberger, email 7/31/2005.

Brucker, Anna Maria
       Relgn: Protestant

Source Title: **Romberger Family information (con't)**

Citation: Romberger Family information, Ron Mitchell, ronnie@@itol.com.

Lehman, Susan
    Marr: June 15, 1798 in Zion Lutheran, Harrisburg, Dauphin Co, PA
Romberger, Balthasar
    Marr: June 15, 1798 in Zion Lutheran, Harrisburg, Dauphin Co, PA

Source Title: **Romberger household**

Citation: Romberger household, 1800 United States Census, Dauphin Co, PA, ancestry.com & Microfilm, PA State Library, Hbg, PA.

Romberger, Susan
    Census: 1800 in father; Upper Paxton, Dauphin Co, PA w

Citation: Romberger household, 1810 United States Census, Dauphin Co, PA, ancestry.com & Microfilm, PA State Library, Hbg, PA.

Romberger, Susan
    Census: 1810 in father; Upper Paxton, Dauphin Co, PA w

Citation: Romberger household, 1820 United States Census, Dauphin Co, PA, ancestry.com & Microfilm, PA State Library, Hbg, PA.

Romberger, Balthasar
    Census: 1820 in Lykens, Dauphin Co, PA (Rimberger)
    Occu: 1820; Manufacturing

Citation: Romberger household, 1830 United States Census, Dauphin Co, PA, ancestry.com & Microfilm, PA State Library, Hbg, PA.

Romberger, Balthasar
    Census: 1830 in Mifflin, Dauphin Co, PA (Blthase)

Source Title: **Rumberger household**

Citation: Rumberger household, 1800 United States Census, Dauphin Co, PA, ancestry.com & Microfilm, PA State Library, Hbg, PA.

Romberger, Balthasar
    Census: 1800 in parents; Upper Paxton, Dauphin Co, PA w

Citation: Rumberger household, 1800 United States cenus, Dauphin Co, PA, ancestry.com & Microfilm, PA State Library, Hbg, PA.

Romberger, John Balthaser
    Census: 1800 in Upper Paxton, Dauphin Co, PA

Citation: Rumberger household, 1810 United States Census, Dauphin Co, PA, ancestry.com & Microfilm, PA State Library, Hbg, PA.

Romberger, Balthasar
    Census: 1810 in Upper Paxton, Dauphin Co, PA age 44

Citation: Rumberger household, 1810 United States cenus, Dauphin Co, PA, ancestry.com & Microfilm, PA State Library, Hbg, PA.

Romberger, John Balthaser
    Census: 1810 in Upper Paxton, Dauphin Co, PA

Source Title: **Rutzel Family**

Citation: Rutzel Family, David Rutzel, leztur@@hotmail.com, awt.ancestry.com.

Benfield, Anna Maria Elizabeth
    Birth: April 01, 1729 in Oley, Philadelphia (Berks) Co, PA

Source Title: **Rutzel Family Genealogy**

Citation: Rutzel Family Genealogy, David Rutzel, leztur@@hotmail.com, awt.ancestry.com.

Angst, Maria Elizabeth
    Marr: 1803 in Oley, Berks Co, PA

Source Title: **Rutzel Family Genealogy (con't)**

Citation: Rutzel Family Genealogy, David Rutzel, leztur@@hotmail.com, awt.ancestry.com.

Benfield, Anna Maria Elizabeth
  Death: February 23, 1804 in Exeter, Berks Co, PA

Trovinger, Elizabeth
  Marr: 1823 in Dauphin Co, PA
  Birth: Abt. 1798 in Somerset County, PA
  Death: Bet. 1860–1870 in Berks Co, PA; Apoplexy (ie, Paralysis due to stroke

Updegroff, John William
  Occu: Abt. 1770; Locksmith, Gunsmith
  Death: Bet. 1800–1804 in Berks Co, PA
  Immigr: 1753

Updegrove, Conrad
  Marr: 1803 in Oley, Berks Co, PA
  Occu: Abt. 1850; Great hunter
  Occu: 1850; Laborer
  Death: April 1865 in Williamstown, Dauphin Co, PA
  Confir: October 09, 1803 in St Jacobs Lutheran, Pine Grove, Berks
    (Schuylkill) Co, PA
  Relgn: St. Johns Lutheran, Mifflin, Dauphin Co, PA

Updegrove, John M
  Marr: 1823 in Dauphin Co, PA

Citation: Rutzel Family Genealogy, Rosie Byard, rbyard@@bigfoot.com.

Updegrove, Conrad
  Occu: Millwright

Source Title: **Samuel Peters**

Citation: Samuel Peters, Descendants of John Peters, Evelyn S. Hartman.

Batdorf, Myrtle Adeline
  Marr: June 15, 1935 in St. Johns (Hill) Lutheran, Lykens, Dauphin Co, PA
  Baptism: October 11, 1918 in Evangelical Lutheran Circuit, Lykens, Dauphin Co,
    PA

Thompson, Harper Bruce
  Marr: June 15, 1935 in St. Johns (Hill) Lutheran, Lykens, Dauphin Co, PA

Source Title: **Sarah Salome Updegrove**

Citation: Sarah Salome Updegrove, Probate files, Roll 43, U4, Dauphin County Courthouse, Reg
of Wills, Harrisburg, PA, Deborah Hershey, Elizabethtown, PA, Mar 2008.

Culp, Sarah "Salome" A
  Prob: Bet. April 02–08 1927 in Harrisburg, Dauphin Co, PA

Source Title: **Schneck household**

Citation: Schneck household, 1810 United States Census, Northumberland Co, PA, ancestry.com
& Microfilm, PA State Library, Hbg, PA.

Schneck, Elizabeth
  Census: 1810 in father; Centre, Northumberland (Union) Co, PA w

Citation: Schneck household, 1820 United States Census, Union Co, PA, ancestry.com &
Microfilm, PA State Library, Hbg, PA.

Schneck, Elizabeth
  Census: 1820 in parents; w

Source Title: **Schnuke household**

Source Title: **Schnuke household (con't)**

Citation: Schnuke household, 1710 United States Census, Northumberland Co, PA, ancestry.com & Microfilm, PA State Library, Hbg, PA.

Schneck, Peter
  Census: 1810 in Centre, Northumberland (Union) Co, PA
    Occu: 1810; Farmer

Citation: Schnuke household, 1830 United States Census, Northumberland Co, PA ancestry.com & Microfilm, PA State Library, Hbg, PA.

Schneck, Peter
  Census: 1830 in Centre, Northumberland (Centre) Co, PA
    Occu: 1830; Farmer

Source Title: **Schofield Family Tree**

Citation: Schofield Family Tree, jenn 13146, ancestry pubic trees, ancestry.com.

Guteman, Jacob
  Marr: April 26, 1801 in Exerter, Berks Co, PA
Voller, Catherine
  Marr: April 26, 1801 in Exerter, Berks Co, PA

Source Title: **Selvage & Peterson Families & More**

Citation: Selvage & Peterson Families & More, Charles J Peterson, PetersonC@@missouri.edu, awt.ancestry.com.

Benfield, Anna Maria Elizabeth
  Death: February 23, 1804 in Exeter, Berks Co, PA
Updegroff, John William
  Birth: February 24, 1732 in Kirchberg Hunsruck, Rhineland-Palatinate, Germany
Updegrove, Conrad
  Birth: November 27, 1771 in Oley, Berks Co, PA
  Death: April 1865 in Williamstown, Dauphin Co, PA

Source Title: **Shadel household**

Citation: Shadel household, 1910 United States Census, Dauphin Co, PA, ED 0133, Visit 0014, www.ancestry.com and 1910 United States Census, Dauphin Co, PA, ED 133, Sheet 1, PA State Library microfilm image.

Culp, Sarah "Salome" A
  Census: 1910 in Williamstown, Dauphin Co, PA (Shadel)
    Res: 1910 in Pottsville St., Williams, Dauphin Co, PA

Source Title: **Snook household**

Citation: Snook household, 1820 United States Census, Union Co, PA ancestry.com & Microfilm, PA State Library, Hbg, PA.

Schneck, Peter
  Census: 1820 in Buffalo, Union Co, PA (Snook)

Source Title: **Strayer & Other Families**

Citation: Strayer & Other Families, Glenda S. Strayer, oolong@@dragonbbs.com, awt.ancestry.com.

Angst, John Daniel
  Birth: December 14, 1749 in East Hanover, Lancaster (Lebanon) Co, PA
Angst, Maria Elizabeth
  Birth: November 11, 1776 in Rockland, Berks Co, PA

Source Title: **Tax lists**

Source Title:	**Tax lists (con't)**

Citation: Tax lists, Germany & Mt. Pleasant Townships, Adams Co County Historical Society.

Hensel, John Casper
      Res: Bet. 1778–1795 in York Co, PA

Citation: Tax lists.

Thomson, Robert
      Baptism: September 15, 1734 in Cranston, Midlothian, Scotland

Source Title:	**The Romberger Line**

Citation: The Romberger Line, Ancestors of Richard Alan Lebo.

Lehman, Susan
      Marr: June 15, 1798 in Zion Lutheran, Harrisburg, Dauphin Co, PA
      Birth: February 19, 1771 in Trappe, Philadelphia (Montgomery) Co, PA
      Res: Abt. 1800 in Harrisburg, Dauphin Co, PA

Romberger, Balthasar
      Marr: June 15, 1798 in Zion Lutheran, Harrisburg, Dauphin Co, PA
      Res: Abt. 1800 in Mifflin, Dauphin Co, PA

Romberger, John Balthaser
      Res: Bet. 1790–1800 in Annville, Dauphin (Lebanon) Co, PA
      Immigr: September 24, 1753 in Germany to USA (ship Neptune)

Romberger, Susan
      Birth: April 16, 1799 in Lykens, Dauphin Co, PA
      Death: February 23, 1857 in Dauphin Co, PA
      Relgn: Upper Paxton, Dauphin Co, PA

Source Title:	**Thompson family information**

Citation: Thompson family information, Films from 1993, Jane L Fouraker, Lancaster Co, PA.

Black, George
      Marr: August 04, 1732 in Inversek, Scotland

Cochran, Isabelle
      Birth: February 07, 1699 in Scotland
      Baptism: February 19, 1699 in Haddington, Scotland

Smith, Mary Helen
      Marr: August 04, 1732 in Inversek, Scotland

Thompson, Alexander
      Occu: Teamster
      Birth: October 22, 1805 in Sauchenside Farm, Cranston, Midlothian, Scotland
      Baptism: November 03, 1805 in Cranston, Midlothian, Scotland
      Occu: Colliery owner

Thompson, Robert
      Occu: Coal Overseer

Thomson, Robert
      Birth: September 13, 1734 in Cranston, Midlothian, Scotland
      Baptism: September 15, 1734 in Cranston, Midlothian, Scotland

Thomson, Robert
      Birth: October 25, 1695 in Cochran, Scotland
      Baptism: November 19, 1695 in Haddington, Scotland

Citation: Thompson family information, Irene C. Stearns, DeKalb, IL.

Goodman, Lydia Ann
      Census: 1880 in Rush, Dauphin Co, PA

Penman, Isabelle Stoddart

Citation: Thompson family information, Irene C. Stearns, DeKalb, IL.

Penman, Isabelle Stoddart
   Birth: May 09, 1816 in Newbattle, Midlothian, Scotland
Russell, Janet
   Marr: April 22, 1791 in Borthwick, Newbattle, Midlothian, Scotland
Thompson, Alexander
   Death: December 04, 1873 in Tower City, Schuylkill Co, PA
Thompson, Robert
   Marr: April 22, 1791 in Borthwick, Newbattle, Midlothian, Scotland

Citation: Thompson family information, James Thompson, jbthompson@@compuserve.com.

Thompson, Alexander
   Immigr: July 09, 1827 in Scotland to New York, NY (ship Nimrod)

Citation: Thompson family information, Jane Fouraker, mjfour@@mindpsring.com.

Russell, Janet
   Marr: April 22, 1791 in Borthwick, Newbattle, Midlothian, Scotland
Thompson, Robert
   Marr: April 22, 1791 in Borthwick, Newbattle, Midlothian, Scotland

Citation: Thompson family information, Jennifer Bachman.

Thompson, Alexander
   Immigr: July 09, 1827 in Scotland to New York, NY (ship Nimrod)

Citation: Thompson family information, Jim Thompson, jbthompson@@compuserve.com, pp 4-11
& Thompson family information, Irene C. Stearns, DeKalb, IL.

Thompson, Alexander
   Birth: October 22, 1805 in Sauchenside Farm, Cranston, Midlothian,
   Scotland

Citation: Thompson family information, Jim Thompson, jbthompson@@compuserve.com, pp
4-11.

Black, Mary
   Marr: Abt. 1760 in Scotland
   Birth: 1737 in Prestonpans, East Lothian, Scotland
Cochran, Isabelle
   Birth: February 07, 1699 in Scotland
   Res: Abt. 1720 in Haddington, East Lothian, Scotland
Moffatt, Christina
   Birth: December 11, 1731 in Dalkeith, Midlothian, Scotland
Penman, Isabelle Stoddart
   Marr: January 01, 1835 in Pottsville, Schuylkill Co, PA
Russell, Janet
   Marr: April 22, 1791 in Borthwick, Newbattle, Midlothian, Scotland
   Birth: December 21, 1766 in Newbattle, Midlothian, Scotland
Thompson, Alexander
   Marr: January 01, 1835 in Pottsville, Schuylkill Co, PA
   Birth: October 22, 1805 in Sauchenside Farm, Cranston, Midlothian,
   Scotland
Thompson, Robert
   Marr: April 22, 1791 in Borthwick, Newbattle, Midlothian, Scotland
   Birth: June 27, 1771 in Edgehead, Cranston, Midlothian, Scotland
   Occu: Abt. 1810; Coalier (Earl of Stair)
Thomson, Robert
   Marr: Abt. 1760 in Scotland

Source Title: **Thompson family information (con't)**

Citation: Thompson family information, Jim Thompson, jbthompson@@compuserve.com, pp 4-11.

Thomson, Robert
        Occu: 1767; Overseer (Coal mine)
        Birth: September 13, 1734 in Cranston, Midlothian, Scotland
        Occu: Abt. 1760 in Collier; Coal miner
        Res: Abt. 1750 in Lasswade, Duddingston, Borthwick, Midlothian, Scotland
Thomson, Robert
        Occu: Abt. 1730; Cap maker

Citation: Thompson family information, John L linden, jllinden@@comcast.net.

Goodman, Lydia Ann
        Birth: February 20, 1856 in Clarks Valley, Dauphin Co, PA
        Death: October 09, 1883 in Tower City, Schuylkill Co, PA; Complications of pregnancy
Russell, Janet
        Marr: April 22, 1791 in Borthwick, Newbattle, Midlothian, Scotland
        Birth: December 21, 1766 in Newbattle, Midlothian, Scotland
Thompson, Robert
        Marr: April 22, 1791 in Borthwick, Newbattle, Midlothian, Scotland

Citation: Thompson family information, Signed November 1, 1836, Jim Thompson, jbthompson@@compuserve.com, pp 4-11.

Thompson, Alexander
        Naturl: July 31, 1834 in Schuylkill Co, PA

Citation: Thompson family information.

Black, George
        Occu: Abt. 1730; Coal miner

Source Title: **Thompson History**

Citation: Thompson History, Jim Thompson, jbthompson@@compuserve.com, pp 4-11.

Cochran, Isabelle
        Marr: November 21, 1718 in Ormiston, East Lothian, Scotland
Thomson, Robert
        Marr: November 21, 1718 in Ormiston, East Lothian, Scotland

Source Title: **Thompson household**

Citation: Thompson household, 1840 United States Census, Schuylkill Co, PA, ancestry.com & Microfilm, PA State Library, Hbg, PA.

Thompson, Alexander
        Census: 1840 in Norwegian, Schuylkill Co, PA

Citation: Thompson household, 1850 United States Census, Schuylkill Co, PA, ancestry.com & Microfilm, PA State Library, Hbg, PA.

Thompson, Alexander
        Census: 1850 in Norwegian, Schuylkill Co, PA
        Occu: 1850; Farming
        Propty: 1850 in $2000
Thompson, Robert Bruce
        Census: 1850 in Norwegian, Schuylkill Co, PA

Citation: Thompson household, 1860 United States Census, Schuylkill Co, PA, PA State library microfilm.

Thompson, Alexander
        Census: 1860 in Porter, Schuylkill Co, PA

Source Title: **Thompson household (con't)**

Citation: Thompson household, 1860 United States Census, Schuylkill Co, PA, PA State library microfilm.

Thompson, Alexander
     Propty: 1860 in $5000 + $230
      Occu: 1860; Farmer

Thompson, Robert Bruce
     Census: 1860 in Porter, Schuylkill Co, PA

Citation: Thompson household, 1870 United States Census, Schuylkill Co, PA, ancestry.com & Microfilm, PA State Library, Hbg, PA.

Thompson, Alexander
     Census: 1870 in Norwegian, Schuylkill Co, PA
      Occu: 1870; Laborer

Thompson, Robert Bruce
     Census: 1870 in father; Norwegian, Schuylkill Co, PA w
      Occu: 1870; Laborer

Citation: Thompson household, 1880 United States Census, Dauphin Co, PA, FHL 1255124, Film T9-1124, p 432B, www.familysearch.org.

Goodman, Lydia Ann
     Occu: 1880; Keeping house

Thompson, Robert Bruce
     Census: 1880 in Rush, Dauphin Co, PA
      Occu: 1880; Coal miner
      Res: 1880 in ? St., Rush, Dauphin Co, PA

Citation: Thompson household, 1900 United States Census, Schuylkill Co, PA www.ancestry.com, Liz McKinnon.

Thompson, Abel Robert
     Census: 1900 in Porter, Schuylkill Co, PA (brother Oliver Thompson)
      Occu: Bet. 1900–1904; Day laborer
      Res: 1900 in Wiconisco St., Sheridan, Schuylkill Co, PA

Citation: Thompson household, 1900 United States Census, Schuylkill Co, PA, T623, Roll 1485, p 189, www.ancestry.com and 1900 United States Census, Schuylkill Co, PA, PA State library microfilm image.

Thompson, Robert Bruce
     Occu: 1900; Supervisor

Citation: Thompson household, 1910 United States Census, Schuylkill Co, PA, www.ancestry.com and 1910 United States Census, Schuylkill Co, PA, ED 62, Sheet 32A, PA State Library.

Thompson, Abel Robert
     Census: 1910 in Porter, Schuylkill Co, PA
      Occu: 1910; Miner (Coal mines)

Thompson, Harper Bruce
     Census: 1910 in Porter, Schuylkill Co, PA

Citation: Thompson household, 1920 United States Census, Schuylkill Co, PA, PA State library, microfilm image.

Thompson, Harper Bruce
     Census: 1920 in Porter, Schuylkill Co, PA

Citation: Thompson household, 1920 United States Census, Schuylkill Co, PA, Roll T625 1651, ED 84, Image 0280, ancestry.com & Microfilm, PA State Library, Hbg, PA.

Thompson, Harper Bruce
     Census: 1920 in Porter, Schuylkill Co, PA

Source Title: **Thompson household (con't)**

Citation: Thompson household, 1920 United States Census, Schuylkill Co, PA, Roll T625 1651, ED 84, Image 0280, www.ancestry.com and 1920 United States Census, Schuylkill Co, PA, PA State library, microfilm image.

Hensel, Augusta "Gussie" Mae
- Census: 1920 in Porter, Schuylkill Co, PA
- Occu: 1920; Seamstress (at home)
- Res: 1920 in 329 Main St., Sheridan, Schuylkill Co, PA

Thompson, Harper Bruce
- Educ: 1920; School

Citation: Thompson household, 1930 United States Census, Schuylkill Co, PA, Roll T626 2146, p 3A, ED 84, Image 0462, ancestry.com & Microfilm, PA State Library, Hbg, PA.

Hensel, Augusta "Gussie" Mae
- Census: 1930 in Porter, Schuylkill Co, PA
- Res: 1930 in 329 Main St., Highway Route 199, Sheridan, Schuylkill Co, PA
- Propty: 1930 in $3500

Citation: Thompson household, 1940 US Federal census, Bruce Thompson, Snyder, PA, www.ancestry.com.

Batdorf, Myrtle Adeline
- Census: 1940 in Tower City, Schuylkill Co, PA

Thompson, Harper Bruce
- Census: 1940 in Tower City, Schuylkill Co, PA
- Occu: Lineman (Bell Telephone Co)

Citation: Thompson household, 1940 US Federal census, Guusie M Thompson, Snyder, PA, www.ancestry.com.

Hensel, Augusta "Gussie" Mae
- Census: 1940 in Porter, Schuylkill Co, PA

Source Title: **Thompson-Batdorf marriage record**

Citation: Thompson-Batdorf marriage record, Register of Wills, Clerk of Orphans Court, Dauphin Co, PA, 1935.

Batdorf, Myrtle Adeline
- Marr: June 15, 1935 in St. Johns (Hill) Lutheran, Lykens, Dauphin Co, PA
- Birth: January 05, 1918 in Big Run, Dauphin Co, PA

Hensel, Augusta "Gussie" Mae
- Occu: 1935; Housewife

Thompson, Harper Bruce
- Marr: June 15, 1935 in St. Johns (Hill) Lutheran, Lykens, Dauphin Co, PA

Source Title: **Thompson-Hensel Marriage**

Citation: Thompson-Hensel Marriage, Office of the Register of Wills, Schuylkill County, PA, June 1904.

Hensel, Augusta "Gussie" Mae
- Marr: June 15, 1904 in Schuylkill Co, PA
- Occu: 1904; Domestic
- Res: 1904 in Tower City, Schuylkill Co, PA
- Birth: February 16, 1885 in Wiconisco, Dauphin Co, PA

Thompson, Abel Robert
- Marr: June 15, 1904 in Schuylkill Co, PA
- Res: 1904 in Porter Tp, Schuylkill Co, PA
- Birth: November 28, 1880 in Sheridan, Schuylkill Co, PA
- Occu: Bet. 1900–1904; Day laborer

Source Title:	**Tower City Centennial**
Citation:	Tower City Centennial.

Thompson, Alexander
        Occu: Bet. 1861–1873; Owner general store

Source Title:	**Updagrove household**
Citation:	Updagrove household, 1830 United States Census, Berks Co, PA, ancestry.com & Microfilm, PA State Library, Hbg, PA.

Updegrove, John M
        Census: 1830

Source Title:	**Updegraf household**
Citation:	Updegraf household, 1840 United States Census, Dauphin Co, PA, ancestry.com & Microfilm, PA State Library, Hbg, PA.

Updegrove, Conrad
        Census: 1840 in Wiconisco, Dauphin Co, PA
Updegrove, John M
        Census: 1840 in Wiconisco, Dauphin Co, PA

Source Title:	**Updagrove Family information**
Citation:	Updegrove Family information, GED imported October 1999, Robin Kornides.

Updegroff, John William
        Birth: February 24, 1732 in Kirchberg Hunsruck, Rhineland-Palatinate, Germany

Citation: Updegrove Family information, p 115, Ed Froeschle, Salem, OR, shared@@teleport.com.

Updegrove, Conrad
        Census: 1820 in Lykens, Dauphin Co, PA

Citation: Updegrove Family information, p 164, Ed Froeschle, Salem, OR, shared@@teleport.com.

Updegrove, Conrad
        Census: 1830 in Lykens, Dauphin Co, PA

Citation: Updegrove Family information, p 358, Ed Froeschle, Salem, OR, shared@@teleport.com.

Updegrove, Conrad
        Census: 1840 in Wiconisco, Dauphin Co, PA

Citation: Updegrove Family information, p 371, Ed Froeschle, Salem, OR, shared@@teleport.com.

Updegrove, Conrad
        Census: 1850 in Wiconisco, Dauphin Co, PA

Citation: Updegrove Family information, p 58, Ed Froeschle, Salem, OR, shared@@teleport.com.

Updegrove, Conrad
        Census: 1810 in Upper Paxton, Dauphin Co, PA

Citation: Updegrove Family information, Robin Kornides, kornides@@usaor.net.

Benfield, Anna Maria Elizabeth
        Birth: April 01, 1729 in Oley, Philadelphia (Berks) Co, PA
        Death: February 23, 1804 in Exeter, Berks Co, PA
Updegroff, John William
        Birth: February 24, 1732 in Kirchberg Hunsruck, Rhineland-Palatinate, Germany

Citation: Updegrove Family information, Rosie Byard, rbyard@@bigfoot.com.

Benfield, Anna Maria Elizabeth

Source Title: **Updegrove Family information (con't)**

Citation: Updegrove Family information, Rosie Byard, rbyard@@bigfoot.com.

Benfield, Anna Maria Elizabeth
      Prob: March 21, 1804 in Exeter, Berks Co, PA

Updegroff, John William
      Res: Bet. 1772–1775 in Western Dt, Berks Co, PA

Updegrove, Conrad
      Burial: 1865 in Dressler Cemetery, Susquehanna, Juniata, PA

Updegrove, John M
      Birth: March 23, 1805 in Pine Grove, Berks (Schylkill) Co, PA
      Death: 1864 in Somerset County, PA

Citation: Updegrove Family information, Updegrove Genealogy, PA State library.

Updegrove, Daniel
      Census: 1870 in Williamstown, Dauphin Co, PA
      Birth: June 28, 1839 in Wiconisco, Dauphin Co, PA
      Death: March 25, 1899 in Williamstown, Dauphin Co, PA

Source Title: **Updegrove genealogy**

Citation: Updegrove genealogy, Vol 10, PA State library.

Updegrove, Conrad
      Occu: Abt. 1850; Great hunter
      Confir: October 09, 1803 in St Jacobs Lutheran, Pine Grove, Berks (Schuylkill) Co, PA
      Res: 1817 in Williams Valley, Dauphin Co, PA

Source Title: **Updegrove household**

Citation: Updegrove household, 1810 United States Census, Dauphin Co, PA, ancestry.com & Microfilm, PA State Library, Hbg, PA.

Updegrove, John M
      Census: 1810 in father; Jonestown, Dauphin (Lebanon) Co, PA w

Citation: Updegrove household, 1820 United States Census, Dauphin Co, PA, ancestry.com & Microfilm, PA State Library, Hbg, PA.

Updegrove, John M
      Census: 1820 in father; Lykens, Dauphin Co, PA w

Citation: Updegrove household, 1820 United States Census, Dauphin Co, PA, Roll M33 102, p 256, Image 104, ancestry.com & Microfilm, PA State Library, Hbg, PA.

Updegrove, Conrad
      Census: 1820 in Lykens, Dauphin Co, PA
      Occu: 1820; Agriculture

Citation: Updegrove household, 1850 United States Census, Dauphin Co, PA ancestry.com & Microfilm, PA State Library, Hbg, PA.

Angst, Maria Elizabeth
      Medical: Deaf

Updegrove, Conrad
      Census: 1850 in Wiconisco, Dauphin Co, PA
      Occu: 1850; Laborer

Updegrove, Daniel
      Educ: 1850; School

Updegrove, John M
      Census: 1850 in Wiconisco, Dauphin Co, PA
      Propty: 1850 in $500
      Occu: 1850; Labor

Source Title: **Updegrove household (con't)**

Citation: Updegrove household, 1850 United States Census, Dauphin Co, PA, PA State library microfilm.

Updegrove, Daniel
   Census: 1850 in Wiconisco, Dauphin Co, PA
Updegrove, John M
   Census: 1850 in Wiconisco, Dauphin Co, PA

Citation: Updegrove household, 1860 United States Census, Lycoming Co, PA, ancestry.com & Microfilm, PA State Library, Hbg, PA.

Updegrove, John M
   Census: 1860 in Clinton, Lycoming Co, PA
   Occu: 1860; Laborer

Citation: Updegrove household, 1870 United States Census, Dauphin Co, PA, PA State library microfilm.

Culp, Sarah "Salome" A
   Census: 1870 in Williamstown, Dauphin Co, PA
   Occu: Bet. 1870–1880; Keeping house
Updegrove, Clara Matilda
   Census: 1870 in Williamstown, Dauphin Co, PA
Updegrove, Daniel
   Census: 1870 in Williamstown, Dauphin Co, PA
   Occu: 1870; Laborer in mine
   Propty: 1870 in $100

Citation: Updegrove household, 1870 United States Census, Dauphin Co, PA, Roll 1335, p 792, Jan.

Updegrove, Daniel
   Census: 1870 in Williamstown, Dauphin Co, PA

Citation: Updegrove household, 1880 United States Census, Dauphin Co, PA, www.ancestry.com and 1880 United States Census, Dauphin Co, PA, FHL 1255125, Film T9-1125, p 312B, www.familysearch.org.

Culp, Sarah "Salome" A
   Occu: Bet. 1870–1880; Keeping house
Updegrove, Clara Matilda
   Census: 1880 in Williamstown, Dauphin Co, PA
Updegrove, Daniel
   Census: 1880 in Williamstown, Dauphin Co, PA
   Occu: 1880; Laborer

Citation: Updegrove household, 1900 United States Census, Juniata, PA, ancestry.com & Microfilm, PA State Library, Hbg, PA.

Culp, Sarah "Salome" A
   Census: 1900

Source Title: **Updegrove household (Updigrove)**

Citation: Updegrove household (Updigrove), 1860 United States Census, Juniata, PA, PA State library microfilm.

Updegrove, Conrad
   Census: 1860 in Susquehanna, Juniata, PA (son Solomon Updegrove)

Source Title: **Uptegraff Family Genalogy Forum**

Citation: Uptegraff Family Genalogy Forum, Rosie Byard, rbyard@@bigfoot.com.

Updegrove, Conrad
   Baptism: December 29, 1771 in St. Josephs Union (Oley Hill), Church, Berks Co, PA

Source Title: **Uptegraff Family Genalogy Forum (con't)**

Source Title: **Warner, Beers & Co**

Citation: Warner, Beers & Co, History of Adams Co County, 1886, p 316.

Hensel, John Casper
      Res: Bet. 1798–1799 in Mt. Pleasant, York Co, PA
      Occu: Bet. 1799–1800; Weaver

Source Title: **Weist household**

Citation: Weist household, 1900 United States Census, Dauphin Co, PA, Roll T623 1404, p 2A, ED 190, ancestry.com & Microfilm, PA State Library, Hbg, PA.

Hensel, Andrew Guise
      Occu: Bet. 1850–1900; Plasterer

Citation: Weist household, 1900 United States Census, Dauphin Co, PA, Roll T623 1404, p 2A, ED 190, ancestry.com & Microfilm, PA State Library, Hbg, PA.

Hensel, Andrew Guise
      Census: 1900 in Wiconisco, Dauphin Co, PA (Weist-Heheel)

Citation: Weist household, 1920 United States Census, Schuylkill Co, PA, ED 143, sheet A, PA State Library, microfilm image.

Culp, Sarah "Salome" A
      Census: 1920 in Tower City, Schuylkill Co, PA (Weist)
      Res: 1920 in 25 West Grand Ave., Tower City, Schuylkill Co, PA

Source Title: **Workman**

Citation: Workman, PA Births, Dauphin County, J. Humphrey.

Workman, Joseph
      Relgn: 1819; St. Johns (Hill) Lutheran, Lykens, Dauphin Co, PA

Source Title: **Workman family information**

Citation: Workman family information, Evelyn Hartman, Evelyn S Hartman, deanh@@voicenet.com.

Romberger, Susan
      Birth: April 16, 1799 in Lykens, Dauphin Co, PA

Workman, Joseph
      Birth: December 03, 1795 in Lykens, Dauphin Co, PA
      Death: May 23, 1857 in Dauphin Co, PA
      Burial: 1857 in Calvary United Methodist, Wiconisco, Dauphin Co, PA

Source Title: **Workman household**

Citation: Workman household, 1820 United States Census, Dauphin Co, PA, ancestry.com & Microfilm, PA State Library, Hbg, PA.

Workman, Joseph
      Census: 1820 in Lykens, Dauphin Co, PA
      Occu: 1820; Agriculture

Citation: Workman household, 1830 United States Census, Dauphin Co, PA, ancestry.com & Microfilm, PA State Library, Hbg, PA.

Workman, Joseph
      Census: 1830 in Lykens, Dauphin Co, PA (James)

Citation: Workman household, 1840 United States Census, Dauphin Co, PA, ancestry.com & Microfilm, PA State Library, Hbg, PA.

Workman, Catherine
      Census: 1840 in family; Not listed w

Workman, Joseph

Source Title: **Workman household (con't)**

Citation: Workman household, 1840 United States Census, Dauphin Co, PA, ancestry.com & Microfilm, PA State Library, Hbg, PA.

Workman, Joseph

Census: 1840 in Wiconisco, Dauphin Co, PA

Citation: Workman household, 1850 United States Census, Dauphin Co, PA, PA State library microfilm.

Workman, Catherine

Census: 1850 in Wiconisco, Dauphin Co, PA

Workman, Joseph

Census: 1850 in Wiconisco, Dauphin Co, PA

Occu: 1850; Farmer

Propty: 1850 in $294

Citation: Workman household, 1850 United States Census, Union Co, PA, FTM CD 305, Disk 4, film 775.

Workman, Joseph

Census: 1850 in Wiconisco, Dauphin Co, PA

About the Author

Marc D. Thompson delved into writing and genealogy at a very early age. He wrote stories, poems, lyrics and family history books. Marc went on to write and research in high school and college, earning a BS degree from Moravian College. He has presented genealogical lectures and authored seven family history volumes and recently published *The Fitness Book of Lists* and *Virtual Personal Training Manual*. His other published works include other genealogical books and a poetry compilation, with poetic appearances in Fighting Chance Magazine, Love's Chance Magazine, Northern Stars Magazine, Offerings, Poetry Motel, Suzerian Enterprises and The Pink Chameleon.

Thompson currently pens a monthly genealogy blog and a fitness blog at ideafit.com. He.is a member of the Association of Professional Genealogists and has founded a PA Genealogy Society. He was the County Coordinator of the Chatham Co, GA USGenweb site and wrote a monthly genealogy column for Atlantic Avenue Magazine. Writing now for over four decades, when he puts pen to paper, eloquent, heat-felt yet real-life truths emerge. He has been influenced by science, art and his relationships, and yet at the same time marvels at the cosmically-driven direction he receives from energy around him. Thompson believes in what he calls Creatalytical Thinking: The fusion of creativity and analysis to view life more fully and fulfill his place in this world.

MARC D. THOMPSON, VIRTUFIT.NET™

www.VirtuFit.net - marc@VirtuFit.net - skype: VirtuFit

ideafit: www.ideafit.com/profile/marc-d-thompson

Index of Individuals

Index of Individuals

Index of Individuals

Index of Individuals

Index of Individuals

Romberger, Joseph: 62,145,170
Romberger, Salome: 62,131,170
Romberger, Samuel: 61,131,170
Romberger, Susan:
32,46,47,60,119,123,129,131,133,136,139,156,159,161,170,2
07,224,231,232,235,243
Rudisill, Living: 180
Russell, James: 69,70,170
Russell, Janet: 38,52,115,129,141,153,170,175,236,237
Russell, John: 69,153,170,203
Russell, Living: 54,170
Russell, Mary (1): 53,170,183
Russell, Mary (1755): 53,153,170
Russell, William (1725): 37,53,70,133,140,141,170,203,229
Russell, William (1755): 53,153,170
Russell, William (2): 53,170,183

S

Sara: 181
Sassaman, Emmanuel: 48,145,170
Schneck (1): 66,170
Schneck (2): 66,170
Schneck, Elizabeth:
35,50,51,65,121,129,134,141,148,158,170,225,233
Schneck, Living: 66,170
Schneck, Peter: 50,66,129,141,148,170,234
Schreckengast?, Anna Maria:
28,42,43,56,117,131,132,136,139,151,170,208,209,226
Semrow, Loretta: 24,160,170,209,210
Shackley, Living: 177
Shackley, Walter: 177
Shadel, Henry L: 37,145,170
Shannon, Living: 7,170,180
Shive, Stanley L: 180
Shomber, Francis W: 181
Shomber, Harry L: 182
Shomber, Living: 182
Shomper, Caroline: 181
Shreffler, Living: 181
Shumber, Mary A: 178
Sidnam: 47,146,170
Sikora, Living (1): 171
Sikora, Living (2): 171
Sikora, Living U: 7,170,180
Singer, Henry: 48,171
Slear, Living (1): 179
Slear, Living (2): 179
Slingwine, Living: 182
Smink, Isaac: 48,146,171
Smith, Mary Helen: 51,68,69,137,153,171,235
Snoke: 56,171
Sophia: 49,146,171
St. Thompson, Living: 7,171,179
Sterner, Catherine: 23,171
Sterner, Living: 24,171
Stoddart, David: 39,54,55,73,130,141,153,171,214,229

Stoddart, Elizabeth:
24,39,40,54,138,141,150,153,156,171,213,214,215,229,230
Stoddart, James: 73,153,171
Stoddart, John: 72,73,141,154,171,226,229
Stout, Harry Daniel: 182
Strohecker, Ida: 177
Strohecker, Maclada: 183
Susan (1790): 60,146,171
Susan (1838): 48,146,171
Susan (1882): 21,146,171,180
Swab, Catherine "Kate": 56,131,146,171
Swartz, David: 45,146,171

T

Tait, Joseph: 176
Tait, Living: 176
Tait, Margaret: 176
Tait, Martin: 176
Thompson, "Carrie" A: 182
Thompson, "Carrie" Isabella: 177
Thompson, "Lillie": 182
Thompson, Abel Franklin: 17,133,146,171,180,201
Thompson, Abel Robert:
6,14,17,23,108,109,110,134,137,149,150,152,155,157,158,17
1,179,201,238,239
Thompson, Abraham L (1865): 183
Thompson, Abraham L (1866): 178
Thompson, Albert: 178
Thompson, Alexander:
6,24,27,40,111,115,126,127,131,134,139,141,149,150,152,15
5,157,160,171,176,202,203,223,235,236,237,238,240
Thompson, Alexander F: 27,146,171,178
Thompson, Allen: 179
Thompson, Allen Herbert: 181
Thompson, Andrew R: 182
Thompson, Anna (1779): 53,154,171,183
Thompson, Anna (1835): 176
Thompson, Anna (1864): 176
Thompson, Arthur W: 181
Thompson, Benjamin: 21,146,171,179
Thompson, Betty: 183
Thompson, Blanche (1883): 21,146,171,180
Thompson, Blanche (2): 183
Thompson, Catherine: 177
Thompson, Charles: 182
Thompson, Charles W: 183
Thompson, Christina (1792): 38,154,171,175
Thompson, Christina (1871): 176
Thompson, Clyde: 181
Thompson, Cora: 181
Thompson, Darryl E: 180
Thompson, David A: 178
Thompson, David Lawson: 176
Thompson, David P: 177
Thompson, David Penman: 27,146,171,176
Thompson, Donald: 177

Index of Individuals

Index of Individuals

Index of Individuals

Updegrove, Daniel:
6,21,35,37,51,114,120,121,126,129,132,134,155,157,159,160,
173,206,212,213,223,241,242

Updegrove, Edward Isaac: 86,128,173

Updegrove, Elizabeth: 65,147,173

Updegrove, Ellen: 43,147,173

Updegrove, Frances: 85,147,173

Updegrove, Jacob: 49,147,173

Updegrove, John Adam: 85,147,173

Updegrove, John J: 49,147,173

Updegrove, John M:
48,49,120,126,130,132,134,149,155,156,159,173,223,233,240
,241,242

Updegrove, Nancy: 49,147,173

Updegrove, Nellie: 65,147,173

Updegrove, Nora Jane: 37,147,173

Updegrove, Peter: 85,147,173

Updegrove, Rebecca: 50,147,173

Updegrove, Sarah: 65,147,173

Updegrove, Solomon (1809): 65,132,173

Updegrove, Solomon (1845): 50,147,173

Updegrove, William Henry: 37,147,174

V

Voller, Catherine: 41,116,133,147,174,234

W

Walter, Maria Salome: 74,75,158,160,174,210

Weir, Elsie: 176

White, Lavinia Eva: 23,147,174

Wilson, Alexander: 176

Wilson, Charles: 176

Wilson, Elizabeth: 38,174,175

Wilson, George: 176

Wilson, Isabelle: 54,71,72,138,155,174

Wilson, James: 38,174,176

Wilson, Living (1): 175

Wilson, Living (2): 176

Wilson, Living (3): 176

Wilson, Living (4): 176

Wilson, Robert (1): 175

Wilson, Robert (1822): 176

Wilson, William: 176

Wittle, Living: 7,174,179

Workman, ?: 48,174

Workman, Benjamin: 60,147,174

Workman, Carolina: 48,147,174

Workman, Catherine:
6,33,34,45,113,118,119,129,133,135,137,142,150,159,174,20
7,219,220,221,243,244

Workman, Elizabeth: 48,132,174

Workman, Jacob (1819): 47,132,174

Workman, Jacob (2): 60,174

Workman, James: 60,174

Workman, John (1823): 47,147,174

Workman, John (2): 60,174

Workman, Joseph:
32,46,47,61,119,123,126,129,132,139,159,161,174,207,224,2
43,244

Workman, Joseph R: 48,147,174

Workman, Nancy: 48,147,174

Workman, Susan: 47,132,174

Y

Yohe, John F: 24,174

Z

Zimmerman, Peter: 65,148,174

www.ingramcontent.com/pod-product-compliance
Lightning Source LLC
Chambersburg PA
CBHW081147270326
41930CB00014B/3061